ACCELERATED ITALIAN

Design, story line and Name Game
by

COLIN ROSE

Translation and Activations
by

GIGI GATTI-DOYLE
and
TERRY DOYLE

Physical Learning Video
by

Libyan Labiosa Cassone

Front cover by Philip Giggle
Front cover photograph by A Becker/Image Bank ©
Memory Maps by Mick Davis

Recorded by Post Sounds Studios Ltd.

Lasersetting and page production
from original diskettes by
Artset Graphics, Chesham, Bucks.

Printed at The Bath Press, Somerset.

ISBN 0 905553 24 1

WELCOME TO

ACCELERATED ITALIAN

There are a lot of new ideas in the Accelerated Learning Language Courses - so it's a good idea to read THE SECRETS OF LEARNING A LANGUAGE first. It will explain what is in the course and why. It may seem like a lot of reading before you actually start learning your new language but the better you understand how to learn languages, the faster you will acquire this one!

Do:

1. Make a conscious effort to relax before each session.

2. Try out Section One of the Physical Learning Video, which follows.

3. Complete Act One.

4. Read through Part One of the Name Game.

5. Move on to Act Two - even if you haven't mastered Act One. It's more interesting and productive to finish and then repeat the whole course than to repeat each Act over and over until you know it perfectly.

   Above all enjoy yourself - then the learning happens automatically!

Colin Rose
Course Designer

INTRODUCTION

This Italian Course has been prepared on the principles of Accelerated Learning to enable you to gain a rapid and enjoyable introduction to Italian. When you have finished the 12 units you will be able to understand and use Italian well enough for everyday travel, business and social situations. Each unit contains a story section and an activation section. We call the story section "Acts" because the Course is constructed like a drama with the characters using practical language in practical situations, just as you will need to do!

You will hear the Act read in several different ways. The different readings have been planned so that each contributes, in its own particular way, to the learning process, and so that learning will be easy and enjoyable.

The activation material in Part 2, will help you practise and recall the language contained in each Act.

Creating memory for language, and being able to recall that language on demand, are two different things. The structure of your Course recognises this.

Each Act starts with a vivid description of the scenes in which the action takes place — because the more you can visualise the scenes, people, action, the better you can create that all important 'mental movie', enabling you to recall vocabulary later in your 'mind's eye'.

The story begins with our young hero, Peter West, arriving in Rome. He has been asked to deliver a package to a certain Signor Bruni. He calls at Signor Bruni's house, meets the beautiful Bella, Signor Bruni's niece, and hands over the package to her. Bella asks Peter to come back to meet her uncle the next day and Peter goes off to spend the night in a nearby hotel where Bella has already reserved a room for him.

After becoming familiar with this first Act, you will be asked to take part in similar dialogues and situations yourself. You will then be introduced to some basic grammar — how to use the Italian for 'a' and 'the', and for 'he' or 'she'; how to handle adjectives in Italian as well as some important parts of the present tense of many useful verbs.

Most important of all you will learn from the start how to **speak** Italian in a series of easy steps. You will learn how to greet people and say goodbye; how to introduce yourself; how to give simple descriptions of other people; how to reserve a room in a hotel. You will also pick up quite a few Italian numbers. You don't have to know your Verdi to know that Italian is a very musical language. This is partly a matter of the pure vowel sounds, partly the intonation, the rhythm, and the close attention to the harmony of the sounds, which also affects spelling. But rather than concern yourself with theories of pronunciation, just **listen** carefully to the Italian speakers on the tapes and enter right from the start into the spirit of imitating them — sing along, if you like, whether **forte** or **pianissimo, adagio** or **allegro con brio.**

So throw away your English reserve and, from Act One on, keep your vowel sounds as pure as possible. That way you will sound like an Italian too.

Buona fortuna!

THE ITALIAN LANGUAGE NAME GAME

Almost everybody likes games and puzzles. As an addition to your Accelerated Learning Course, let us introduce you to a fascinating game. It's a game with a very valuable payoff.

At the end of the **Name Game** you will be able to see the meaning of a significant proportion of the Italian language without consciously trying to learn a single word! Just treat the language as a fascinating but easily soluble puzzle.

But first let us give you three very simple and apparently unrelated puzzles:-

1. 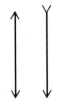
Q. Which vertical line is the longest?

A. They are both the same. Sometimes things only <u>look</u> different superficially.

2. 4 8 12 16 20
Q. What is the next figure in the sequence?

A. 24. Because there is a principle involved. Once you know the principle you can work out hundreds of similar puzzles. Working out the principle is always more efficient than learning thousands of individual facts.

3. VINE — YARD
Q. Can you change **VINE** into **YARD** by just changing one letter at a time? Each new word must make sense.

A.
<u>VINE</u>
WINE
WIND
WAND
WARD
<u>YARD</u>

The principle is that quite small individual changes can add up over time to a big change. And that is what happens to languages over the centuries.

The purpose of these little games is to show that after you have played even once, you can solve any similar puzzle in the future because you know the principle involved.

Well, you can play just such puzzle games with the Italian language.

The central point to realise is that the Italian language was not invented word by word on a random basis. It has evolved over the last 2,000 years in quite a logical way – just as English has evolved.

And here is the good news:–

A large portion of Italian and English have evolved from the same language, originally Latin. So in a real sense, English and Italian are like dialects of each other. The fact that they do not always look alike at first sight is partly because even our own language has changed substantially over time, and partly because English actually has two roots – the Indo-Germanic, and the Latin. This double origin accounts for the fact that English is a very rich language, and there are very often two words in English that essentially mean the same.

The 'posh' word will descend from Latin, via Old French, which was for centuries the language of the Court, and of diplomacy. The more basic word will have come from Germanic. An example would be 'aspire' and 'hope'. The Italian for 'to hope' is **sperare,** relating to the English 'aspire', while the German is **hoffen,** with a direct connection to 'hope'.

Another good example is the word 'speech'. The basic word is associated with the German **Sprache,** but the posher English word might be 'discourse', which leads to the Italian **discorso.**

Now, as you would expect, over the 2,000 year period in which the two dialects, Italian and English, developed, the two words 'discourse' and discorso are certainly not the same, but you can see the association; and the single most important principle of Acclerated Learning is association. When you associate two items together – one that is new, and one that you already know – you have formed the basis of strong memory.

Incidentally, as you might have begun to suspect, the Italian for 'accelerate' (a 'posh' word in English) is **accelerare,** and 'association' is **associazione.** The second most important aspect of Accelerated Learning is that it is easier to learn one basic principle that can apply to hundreds of future situations, than tediously learn each new individual example.

The **Name Game** is helpful for another reason. We talk of 'learning a language' as if it were one skill — in fact there are really FOUR types of skill. They overlap, but they are distinct.

The easiest skill for most adults is reading, because you can take your own time, and the context helps a lot. Then comes the ability to follow a conversation that has been deliberately simplified and carefully enunciated for you. The third skill is speaking, because you pick your own words and speed. The fourth and highest skill is to follow a 'real-life' native conversation, because the pronunciation is typically fast, indistinct and 'blurred' to novice ears.

An Accelerated Learning course provides you with all four skills. Indeed we believe that as an adult, to try to learn a language from, say, audio tapes alone is a misleading simplification of the task, and cuts down a lot on the enjoyment and indeed pride of being able to read effectively as well as talk and understand. Reading is by far the fastest way to build vocabulary, and the **Name Game** gives you lots of help to see the patterns in the Italian language.

ITALIAN IS BEAUTIFUL – AND EASY!

As we said above, Italian, in common with French, Spanish, Portuguese and English, evolved from Latin, but it was the Latin that was spoken by the Roman soldiers and colonisers, rather than the more formal written language. Indeed modern Italian is actually based on the dialect spoken in Florence.

Florence became influential, partly because it was the main printing centre, and partly due to the writers who congregated there, such as Dante, Petrarch and Boccaccio. Perhaps it is from them that Italian gets such an attractive rhythm and 'music'!

As an English speaker learning Italian, you'll be pleased to know that about 55% of English words derive ultimately from the Latin root, with about 30% being Germanic (the rest are from various sources!).

The good news is that most of the more sophisticated English vocabulary relates very directly to Latin/Italian, so you'll become fluent surprisingly fast.

Well, that's enough introduction – let's get on with the **Name Game!**

Here we go ...

Italian	English
Il deserto è arido.	The desert is arid.
La caverna è umida.	The cave is damp.

These little sentences contain a surprising amount of information!

Principle 1

There are thousands upon thousands of words that are almost identical in Italian and English. I call them gifts! Naturally there are a few small differences, in spelling or in pronunciation, but you'll rapidly get the feel for what these differences are likely to be.

Here are just a few:–

passaporto
studente
professione
vegetariano
occasione
idea
importante
necessario

continuare
traffico
telefonare
elegante
cinema
hotel
intelligente
monumento

Principle 2

In common with almost all European languages, Italian has masculine and feminine words, ie. gender. So it's **il deserto** and **la caverna.** The word endings frequently give you the clue.

If it ends in **o** or **e** it's usually masculine; if **a** it's usually feminine.

By just reading and listening you'll find that you need to make no special effort to remember which is which. Above all, you need to remember that our aim is to communicate. Saying 'il' when it should be 'la' in the early stages is no big problem – you'll still be understood. Later you'll get it exactly right.

Principle 3

Did you notice the endings of the words that described 'il deserto' and 'la caverna'? The adjective "agrees" with the object it describes. So it's **il deserto arido** because the desert is masculine, but **la caverna umida** because cave is a feminine word.

Principle 4

Italian words rarely contain an 'h'. This simple principle sheds immediate light on quite a few words which otherwise appear unfamiliar ...

umido	humid	**il metodo**	method
l'orizzonte	horizon	**umano**	human
l'autore	author	**esitare**	to hesitate
il teatro	theatre	**umile**	humble
l'abitante	(in)habitant		

And how about...

la storia	history	**il tuono**	thunder
l'ora	hour	**onesto**	honest
l'arringa	herring	**uomo**	man (as in homo-)

Useful, isn't it?

How about some more 'gift' words before we move on? Remember, always cover up the English so you can guess the Italian meaning. Even if you guess it wrong, you'll almost certainly see why you made a different deduction, and that teaches you too.

la vista	view	**l'est**	east
la valle	valley	**il sud**	south
la costa	coast	**l'ovest**	west
il capo	cape	**il nord**	north
la lampada	lamp	**il centro**	centre
il clima	climate		

Principle 5

Il prodotto è perfetto.   The product is perfect.

Il latte ha sapore buono.   The milk has a good taste.

Words that in English contain 'ct' or 'pt' are usually represented by **tt** in Italian. So ...

il fatto	fact	**il difetto**	defect
corretto	correct	**diretto**	direct
la condotta	conduct	**il rispetto**	respect
attuale	actual	**l'insetto**	insect
l'attore	actor	**il dottore**	doctor
il concetto	concept	**il contatto**	contact
intatto	intact	**l'ottimismo**	optimism
adattare	adapt		

The same principle is behind some slightly less obvious words, like...

il tatto	touch (derivation: tactile)
il latte	milk (think of <u>lact</u>ate)
otto	eight (links with <u>oct</u>agon)

Because **la pittura** is a picture, you'll see that **il pittore** is a painter, and how **stretto** means narrow (originally 'strict').

You're probably now full of **ottimismo** about your prospects **(prospettive!)** for learning Italian quickly and enjoyably. And it's not now difficult to see why **latte** means milk, but we'll have to dig a little deeper to discover the connections which show why **sapore** means taste.

Principle 6
_____

The clue is the comparatively common interchange over the centuries between **b, v** and **p.** So ...

il sapore	taste	relates to savour
la capanna	hut	from cabin
il lavoro	work	relates to labour
le febbre	fever	b=v
la tavola	table	v=b

And because you can now deduce that **scrivere** means to write (scribe), the double use of Principles 5 and 6 gives you the meaning of **scrittura** as writing (literally scripture!).

Similar sound changes also explain **coperta** = covered, and **scoperta** = discovered.

Now if you're starting to develop the enquiring mind that will make absorbing new words easy, because they become so much more memorable, you might have asked yourself whether there is another principle behind **scoperta** meaning <u>dis</u>covered. Well, yes!

Principle 7
_____

Il peso forte sbilancia la tavola. The heavy weight unbalances the table.

The principle, of course, is that where English would often use 'dis-' or 'un-' before a word to give it the opposite meaning, Italians use **s.**
So ...

sbandare	disperse (disband)
sbarbare	shave (disbeard!)
sbarcare	land (disembark)
sfavore	disfavour
sfidare	challenge (ie. take away faith)
smoderato	immoderate
slogare	dislocate
sdegnare	disdain

But wait, the last word is interesting. Does the g have a special implication?

Principle 8

Sua figlia ama il lavoro.   His daughter likes work.

At first sight the connection between **figlia** and daughter is not so obvious, until you remember the phrase "filial affection", the love of a son or daughter.

So, by recognising that Italian often adds a **g** before the combination li, you can see why ...

la foglia	leaf (folio)	**meglio**	better (ameliorate)
il figlio	son	**la paglia**	straw (palliasse)

And here's an interesting one! **La chiglia** is a keel. Which leads to the next principle ...

Principle 9

È un grande rischio.   It's a great risk.

The principle is that **ch** is pronounced like a hard 'c' or 'k'. It replaces the English 'k' which does not exist in Italian except in some foreign words, 'q' (sometimes), and 'c', when a hard 'c' sound is wanted before **e** or **i**.

il chiosco	kiosk	**la richiesta**	request
il chilogrammo	kilogram	**l'inchiesta**	inquest

Here's another one: **il chiostro** means cloister. But wait a minute! That last word isn't so obvious. Maybe there's another principle here.

Principle 10

La donna bionda è graziosa.   The blonde woman is pretty.

Very often English now has an 'l' where Italian retains an **i**, usually after **p, f** or (as in chiostro), **ch**. So it's ...

il fiore	flower	**chiaro**	clear
il piano	plan or plane	**il pianeta**	planet
il tempio	temple	**la fiamma**	flame
la pianta	plant	**la piattaforma**	platform
il piatto	plate	**il piattino**	saucer
chiaro	clear		

And here are a few interesting ones which require a little more detective work.

chiuso	closed (**ch** = 'c', **i** = 'l')
la piaga	wound (see the connection with plague?)
la chiave	key (relates to clef)
piacere	to like (placate)
bianco	white (think of 'blanch')
doppio	double

Principle 11

La giornalista è estremamente sexy.   The (lady) journalist is extremely sexy.

Italian only has 21 letters in its alphabet. The **j k w x** and **y** do not occur naturally, although some foreign words retain them.

We've already seen: ENGLISH k = ITALIAN **c** or **ch**

The others are: **j** =   **g**
                             x =   **s**
                             y =   **g** or **i**

j = g

la giacca	jacket	**il gioielliere**	jeweller
la gelosia	jealousy	**la gioia**	joy
giusto	just	**gioviale**	jovial

x = s

la mistura	mixture	**esterno**	external
il sesso	sex	**la tassa**	tax
prossimo	near	**fissare**	fix
esatto	exact	**esaminare**	examine
esagerare	exaggerate	**escludere**	exclude
esistere	exist	**aspettare**	wait (expect)

y = g

pagare	pay	**il raggio**	ray
grigio	grey	**pregare**	pray
distruggere	destroy		

y = i

ariano	Aryan	**asimmetrico**	asymmetrical
la siringa	syringe	**il sistema**	system
la cripta	crypt	**il tiranno**	tyrant

And here's a word that combines a few principles:

l'impiegato	employee

BONUS!

How would you like to recognise thousands of Italian words <u>at a glance?</u>

Instead of you figuring it out from a sentence, we are going to give you some very simple principles that provide you with thousands of easy-to-remember words.

If the Italian word ends in **-zione,** its equivalent is -tion.

nazione	nation	**condizione**	condition
associazione	association	**abbreviazione**	abbreviation

If it ends in **-tà** its equivalent is -ty.

velocità	velocity	**pietà**	piety
libertà	liberty	**difficoltà**	difficulty
crueltà	cruelty	**autorità**	authority
città	city	**cattività**	captivity

If it ends in **-ìa** or **-ia** its equivalent is -y.

geometrìa	geometry	**psicopatìa**	psychopathy
scortesìa	rudeness (discourtesy)		
tirannia	tyranny	**melodìa**	melody
storia	history		

If it ends in **-ezza** its equivalent is -ness.

tristezza	sadness	**ricchezza**	wealth (rich-ness)
grandezza	size (grand-ness)	**larghezza**	width (large-ness)
bellezza	beauty	**dolcezza**	sweetness

If it ends in **-enza** its equivalent is -ence.

esistenza	existence	**pazienza**	patience
indifferenza	indifference	**conferenza**	conference

If it ends in **-izia** it can equate to -ship.

amicizia	friendship

And here's another bonus! All the endings above are feminine, so they all take "la" (or l' if the first letter is a vowel).

INTERLUDE

Sometimes you have to do some interesting detective work to really uncover the hidden connection. So, since we've just had a really easy bonus section, let's see how you can sharpen your skills as a linguistic Miss Marple.

Do continue to treat it as a game. Cover up the right hand column, and try to work out what the Italian word means. Remember the Chinese proverb:

"I forget what I hear, I remember what I see, but I learn what I <u>do</u>."

Here's a list of some teaser words. The linguistic links are given in the third column.

Italian	English	Linguistic link
trovare	find	as in treasure trove
il fumo	smoke	fume
la farina	flour	farinaceous
il filo	thread	filament
polvere	to dust	pulverise
la luce	light	lucid
il fulmine	lightning	fulminate
l'ombra	shade	umbrella
il sole	sun	solar
l'onda	wave	undulate
la terra	earth	terrestrial
la penna	feather pen	think of a quill pen!
la fabbrica	factory	fabricate
il fratello	brother	fraternity
il muro	wall	mural
la scala	staircase	scale
il maestro	teacher	master
la firma	signature	affirm = sign
il dorso	back	dorsal (fin)
l'osso	bone	ossify
il cervello	brain	cerebral
l'occhio	eye	ocular
il pugno	fist	pugnacious
il piede	foot	pedestrian
il rene	kidney	renal
il collo	neck	collar
il sarto	tailor	sartorial
il ritardo	delay	retard
il posto	seat, place	posterior
il pollo	chicken	pullet
la fame	hunger	famished
il furto	theft	furtive
tenere	to hold	tenacious
sperare	to hope	aspire
parere	to seem	appear
la mente	mind	mental
dimenticare	to forget	"out of mind"
sposato	married	espoused

chiamare	to call or name	clamour
sedere	to sit	sedentary
parlare	to speak	parlance
cantare	to sing	a cantor chants
dormire	to sleep	dormitory
minacciare	to threaten	menace
la mattina	morning	matins
la notte	night	nocturnal
salvare	to save	salvation
tardi	late	tardy
aperto	open	aperture
corto	short	curt
portare	to carry	portable
ballare	dance	ball
saggio	wise	sage
giòvane	young	juvenile
rubare	to steal, rob	robber
gustare	to taste	gusto
pensare	to think	pensive
gettare	to throw	jettison
la mano	hand	manual
volere	to want, wish	voluntary
legare	to tie	ligament
lavare	to wash	lavatory
mandare	to send	mandate
seguente	following	sequence
sicuro	safe	secure
cadere	to fall	cadence
fedele	faithful	fidelity
freddo	cold	frigid
la coda	tail	a coda is added

BEWARE FALSE FRIENDS!

Now and again you'll run across a false friend. A word that looks a gift, only to deceive you. So **comprare** is to buy – **confrontare** is the word that means to compare!

La riva is a river<u>bank</u> – **il fiume** is a river.

Il temporale is a storm – **il tempo** means time, or weather.

Principle 12

Lo scalatore scala la montagna.   The climber climbs the mountain.

In English it's usually very easy to make the word for someone who is the person acting out the verb: you simply add '-er' or '-or' to the stem of the verb.

It's the same principle in Italian: just add **-tore** to the stem of the verb. To climb is **scalare,** so a climber is **scalatore.**

lavoratore	worker	**scrittore**	writer
visitatore	visitor	**esecutore**	performer (executor)
attore	actor	**disertore**	deserter
detonatore	detonator	**inventore**	inventor

xvi

Principle 13

This easy principle is that the sounds of vowels change quite a lot over time between languages deriving from the same roots (remember Italian and much English both derive from Latin originally).

So by just substituting a different vowel sound, the Italian word is often easily identified ...

Italian **o** can be English 'ou'.

l'incontro	encounter	**lo sconto**	discount
incoraggiare	encourage	**la trota**	trout
il monte	mount	**contare**	to count

Italian **ri–** is often English 're-'.

riflettere	to reflect	**la riforma**	reform
rilassare	to relax	**il ritorno**	return
la riunione	reunion	**il ristorante**	restaurant
riparare	to repair	**riluttante**	reluctant

Italian **i** can be English 'e', and Italian **e** can be English 'i'.

l'impero	empire	**incantare**	to enchant
imbarcarsi	to embark	**distruggere**	to destroy
dimostrare	demonstrate		

Italian **o** can be English 'u'.

il polso	pulse	**corrente**	current
corto	short (curt)	**soffrire**	suffer
incrostare	encrust	**soprannaturale**	supernatural
la soprastruttura	superstructure		

As you can see, **sopra** means above, and equates directly to 'super-' in English. Similarly, **sotto** means under or below, and equates to 'sub-'. That gives you lots of words!

sottocutaneo	subcutaneous	**sopravvivere**	to survive
sottomano	underhand	**sottolineare**	to underline
sottoscritto	undersigned	**soprattassa**	super-tax
sottomarino	submarine	**sotterfugio**	subterfuge
sotterraneo	subterranean	**sottolineare**	to underline

sottosopra means upside-down or topsy-turvy!

However, all this is a bit of a digression. The principle we should look at next is contained in the words:

Principle 14

finire = to finish   **finito** = finished

Can you figure it out? It's that you can usually form the past participle (for use in the past tense) in Italian by removing the infinitive ending and adding **-ito** or **-ato.**

So if **cantare** = to sing   **cantato** = sung
and **partire** = to leave   **partito** = left (departed)
andare = to go   **andato** = gone

Principle 15

L'oggetto è osceno.   The object is obscene.

The simple word **oggetto** actually illustrates three principles! Remember **tt** = 'ct', and **g** = 'j'? The one we haven't met before is that where in English we often encounter 'obj-' and 'obs-', as well as 'abj-' and 'abs-', in Italian the 'b' is dropped. So ...

l'oscurità	obscurity	**l'oggettività**	objectivity
l'ostacolo	obstacle	**assurdo**	absurd
l'astinenza	abstinence	**ostinato**	obstinate

Principle 16

Il prezzo è troppo caro.   The price is too dear.

Very often a **z** or **zz** in Italian will relate to '-ce' in English. So it's

la razza	race	**la forza**	force
il pezzo	piece	**la scienza**	science
lo spazio	space	**la piazza**	square (place)

For those readers looking for a connection between dear and **caro,** there isn't an easy one. However there is a linguistic link, but it's to the French word for expensive – 'cher'.

You may have already noticed that a **c** in Italian often replaces 'ch' in English or French. So **cantare** is to sing (chant), **toccare** is to touch, and **la camera** is a room, but linked to chamber. You'll now see why ...

il campione	champion	**il capitolo**	chapter
la carità	charity	**la carta**	map (chart)
castigare	to chastise		

If that was all a bit roundabout, here's a delightfully simple principle.

Principle 17

Il filosofo è filantropico.   The philosopher is philanthropic.

Italian pronunciation follows pretty standard rules, and 'ph' does not exist. So ...

la foto	photo	**la fobia**	phobia
fotogenico	photogenic	**la fase**	phase
		la frase	sentence (phrase)

But a doctor (physician) is **il medico!**

Principle 18

Many adjectives (descriptive words) are formed in Italian from the same stem as the corresponding English words. It's just the endings that are slightly different.

So where English ends an adjective in '-ous', Italian changes the ending to **-oso** to agree with masculine nouns, and **-osa** for feminine.

amoroso	amorous	**generoso**	generous
calloso	callous	**prezioso**	precious
curioso	curious	**numeroso**	numerous
		glorioso	glorious

Where English ends in '-ic', Italian ends in **-ico** or **-ica**.

eclettico	eclectic	**cosmico**	cosmic
accademico	academic	**meccanico**	mechanic
statico	static	**elettrico**	electric
pubblico	public	**tragico**	tragic

And where English ends in '-al', Italian ends in **-ale**.

asessuale	asexual	**letterale**	literal
illegale	illegal	**bronchiale**	bronchial
rurale	rural	**plurale**	plural

Talking of plurals leads us to the next principle – how to form a plural in Italian.

Principle 19

Il libro vecchio.	The old book.	—	**I libri vecchi.**	The old books.
La tavola piccola.	The small table.	—	**Le tavole piccole.**	The small tables.

You may have noticed that nearly all Italian words end in a vowel, in fact they normally end in **a e i** or **o**. That's why spoken Italian has such an attractive sound.

So plurals of Italian words cannot simply end in 's' like most English ones do. They follow different rules depending on the ending of the original noun.

Nouns ending in **o** or **e** form plurals by changing the **o** or **e** to an **i**.

libro	—	**libri**	**anno**	—	**anni**
voce	—	**voci**	**cameriere**	—	**camerieri**

Nouns ending in **a** change the **a** to an **e**.

donna	—	**donne**	**scuola**	—	**scuole**

When the noun ends in **-ca** or **-co,** the plural is formed in the same way, except that in order to maintain the hard '**c**' sound before the plural ending of -e or -i, an **h** is added.

So it's   **banco — banchi**   (pronounced ban-kee)
                     barca — barche   (pronounced bar-kay)

Adjectives still have to agree in the plural. So if the plural ending of the noun is **-i,** the adjective ending is **-i,** and if it is **-e,** then the adjective ends in **-e.**

La sala bianca.	The white hall. —	**Le sale bianche.**	The white halls.
Il tappeto rosso.	The red carpet. —	**I tappeti rossi.**	The red carpets.
Un melone dolce.	A sweet melon. —	**I meloni dolci.**	Sweet melons.

Principle 20
_____

     Lavora sempre lentamente.   He always works slowly.

The principle here is that whereas in English we add -ly to make up lots of adverbs, in Italian you take the feminine ending of the descriptive word and add **-mente.**

So a slow man is **un uomo lento.** A slow woman is **una donna lenta.**
And slowl<u>y</u> is **lentamente.**

This principle gives you lots of words ...

rapidamente	rapidly	**dolcemente**	sweetly
continuamente	continually	**frequentemente**	frequently
onestamente	honestly	**stupidamente**	stupidly

We're now coming to the end of what I hope you'll agree is a new approach to vocabulary. Treating it as a game, applying a detective's mind to new words, always asking yourself, 'I wonder if ...'.

By now if you saw the word **amichevole** in a sentence, I hope you'd use both the context as a clue, and your curiosity.

You might even come to equate '**-vole**' with the English '-full' and see that **amichevole** means friendly (literally, full of friendship).

Once you'd worked that out, and saw that **colpevole** meant guilty, you'd make the connection with culpable, or full of blame.

Again, you might be reading a sentence, and see **cascata.** The deduction that this means cascade could lead to the thought that 'd' and 't' may be used in a similar way, so that when you meet the word **malattia** you could see the link with malady, and guess that malattia means illness.

Moreover, when you see that **la pinna** means fin, it's not so hard to see how **il pesce** has transformed itself into fish in English.

As you develop your linguistic linking ability, you'll start to make predictions, some easy, some more sophisticated. So when you see that **gruppo** is group, you could predict that **zuppa** is soup.

Looking for linguistic links is just one way in which you can make learning a language fun – but it's an excellent way!

THE GRAMMAR GAME
SOMETIMES THINGS JUST LOOK COMPLICATED!

E	G	P	L
J	A	K	B
Q	T	S	R
I	W	Z	Y

Look at the square of letters above. Can you make out a word in there? At first it looks like a jumble of letters – but if we were to tell you to look at the diagonal line starting at the top left and running to the bottom right, you would soon see a word emerge.

When you start the Accelerated Learning Italian Course proper you are likely to notice two things: learning the vocabulary is probably <u>easier</u> than you expected, while the make-up of verbs involves tenses, as in English, and <u>appears</u> somewhat less easy than you may have expected.

Actually this is lucky because the first priority is to make yourself understood. <u>Then</u>, after you begin to have confidence and fluency with the language, you can perfect the grammar.

So feel free to ignore this section completely at this stage, because you will absorb all the grammar rules naturally as you listen to the tapes and follow the radio play in your book.

If you have read the book ACCELERATED LEARNING, you may also recall that one of the elements that makes learning much easier is to have an overview of the subject before you start. Then you can see how things fit together, just as a jigsaw puzzle is much easier to do if you have the picture on the box lid in front of you.

So if you feel you'd like an overview of Italian grammar, by all means read and respond to the questions below. But <u>don't</u> try to learn any of the rules – just get the 'big picture'.

As we have said many times, you remember best those things you are involved in, things you work out for yourself. So let's turn this into a **Grammar Game.** We will give you several words of Italian, and then ask you a question. Your task is to answer this question and to figure out the principle involved. If you do, you will remember the make-up of Italian verbs with little effort.

GAME 1.

> If to love is **amare**
> and I love is **amo**
> and to sing is **cantare**
> what is I sing?

ANSWER: **canto**

Principle   Italians do not use pronouns like I, you, he, she, we or they very often. They indicate who is loving or singing by changing the end of the verb (as was the case in Latin).

Why not take the list below, cover up the last column and see how you get on?

vendere	=	to sell	so	I sell	=	**vendo**
dividere	=	to divide		I divide	=	**divido**
fumare	=	to smoke		I smoke	=	**fumo**
partire	=	to leave		I leave	=	**parto**
finire	=	to finish		I finish	=	**finisco**

We can conclude therefore that <u>normally</u> to say I do something, we just add an **o** to the stem of the verb. Of course there are always exceptions, but you'll learn those automatically as you progress.

GAME 2.

| **pagare** | = | to pay | **vendere** | = | to sell | **partire** | = | to leave |
| **paga** | = | he pays | **vende** | = | he sells | **parte** | = | he leaves |

So if

amare	=	to love	**dividere**	=	to divide	**vivere**	=	to live
what is	....	he loves?	What is	....	he divides?	What is	....	he lives
ANSWER	**ama**		ANSWER	....	**divide**		ANSWER	**vive**

Principle

You'll have worked out that to say he (or she, or it) does something merely requires that you add an **a** or and **e** to the stem of the verb.

REMINDER: Don't deliberately try to learn this. You will absorb it all from the text later, but a run-through of these principles now will make that absorption even easier.

GAME 3.

Canto, canti, cantiamo tutti, per gelati!

This is a <u>very</u> loose version of: "I scream, you scream, we all scream, for ice cream", except that we have translated it as sing instead of scream.

The purpose is to let you figure out the way to say 'you sing' and 'we sing'. Got it? So if we tell you that 'they sing' is **cantano,** and 'you (plural) sing' is **cantate,** you've now got the whole Italian present tense figured out.

Here's a confirmation:

	cantare	vendere	partire
I	canto	vendo	parto
you	canti	vendi	parti
he/she	canta	vende	parte
we	cantiamo	vendiamo	partiamo
you (pl)	cantate	vendete	partite
they	cantano	vendono	partono

Again, you don't have to learn this. You'll pick it up later from the course proper, but it's a useful overview to help you see the pattern.; Note the difference between verbs ending in -are, -ere or -ire.

GAME 4.

Strictly speaking, this is more of a bargain than a game! Because we're going to show you how to make a past tense in Italian – all in 5 minutes! And when you've finished, you've been introduced to a good proportion of the grammar rules you'll need.

Here's the sequence. The Italian for 'to have' is **avere.** It is an irregular verb as the following shows:

I have	=	ho
you have	=	hai
he has	=	ha
we have	=	abbiamo
you (pl) have	=	avete
they have	=	hanno

To say 'I have sung' is **ho cantato.** To say 'you have sung' is **hai cantato.** Can you guess what 'he has sung' is?

If you said **ha cantato** then give yourself a pat on the back! The ending **-ato** is directly equivalent to the '-ed' in English, and the verb 'to have' (avere) is used exactly as in English.

So to put **pagare** (to pay) into the past tense, you simply say:

ho pagato	I have paid
hai pagato	you have paid
ha pagato	he has paid
abbiamo pagato	we have paid
avete pagato	you (pl) have paid
hanno pagato	they have paid

The same principle holds good , with a slight change, for verbs ending in **-ere** or **-ire,** like **vendere** or **finire.** In these cases the English '-ed' becomes either **-uto** or **-ito.**

ho venduto	**ho finito**
hai venduto	**hai finito**
ha venduto	**ha finito**
abbiamo venduto	**abbiamo finito**
avete venduto	**avete finito**
hanno venduto	**hanno finito**

So in a 10-minute overview, you've seen how to use the present tense and a past tense! Have a check to see how easily you've absorbed it.

What is?		
	I sell	**vendo**
	we sing	**cantiamo**
	he has finished	**ha finito**
	they have paid	**hanno pagato**

So now you're almost ready to start the course proper. Have fun!

WHAT TO DO WHEN THERE IS NO LINGUISTIC ASSOCIATION!

Despite the fact that the **Name Game** section of the Accelerated Learning Course will make a significant proportion of Italian words understandable to you from the beginning, there will clearly still be many words that simply do not have an English association. And we know that if there are no associations, it takes a lot more effort to create a lasting memory, ie. to learn.

Now the whole point of the unique techniques built into Accelerated Learning is to maximise the chance of strong associations being formed quickly and easily in your mind. Hence the novel memory maps to create visual associations and thus memory. Hence the unique use of Baroque music to create sound and emotional associations and thus memory. Hence the emphasis on gesturing and acting out the scenes to create physical associations. Hence the use of games to involve you. Indeed involvement is the most powerful learning tool of all.

Despite this unique combination of memory aids, there will realistically still be words that are not easy to lock into your long term memory store.

When this happens, take a tip from a professional 'memory man'. Create your own 'mnemonic dictionary'. (Mnemonic merely means a memory aid and is described in full in the ACCELERATED LEARNING book.)

Creating a mnemonic dictionary is simple, but it does require a little imagination. However, it is fun, and we guarantee it works. Here's what to do.

Take the new Italian word and find a strong visual image to associate with it. The image should deliberately be as odd, comic or bizarre (even vulgar!) as possible. If there is a rhyming association, so much the better.

Let's take a look at a few examples of what you might do, taken from the lessons you are about to start on.

MNEMONIC DICTIONARY

capelli = hair

The prime principle of Accelerated Learning is the power of association – operating a memory link between the new and the already familiar.

A mnemonic for this link would be to imagine a girl called Ellie with a 'cap' of hair, giving you cap on Ellie, or **capelli.**

comodo = comfortable

Imagine sitting 'comfortably' on a commode! Which leads simply to **comodo.** We did say that vulgar associations are often memorable!

stanco = tired

Think what it feels like to be 'oh, so stinking tired' after a long day shopping.

piacevole = pleasant

Here's a very visual link. Imagine a sweet little vole sitting under an arch eating a pea, looking very pleased with himself, giving you pea – arch – vole = **piacevole.**

It is not our intention to give lots of examples here because a thousand different people will have a thousand different ways of making up their own mnemonic dictionaries.

The point is to have fun, and invest a bit of yourself in the ideas.

One last example. The Italian for 'hot' and 'cold' can be confusing to the English learner, as they seem to be the wrong way round!

caldo	=	hot	(you'd think it should be 'cold')
freddo	=	cold	

So why not make a mnemonic couplet: Freddy's freezing cold, but Callie's scalding hot.

Over to you!

TIPS FOR RAPID LEARNING

1. An excellent way to acquire vocabulary is to write words you especially want to remember on post cards with the translations on the back. You can use otherwise wasted time to 'revise' these words.

    Just 10 words a day learned gives you over 3,000 words in a year - the basis of an entire language.

2. Make sure you act out the dialogues as expressively as possible - the more you physically act out the language the better you'll learn it.

3. Make up post-it notes of objects you see around the house in Italian. Every time you see the object it's a reminder of the word, e.g. door, kitchen, bathroom. Use your dictionary or the glossary.

4. Look back over the Radio Play and pick out 10 words to represent visually. The quality of the drawing doesn't matter - it's the action of pictorialising the word that creates memory for the vocabulary.

5. Go back over the Radio Play and select the 10 Italian words you think will be the most useful - then rank them in order of importance.

6. Underline or highlight the particular words and phrases you want to fix in your memory. And remember that <u>writing</u> down words and sentences while you say them aloud combines visual, auditory and physical memory. Such words are well remembered.

7. When you've finished each Act, close your eyes and visualise the scenes - then describe <u>out loud</u> in your new language what happened. Use your own words, don't try to repeat phrases 'parrot fashion'. It's vital you take every opportunity to talk <u>out loud</u> in your new language.

IMPORTANT  **You should do these seven additional exercises for each and every Act.**

Act 1   **Atto 1**

<table>
<tr><td>Scene 1</td><td>**Scena 1**</td></tr>
<tr><td>Peter arrives in Rome.</td><td>**Peter arriva a Roma.**</td></tr>
</table>

Peter looks at the house.	**Peter guarda la casa.**
It is large and beautiful,	**È grande e bella,**
with two ancient columns	**con due colonne antiche**
and a little fountain in front.	**e una piccola fontana davanti.**
He goes up to the front door,	**S'avvicina alla porta,**
rings the bell and waits.	**suona il campanello, e aspetta.**
An old lady opens the door.	**Una signora anziana apre la porta.**

"Good evening.	**"Buona sera.**
What is it you want?"	**Che cosa desidera?"**
asks the lady.	**domanda la signora.**
"Good evening," says Peter.	**"Buona sera, signora," dice Peter.**
"Is this Mr. Bruni's house?"	**"È questa la casa del Signor Bruni?"**
"Yes, it is," replies the lady.	**"Sì, certo," risponde la signora.**
"I'm looking for Mr. Bruni,"	**"Cerco il Signor Bruni,"**
"You are Mr. ...?"	**"Lei è il Signor ...?"**
"I am Mr. West." replies Peter.	**"Sono il Signor West," risponde Peter.**
"Ah yes, come in Mr. West.	**"Ah, sì, entri Signor West.**
Please make yourself at home."	**Prego, si accomodi."**

Peter goes into the house,	**Peter entra in casa,**
and waits in a large white hall.	**e aspetta in una grande sala bianca.**

Scene 2	**Scena 2**
A young woman	**Una donna giovane**
comes down the stairs.	**scende le scale.**
She is tall and beautiful.	**È alta e bella.**
She has blue eyes	**Ha gli occhi azzurri**
and black hair.	**e i capelli neri.**
She goes up to Peter	**S'avvicina a Peter**
and says with a smile:	**e dice con un sorriso:**

"Good evening. Can I help you?"	**"Buona sera, signore. Desidera?"**
"Good evening.	**"Buona sera, signorina.**
My name is Peter West.	**Il mio nome è Peter West.**
I've come from England.	**Vengo dall'Inghilterra.**
I have a package for Mr. Bruni."	**Ho un pacchetto per il Signor Bruni."**
"Have you any identification?"	**"Ha un documento d'identità?"**
asks the young woman.	**domanda la giovane donna.**
"It's important."	**"È importante."**
"Yes, of course,	**"Sì, certo,**
here's my passport."	**ecco il mio passaporto."**

The young woman takes the passport.	La giovane prende il passaporto.
"So, your name is Peter West. You're English..."	"Dunque, si chiama Peter West. Lei è inglese ..."
"Yes," he says, "I'm English."	"Sì," dice lui, "Sono inglese."
Then he smiles and goes on:	Poi sorride e continua:
"I'm a student, I'm 23 years old, and I live in London."	"Sono studente, ho ventitre anni, e abito a Londra."
"Fine," she says.	"Bene," dice lei.
"I'm pleased to see you. I am Bella Bruni. I'm Mr. Bruni's niece. The package is for my uncle. Welcome to Rome, Mr. West."	"Molto piacere. Io sono Bella Bruni. Sono la nipote del Signor Bruni. Il pacchetto è per mio zio. Benvenuto a Roma, Signor West."
"Thank you, here's the package. Is that all?"	"Grazie, ecco il pacchetto. È tutto?"
"No," she replies.	"No," risponde lei.
"My uncle is out of town. He's coming back tomorrow. There's a room reserved for you at the Three Palms Hotel, in via Milano. It's a small hotel, but it's comfortable and quiet. Come back tomorrow morning at ten."	"Mio zio è fuori città. Ritorna domani. C'è una camera riservata per Lei all'Hotel Tre Palme, in via Milano. È un albergo piccolo, ma è comodo e tranquillo. "Ritorni domani mattina alle dieci."
"Thank you," says Peter.	"Grazie," dice Peter.
"Is the hotel far?"	È lontano l'albergo?"
"It's 200 metres away. You take the first street on the right, cross the square, and via Milano is there on the left."	"È a duecento metri. Lei prende la prima strada a destra, attraversa la piazza, e via Milano è lì a sinistra."
"Many thanks," says Peter.	"Mille grazie," dice Peter.
"Goodbye."	"Arrivederci."
"Goodbye," replies Bella.	"Arrivederci," risponde Bella.
"See you tomorrow."	"A domani."

È questa la casa del signor Bruni?

Scene 3	**Scena 3**
Peter arrives	**Peter arriva**
at the Three Palms Hotel.	**all'Hotel Tre Palme.**
"Good evening,"	**"Buona sera,"**
says Signora Alberti	**dice la Signora Alberti,**
the owner.	**la proprietaria.**
"Can I help you?"	**"Desidera?"**
"Good evening," replies Peter.	**"Buona sera," risponde Peter.**
"You have a room reserved	**"Ha una camera riservata**
in my name.	**a mio nome.**
My name is Peter West.	**Mi chiamo Peter West.**
I've come from England."	**Vengo dall'Inghilterra."**
"Mr. West ... Ah, yes,"	**"Signor West ... Ah, sì,"**
says Signora Alberti,	**dice la Signora Alberti,**
"One single room with bath.	**"Una camera singola, con bagno.**
Will you give me your passport,	**Mi dà il passaporto,**
please?"	**per favore?"**
"Yes, here it is," says Peter.	**"Sì, eccolo," dice Peter.**
"Thank you, here is the key,	**"Grazie, ecco la chiave,**
Mr. West.	**Signor West.**
Room number seven.	**Camera numero sette.**
On the first floor."	**Al primo piano."**
"Thank you," says Peter.	**"Grazie," dice Peter.**
"Good night, Mr. West,"	**"Buona notte, Signor West,"**
says Signora Alberti.	**dice la Signora Alberti.**
"Good night," says Peter,	**"Buona notte, signora," dice Peter**
and goes upstairs.	**e sale le scale.**
He finds room number seven.	**Trova la camera numero sette.**
Opens the door.	**Apre la porta.**
Goes in.	**Entra.**
The room is pleasant and quiet.	**La camera è piacevole e tranquilla.**
The bed is comfortable.	**Il letto è comodo.**
Peter is tired but happy.	**Peter è stanco, ma felice.**
"What a great adventure,"	**"Che bella avventura,"**
he thinks,	**pensa,**
"My first journey to Rome!"	**"Il mio primo viaggio a Roma!"**

Trova la camera numero sette.

3

POSITIVE THOUGHTS TO LEARN A LANGUAGE

We have chosen these sentences for you to learn.
Learn each Positive Thought (they are sometimes called affirmations)
and repeat them over and over to yourself. You are not only learning
your new language - you are helping to program your mind to become
a confident language learner!

1	Italian is interesting to learn	**E'interessante imparare l'italiano**
2	I am delighted at how much I understand	**Sono molto contento di quanto io capisca**
3	I can speak more and more	**Posso parlare sempre di piu'**
4	I enjoy listening to the cassettes	**Mi piace ascoltare le cassette**
5	I am confident when I speak Italian	**Sono sicuro di me stesso quando parlo l'italiano**
6	I notice satisfying progress every week	**Noto un soddisfacente progresso ogni settimana**
7	Learning is easy	**Imparare e'facile**
8	I like to read Italian	**Mi piace leggere l'italiano**
9	I am proud that I am becoming a good Italian speaker	**Sono orgoglioso del fatto che mi viene sempre piu' facile parlare l'italiano**
10	I tell myself I can, and I can	**Dico a me stesso che posso, e posso**
11	I have faith in myself and my skills	**Ho fiducia in me stesso e nelle mie abilita'**
12	I have an ever-increasing vocabulary	**Il mio vocabolario aumenta sempre di piu'**
13	I enjoy remembering Italian	**Mi piace ricordare l'italiano**
14	I remember Italian quickly	**Ricordo l'italiano alla svelta**

ATTO 1 (i)

Peter guarda la casa.

È grande e bella con due colonne antiche

e una piccola fontana davanti.

S'avvicina alla porta,

suona il campanello, e aspetta.

Buona sera, che cosa desidera?

Una signora anziana apre la porta.

È questa la casa del Signor Bruni?

Peter entra in casa.

Una donna giovane scende le scale.

Ha gli occhi azzurri e i capelli neri.

Buona sera, signore. Desidera?

Il mio nome è Peter West. Vengo dall'Inghilterra.

S'avvicina a Peter e dice con un sorriso:

Ho un pacchetto per il Signor Bruni.

PASSAPORTO
Peter West
Studente
Ventitre Anni
Londra.

Sì, certo, ecco il mio passaporto.

C'è una camera riservata per Lei all'Hotel Tre Palme.

Il pacchetto è per mio zio.

È un albergo piccolo,

ma è comodo
e tranquillo.

È lontano l'albergo?

VIA
MILANO

Via Milano è lì a sinistra.

A domani.

Peter arriva all'Hotel Tre Palme.

Ha una camera
riservata
a mio nome.

Una camera
singola, con
bagno.

RICEVIMENTO

Grazie, ecco la chiave,
Signor West.

ATTO 1 (iv)

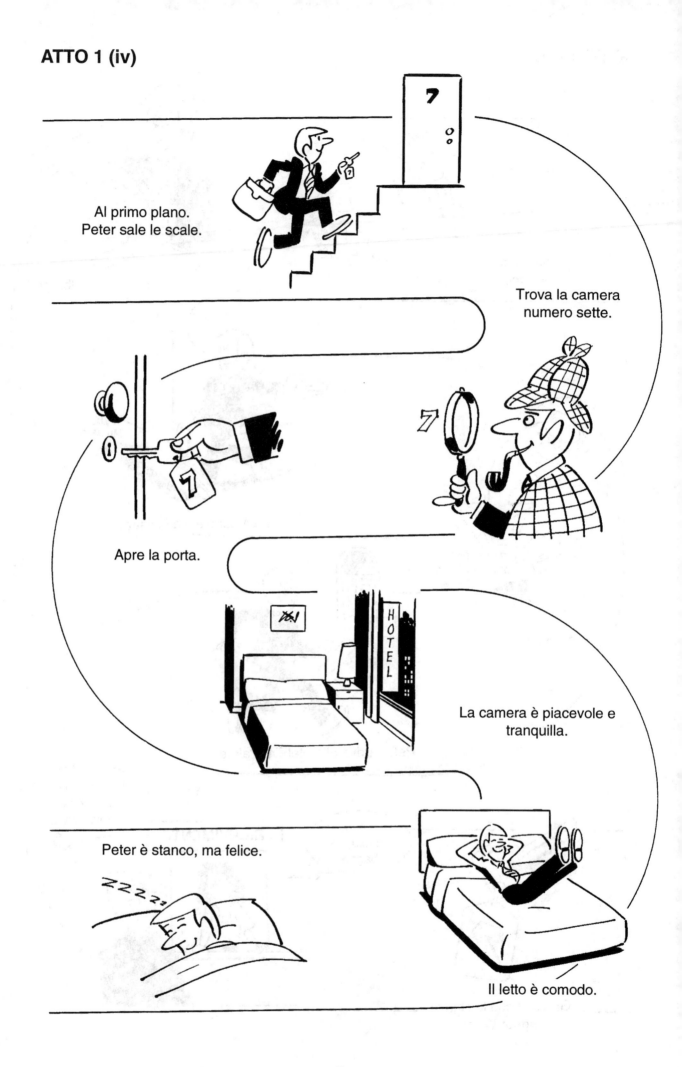

Al primo plano.
Peter sale le scale.

Trova la camera
numero sette.

Apre la porta.

La camera è piacevole e
tranquilla.

Peter è stanco, ma felice.

Il letto è comodo.

Intonation and Pronunciation

a) Tune in to the rhythm and flow of the Italian language, and listen carefully to the intonation patterns. See if you can spot the difference between question and answer patterns.

Repeat after the tape:

> **RIPETA:**
> 1. **È questa la casa del Signor Bruni?**
>   **Sì, questa è la casa del Signor Bruni.**
>
> 2. **Ha una camera?**
>   **Sì, ho una camera.**
>
> 3. **Lei è Peter West?**
>   **Sì, sono Peter West.**
>
> 4. **Lei è inglese?**
>   **Sì, sono inglese.**

b) In English you are familiar with the way we pronounce the letter 'o' in words like 'phone', 'don't' (at least in the South!). Now listen carefully to the way Italians pronounce the letter **o** in this sentence:

Sono Bella Bruni.

Quite different, isn't it! Now listen carefully to these sentences and repeat them:

> **RIPETA:**
> 1. **Sono Bella Bruni.**
> 2. **Abito a Roma.**
> 3. **Via Milano numero quattro.**
> 4. **Porto un pacchetto.**
> 5. **Ha un passaporto.**
> 6. **Arrivo a Roma.**

c) In Italian, the letter **c** is pronounced either 'hard' as in the English sound in 'come': **la casa; che cosa;** or **ch** as in the English sound in 'cheese', **cento, città**. This is the way it is pronounced before the letters **e** and **i**.

Try repeating these sentences:

> **RIPETA:**
> 1. **Peter guarda la casa.**
> 2. **S'avvicina alla porta.**
> 3. **Che cosa desidera?**
> 4. **Si, certo.**
> 5. **Ecco il pacchetto.**
> 6. **Mio zio è fuori città.**

S'avvicina alla porta.

d) RHYMES AND PROVERBS

Finally here are some Italian rhymes and proverbs to practise these sounds:

> 1. **Chi va piano, va sano e va lontano.**
>   (Better safe than sorry.)*Lit: He who goes slowly, goes healthily and goes a long way.
>
> 2. **Chi cerca, trova.**
>   (He who seeks shall find.)
>
> 3. **Tutto il mondo è paese.**
>   (All the world's a village.)
>
> 4. **Meglio tardi che mai.**
>   (Better late than never.)

Functional Dialogues

Now you will learn how to use the vocabulary you already know in real-life dialogue.

1.

	Peter arrives at 5 via Milano.	**Peter arriva in via Milano, numero 5.**
	An old lady opens the door.	**Una signora anziana apre la porta.**

Signora:	What is it you want?	**Che cosa desidera?**
Peter:	Good evening.	**Buona sera, signora.**
	Is this Signor Bruni's house?	**È questa la casa del Signor Bruni?**
Signora:	Yes. it is.	**Sì, certo.**
Peter:	I'm looking for Mr Bruni.	**Cerco il Signor Bruni.**
Signora:	And you are ...?	**Lei è il Signor ...?**
Peter:	I'm Mr West.	**Sono il Signor West.**
Signora:	Ah yes, come in Mr West.	**Ah sì, entri Signor West.**
	Please make yourself at home.	**Prego, si accomodi.**
Peter:	Thank you.	**Grazie, signora.**

2.

	Peter introduces himself to Bella.	**Peter si presenta a Bella.**

Bella:	Good evening, can I help you?	**Buona sera, signore, desidera?**
Peter:	Good evening.	**Buona sera, signorina.**
	My name's Peter West.	**Il mio nome è Peter West.**
	I've come from England.	**Vengo dall'Inghilterra.**
Bella:	Have you any identification?	**Ha un documento d'identità?**
Peter:	Here's my passport. Look.	**Ecco il mio passaporto. Guardi.**
Bella:	So, your name's Peter West.	**Dunque, si chiama Peter West.**
	You are English.	**Lei è inglese.**
Peter:	Yes, I'm twenty-three years old.	**Sì, ho ventitre anni.**
	I'm a student,	**Sono studente,**
	and I live in London.	**e abito a Londra.**
Bella:	Fine, I'm pleased to see you.	**Bene. Molto piacere.**
	Welcome to Rome.	**Benvenuto a Roma.**
Peter:	Thank you.	**Grazie, signorina.**

Ecco il mio passaporto.

3. Peter is phoning a girl-friend in London. He's talking about Bella.

Peter telefona a un'amica a Londra. Parla di Bella.

Girlfriend

Amica

Amica:	Does she live in Rome?	**Abita a Roma?**
Peter:	Yes, she lives in a big house.	**Sì, abita in una grande casa.**
Amica:	Beautiful?	**È bella?**
Peter:	The house?	**La casa.**
Amica:	No, Bella.	**No, Bella.**
Peter:	Oh! Yes, she's got blue eyes and black hair.	**Ah! Sì! Ha gli occhi azzurri e i capelli neri.**
Amica:	Is she young?	**È giovane?**
Peter:	Yes, she's twenty four.	**Sì, ha ventiquattro anni.**

4. Bella is reserving a room for Peter at the Three Palms Hotel.

Bella riserva una camera per Peter all'Hotel Tre Palme.

Signora Alberti = S.A.:

Bella:	Good morning.	**Buongiorno, signora.**
S.A.:	Good morning. Can I help you?	**Buongiorno, signorina, desidera?**
Bella:	Have you a room, please?	**Ha una camera, per favore?**
S.A.:	For one night?	**Per una notte?**
Bella:	Yes.	**Sì, signore.**
S.A.:	Single or double?	**Singola o doppia?**
Bella:	Single, please.	**Singola, per favore.**
S.A.:	Is it for you?	**È per lei?**
Bella:	No it's for Mr West. He's arriving this evening from England.	**No, è per il Signor West. Arriva questa sera dall'Inghilterra.**
S.A.:	There's room number seven on the first floor. It's a single room. It's nice and quiet.	**C'è la camera numero sette al primo piano. È una camera singola. È piacevole e tranquilla.**
Bella:	Good. Thank you. Goodbye.	**Bene. Grazie. Arrivederci.**
S.A.:	Goodbye.	**Arrivederci, signorina.**

Al primo piano.

5. Peter arrives at the hotel. **Peter arriva all'albergo.**

S.A.:	Good evening. Can I help you?	**Buona sera, signore. Desidera?**
Peter:	Good evening.	**Buona sera, signora.**
	There's a room reserved for Mr West.	**Ha una camera riservata per il Signor West.**
S.A.:	Are you Mr West?	**Si. Lei è il Signor West?**
Peter:	Yes.	**Sì, signora.**
S.A.:	Room number seven on the first floor. Here's the key.	**Camera numero sette al primo piano. Ecco la chiave.**
Peter:	Thank you. Goodnight.	**Grazie, signora. Buona notte.**
S.A.:	Goodnight.	**Buona notte, signore.**

Peter arriva all'Hotel Tre Palme.

Personalised Dialogues

1. You are visiting Signora Visentini for the first time. An old lady has answered the door-bell.

Signora: **Desidera?**
Lei: Say Good evening and ask if this is Signor Visentini's house.
Signora: **Si, è questa. Che cosa desidera?**
Lei: Say you're looking for Signor Visentini.
Signora: **Lei è ...?**
Lei: Say your name.
Signora: **Ah, si. Entri. Prego, si accomodi.**
Lei: Say Thank You.

2. You are introducing yourself to Signora Visentini, who is expecting you but who has never seen you before.

Signora V: **Lei si chiama ...?**
Lei: Say your name.
Signora V: **Viene da Londra?**
Lei: Say which town you have come from.
Signora V: **Ha un documento d'identità?**
Lei: Show your passport and point out your name and nationality.
Signora V: **È studente?**
Lei: Tell her your profession and add your age.
Signora V: **Bene. Molto piacere. Benvenuto a Roma.**
Lei: Say Thank You.

3. You are talking to a friend about Bella.

Amica: **È inglese?**
Lei: Say No, she's Italian.
Amica: **Abita a Londra?**
Lei: Say No, she lives in Rome.
Amica: **È bella?**
Lei: Say Yes, and describe the colour of her eyes and hair.
Amica: **È giovane?**
Lei: Say how old she is.

4. Reserving a room at a hotel.
   (**Proprietaria**/Proprietor)

Proprietaria: Buongiorno. Desidera?
Lei: Say Hello and ask if she has a room.
Proprietaria: Una camera singola o doppia?
Lei: Say Single, please.
Proprietaria: È per lei?
Lei: Say Yes and give your name.
Proprietaria: Bene. C'è la camera numero cinque.
Lei: Say Thank you and Goodbye.

5. Checking in at the Hotel Tre Palme.

Mi chiamo Peter West.

Proprietaria: Buona sera. Che cosa desidera?
Lei: Say Good evening and that there's a room reserved for you.
Proprietaria: Si chiama ...?
Lei: Say your name.
Proprietaria: Ah, sì. C'è la camera numero cinque.
Lei: Ask if it is a quiet room.
Proprietaria: Sì. Ecco la chiave.
Lei: Say Thank you and Goodnight.

Grammar

You will be surprised how many of the rules of Italian grammar you have already absorbed without realising it. The following points merely bring specific rules to your conscious attention. We have put some of them into rhyme or jingle, as it's easier to remember that way. Remember, too, that these grammar notes are selective – if you want to know more, refer to a full Italian grammar.

1. SAYING 'the': **il, la** or **l'**

RULE: ''In Italian
You will find,
Gender marries
Its own kind.''

So you say: **il signore** because he is male
and: **la signora** because she is female.

At first sight it is not always obvious why some things are masculine and others are feminine: it's **il pacchetto** and **la porta**. But from these two examples you will have picked up a useful clue: in Italian, most nouns ending in **o** are masculine, and most nouns ending in **a** are feminine:

il passaporto	**la casa**
il letto	**la piazza**

Some nouns ending in **-e** are masculine, some are feminine:

il signore	**la nipote**
il nome	**la chiave**

'The' is **l'** with all nouns beginning with a vowel, or vowel sound, whether masculine or feminine:

Masculine	Feminine
l'albergo	**l'Inghilterra**
l'hotel	**l'avventura**

In the plural: **il** becomes **i**:   **i capelli**
                 la becomes **le**:   **le scale**
and   **l'** becomes **gli**:   **gli occhi**
                 or **le**:   **le avventure**

2. SAYING 'a' or 'an': **un** or **una**

You have seen **il** is the masculine form of 'the' and **la** is the feminine form. So how do you say a (or 'an') in Italian?

RULE: ''**Un** goes with **il** –
they're masculine, you see,
Una goes with **la**,
more feminine to be ...''

So you say: **il signore**   and **un signore**
               il pacchetto and **un pacchetto**
               la signora   and **una signora**
               la porta   and **una porta**

3. SAYING 'he' or 'she'

In Italian the ending of the verb usually tells you who is speaking or acting, so you generally only use the words for 'he' or 'she' for the sake of emphasis or clarity.

So we have: **Un signore arriva.**
Si chiama Peter. (No word for 'he').

and: **Una signora arriva.**
Si chiama Bella.(No word for 'she').

But to distinguish between two people talking we have:

"Sì," dice lui, "sono inglese,"

and: **"Bene," dice lei, "molto piacere."**

Lei, as you've seen, is used to mean either 'she' or 'you', depending on the context. When it means 'you' it is sometimes written with a capital **L**: **Lei**, as in this chapter only, for the sake of clarity.

So for emphasis, we have:

Lei è il Signor ...?
Lei è inglese.

Otherwise, you simply say:

È il Signor West.
È inglese.

Similarly, in the case of objects, there is no need to use a word for 'it':

La casa è grande.
È grande. (No word for 'it')

RULE: ''He, she and it
are a piece of cake:
only use them
for clarity's sake!''

Signore, Signora, Signorina
Note that before a name Signore is shortened to Signor (Signor West). When addressing someone, it's usually, though not always, written with a capital 'S'.

4. ADJECTIVES

In Italian the ending of the adjective needs to "agree" with the noun.

In most cases adjectives with masculine nouns end in **-o**.

Those with feminine nouns end in **-a**.

So: **Peter è contento.**
but: **Bella è contenta.**

or: **il pacchetto è piccolo.**
but: **la casa è piccola.**

Adjectives ending in **-e** are the same with both masculine and feminine nouns:

Peter è felice.
Bella è felice.
Il pacchetto è grande.
La casa è grande.

RULE: "Adjectives, you can't help seeing,
with nouns and pronouns are always agreeing,
so   **o** is **o**
and **a** is **a**
and **e** is always **e**-ing."

In Italian most adjectives come after the noun, i.e. the order is usually the opposite of English:

Ha gli occhi azzurri
e i capelli neri.

In general, however, word order in Italian is much more flexible than in English.

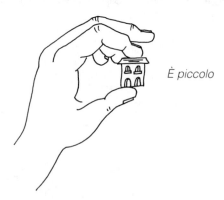

È piccolo

16

5. SAYING 'to the' or 'at the'; 'from' and 'of.'

The Italian word **a** means either 'to' or 'at'. It combines with **il** or **la** to mean 'to the' or 'at the' as follows:

a + il = al
a + la = alla
a + l' = all'

So:
La camera numero sette è al primo piano.
Peter s'avvicina alla porta.
Peter arriva all'Hotel Tre Palme.

The Italian word **da** (from) combines with **il** or **la** in the same way:

da + il = dal
da + la = dalla
da + l' = dall'

So:
Vengo dall'Inghilterra.

The word **di** (of) combines as follows:

di + il = del
di + la = della
di + l' = dell'

So:
La casa del Signor Bruni.
Sono la nipote del Signor Bruni.

6. VERBS

In Italian, just as in English, you can have a different form of a verb depending on whether you are saying 'I', 'You', 'He, 'She' etc. So in English you say 'I do', 'You do' but 'He/She does'. Italian is quite straightforward. If you look up verbs in a dictionary you will find they end in **–are, –ere** or **-ire**:

e.g.
parlare (to speak)
prendere (to take)
aprire (to open)

If the verb ends in **-are** you say:

parlo (I ...)
parla (he/she, you ...)

If the verb ends in **-ere** you say:

prendo (I ...)
prende (he/she, you ...)

If the verb ends in **-ire** you say:

apro (I ...)
apre (he/she, you ...)

17

Most verbs are regular, and follow these basic patterns, but as in English, some verbs do not follow these regular rules. Many irregular verbs are the most common and most useful!

So 'to be' is:	**sono**	(I ...)
	è	(he/she, you ...)
and 'to have' is:	**ho**	(I ...)
	ha	(he/she, you ...)

If you think back over your first lesson, you will find you already know all this:

REMEMBER:
Sono il Signor West.
Il mio nome è Peter West.
È grande e bella.
Lei è il Signor ...?

Ho un pacchetto per il Signor Bruni.
Ha gli occhi azzurri.
Ha una camera riservata a mio nome.

If you go over the above rule section again, you will find that you have already learned a good deal of the basic Italian grammar.

And while we're on verbs, a few more Italian idioms and sayings:

Chi dorme non piglia pesci.

(The early bird catches the worm.)

Lit: He who sleeps does not catch fish.

Volere è potere.

(Where there's a will there's a way.)

Lit: To want is to be able.

**Tra il dire e il fare c'è
in mezzo il mare.**

(There's many a slip 'twixt cup and lip.)

Lit: Between saying and doing,
the sea is in the middle.

Multipliers

In every language a small number of common words or phrases allow you to generate a great deal of everyday communication. You will build up a stock of useful language really quickly if you concentrate on using these.

Such words and phrases can be used again and again in a variety of situations. We'll call them multipliers. Here are a few from Act 1.

1. CHE COSA ...?

If you want to ask WHAT somebody wants, or is looking for, and so on, use this phrase at the beginning of the sentence:

Che cosa desidera?   What do you want?
Che cosa trova Peter?   What does Peter find?

2. A

You've seen that **a** can mean 'to', 'at' (or even 'in': **a mio nome** – in my name.) You can also use it when you are arranging to meet someone later on, like this:

A domani.   See you tomorrow.
A stasera.   See you this evening.
Alle dieci.   At ten o'clock.

     (= **a** + **le**)

3. C'è

C'è means 'there is':

C'è una camera riservata per Lei.
There's a room ...

C'è un pacchetto per il Signor Bruni.
There's a package ...

If you change the intonation it also means 'is there?'

C'è una camera riservata per il Signor West?
C'è un albergo in via Milano?

4. ECCO

If you are handing something over to somebody, or acknowledging the arrival of someone, you would begin with **ecco** ... here is:

Ecco il mio passaporto.
Here's my passport.

Ecco la chiave.
Here's the key.

Ecco mio zio.
Here's my uncle.

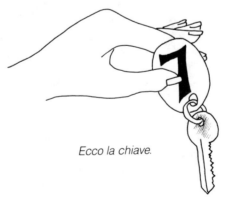

Ecco la chiave.

If you do not want to repeat the noun, simply say:

eccolo	here it is (**il passaporto**)
eccola	here it is (**la chiave**)
eccolo	here he is (**mio zio**)
eccola	here she is (**Bella**)

Games

1. WORD CARDS

Using the word cards, see if you can make up the Italian version of these English sentences. Write down each sentence which you have composed and check the correct answer at the back of the book.

1. 1   Peter looks at the house.

1. 2   The house is large and beautiful.

1. 3   An old lady opens the door.

1. 4   I'm looking for Mr. Bruni.

1. 5   Peter goes into the house.

1. 6   The young woman takes the passport.

1. 7   I live in London.

1. 8   My name is Bella Bruni.

1. 9   Here is the package.

1.10.   It's a small hotel but it's comfortable.

Now see how many more sentences you can make up on your own in five minutes, using the word cards only.

Peter guarda la casa.

20

2. Fill in the spaces with adjectives in Italian corresponding to the clues. If you get the right answers the letters in the shaded column will give another adjective to be found in the text.

Game 1

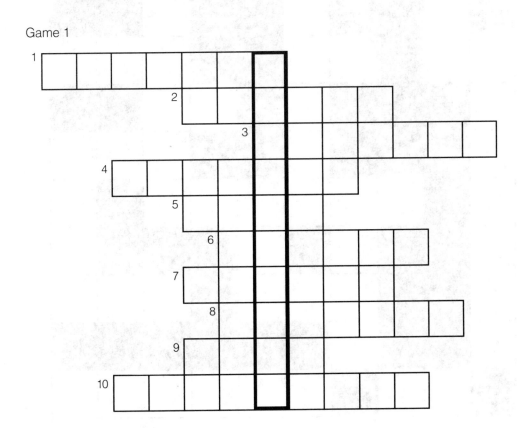

1.   **Bella ha gli occhi** _ _ _ _ _ _ _ _.

2.   **Il letto è** _ _ _ _ _ _ _.

3.   **L'albergo è** _ _ _ _ _ _ _ _.

4.   **Una camera** _ _ _ _ _ _ _ _ **con bagno**.

5.   **Bella ha i capelli** _ _ _ _.

6.   **Peter è** _ _ _ _ _ _ _ **ma felice**.

7.   **La casa è** _ _ _ _ _ _ _.

8.   **Una signora** _ _ _ _ _ _ _ _ **apre la porta**.

9.   **Bella è** _ _ _ _ _ **e bella**.

10. **La camera è** _ _ _ _ _ _ _ _ _ _ **e tranquilla**.

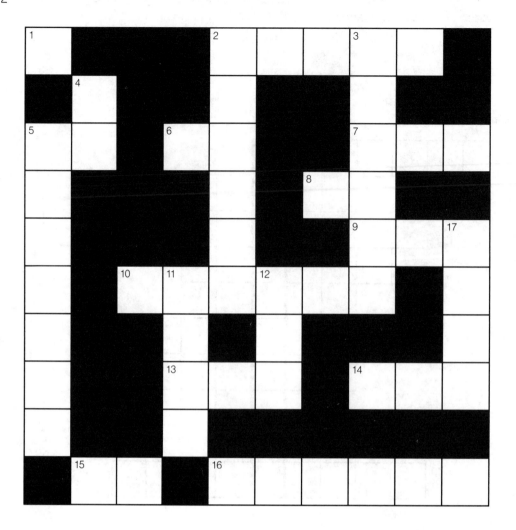

CLUES

ACROSS

1. **È grande__bella.**

2. **La camera è al primo __ __ __ __ __.**

5. **__ __ = Yes.**

6. **__ __ gli occhi azzurri.**

7. **C'è una camera riservata __ __ __ Lei.**

8. **__ __ = No.**

9. **Hotel __ __ __ Palme.**

10. **__ __ __ __ __ __ __ = Thank you.**

13. **Il __ __ __ nome è Peter West.**

14. **__ __ __ = one.**

15. **Signora Alberti, __ __ proprietaria.**

16. **È __ __ __ __ __ __ __ la casa del Signor Bruni.**

DOWN

2. **Attraversa la __ __ __ __ __ __.**

3. **__ __ __ __ __ __ __ = niece.**

4. **Prego, __ __ accomodi.**

5. **__ __ __ __ __ __ __ __ = smile.**

11. **Benvenuto a __ __ __ __ __.**

12. **Il pacchetto è per mio __ __ __.**

17. **__ __ __ __ __ il mio passaporto.**

	VERO	FALSO
1		
2		
3		
4		
5		
6		
7		
8		
9		
10		

Vero o Falso (True or False)

1. **La casa è grande e bella.**

2. **Una donna giovane apre la porta.**

3. **È la casa del Signor Bruni.**

4. **Una signora anziana scende la scala.**

5. **Bella ha gli occhi neri e i capelli azzurri.**

6. **Il Signor Bruni ritorna a Roma domani.**

7. **Peter ha una camera riservata per una notte.**

8. **L'Hotel Milano è in via Tre Palme.**

9. **L'albergo è piccolo ma comodo.**

10. **Peter sale le scale.**

What if...? **Se invece...**

What if Peter didn't go to Rome at all, but to Venice, Naples or Palermo?

What if his name wasn't even Peter, but Steve, or Jack? What if Peter were you?

What if Bella wasn't beautiful at all, but ugly, deformed, or just plain normal? With blonde hair perhaps, and brown eyes; with a big nose? Now's your chance to invent an alternative story, Act by Act, Scene by Scene. Use the alternatives provided below, or find your own in a dictionary. Above all think in Italian, feel your way through the characters and situations, listen to the sounds, and catch the smells, create your own pictures.

Your story may be realistic or it may be fantasy: the characters may inhabit the figures and landscapes of Canaletto, Botticelli or Chagall. Their music may be Vivaldi or Stravinsky, their creator Kafka, Lewis Carroll or Cervantes.

A world where pink elephants fly, or the Mafia underworld schemes ...

Use only the structures and phrases that you already know and build on them gradually as you go, adding new vocabulary and place names as you wish. Watch the story grow from Act to Act.

The Italian word for 'if' is **se** ... and **invece** means 'instead'.

1.   **Il signore inglese non si chiama Peter.**

            Invece si chiama: – Steve
                                  – Jack
                                  – your name
                                  – other

2.   **Peter non è inglese.**

            Invece è: – **americano**
                                 – **sud-americano**
                                 – **canadese**
                                 – **o ...**

3.   **La casa non è grande e bella.**

            Invece è: – **piccola**
                                 – **enorme**
                                 – **un castello**
                                 – **o ...**

4.   **Bella non è alta e bella.**

            Invece è: – **piccola**
                                 – **stupida**
                                 – **vecchia**
                                 – **o ...**

5. **Peter non arriva dall'Inghilterra.**

    Invece arriva: – **dall'America**
                               – **dall'Australia**
                               – **da Brasilia**
                               – **o ...**

6. **Peter non è studente.**

    Invece è: – **giornalista**
                           – **dottore**
                           – **mafioso**
                           – **o ...**

7. **Bella non è la nipote del Signor Bruni.**

    Invece è: – **la moglie**
                           – **la sorella**
                           – **l'amante**
                           – **o ...**

8. **Bella non abita a Roma.**

    Invece abita a: – **Venezia**
                                – **Napoli**
                                – **Palermo**
                                – **o ...**

9. **Peter non abita a Londra.**

    Invece abita a: – **New York**
                                – **Sydney**
                                – **Rio de Janeiro**
                                – **o ...**

10. **La Signora Alberti non è la proprietaria dell'albergo.**

    Invece è: – **la moglie del proprietario**
                           – **la cameriera**
                           – **una mafiosa**
                           – **o ...**

11. **Non è il primo viaggio di Peter a Roma; l'avventura non è bella, ma strana, misteriosa, stupida, o ..., o ...**

Continua ... Buona fortuna!

A REMINDER

Are you still doing the 'extra exercises' we described on page xxvii :

1. Making up post cards to revise with.

2. Acting out the Dialogues expressively.

3. Putting up post-it notes around the house or office or even in the car!

4. Representing at least 10 words visually.

5. Selecting the 10 most useful words per Act. (That gets you reviewing them all!)

6. Underlining, highlighting and <u>writing down</u> key words and sentences.

7. Describing the scenes out loud in your new language.

8. Making a Word Web for each Act.

Act 2	**Atto 2**
Scene 1	**Scena 1**
Peter wakes up in the hotel,	**Peter si sveglia all'hotel,**
he has breakfast.	**fa colazione.**
The next morning,	**La mattina dopo,**
when he wakes up,	**quando si sveglia,**
Peter looks around him.	**Peter si guarda intorno.**
The furniture in the room	**I mobili della camera**
is old and beautiful.	**sono vecchi e belli;**
On the floor	**sul pavimento**
is a dark red carpet.	**c'è un tappeto rosso scuro.**
From the street	**Dalla strada**
comes the noise of traffic.	**viene il rumore del traffico.**
Peter gets out of bed,	**Peter si alza,**
opens the window,	**apre la finestra,**
then the shutters.	**poi apre le persiane.**
The street below is wet with rain,	**Sotto, la strada è bagnata di pioggia,**
but now it has stopped raining.	**ma ora non piove più.**
Peter goes back to bed.	**Peter ritorna a letto,**
The sheets are still warm,	**Le lenzuola sono ancora calde,**
they smell of lavender.	**hanno profumo di lavanda.**
A little later	**Dopo un poco**
he gets up,	**si alza,**
opens his suitcase,	**apre la valigia,**
takes out his toothpaste	**prende il dentifricio**
and toothbrush.	**e lo spazzolino da denti.**
Then he takes his soap, his razor,	**Poi prende il sapone, il rasoio,**
his comb,	**il pettine,**
goes into the bathroom,	**va nel bagno,**
and puts on the light.	**e accende la luce.**
The bathroom is very clean.	**Il bagno è pulitissimo.**
There is a bath,	**Ci sono la vasca da bagno,**
a bidet, a shower, and a toilet.	**il bidè, la doccia, e il gabinetto.**
The towels are large	**Gli asciugamani sono grandi**
and soft.	**e morbidi.**
Peter shaves,	**Peter si fa la barba,**
then takes a shower,	**poi fa la doccia,**
and washes his hair.	**e si lava i capelli.**
He thinks about the package.	**Pensa al pacchetto.**
Why is Signor Bruni making him	**Perchè lo fa rimanere a Roma**
stay in Rome?	**il Signor Bruni ...?**
Well, after all, it really is	**Beh, dopotutto, è veramente**
a nice adventure	**una bella avventura,**
and a free holiday too!	**e poi è anche una vacanza gratuita!**
Peter gets dressed quickly	**Peter si veste in fretta,**
and goes down to breakfast.	**e scende a fare colazione.**

	Scene 2	**Scena 2**
	"Good morning, sir."	**"Buongiorno, signore,"**
	says the waitress,	**dice la cameriera,**
	with a friendly smile.	**con un sorriso simpatico.**
	She's a rather plump girl	**È una ragazza grassoccia,**
	with brown eyes	**con gli occhi marroni**
	and blonde hair.	**e i capelli biondi.**
	She's wearing a white blouse	**Porta una camicetta bianca**
	with a short black skirt.	**con una gonna nera corta.**
Peter:	Good morning.	**Buongiorno.**
	What's for breakfast?	**Che cosa c'è per colazione?**
Waitress:	There's rolls, brioches and coffee.	**Ci sono panini, brioches e caffè.**
	Peter smells the fresh rolls	**Peter sente l'odore dei panini freschi**
	and the aroma of freshly made coffee.	**e l'aroma del caffè appena fatto.**
Peter:	"What a lovely smell," he thinks.	**"Che buon odore" pensa,**
	"It's making me hungry!"	**"mi fa venir fame."**
	The waitress brings him breakfast.	**La cameriera gli porta la colazione.**
	Peter eats the warm rolls	**Peter mangia i panini caldi**
	with butter and jam.	**con burro e marmellata.**
Peter:	They're very good.	**Sono buonissimi.**
Waitress:	Do you want some more coffee?	**Vuole ancora caffè?**
Peter:	Yes, please.	**Sì, grazie.**
Waitress:	Where do you come from, sir?	**Da dove viene, signore?**
Peter:	I come from London. I'm English.	**Vengo da Londra, sono inglese.**
Waitress:	I'd love to visit London.	**Vorrei tanto visitare Londra.**
	Is it a beautiful city?	**È una bella città?**
Peter:	Yes, it's beautiful, and very big.	**Sì, è bella, e molto grande.**
Waitress:	What do you do for a living?	**Che cosa fa di professione?**
Peter:	I'm a student.	**Sono studente.**
Waitress:	Is it your first visit to Rome?	**È la prima volta che viene a Roma?**
Peter:	Yes, I arrived yesterday by plane.	**Sì, sono arrivato ieri in aereo.**
Waitress:	You speak very good Italian.	**Parla italiano molto bene.**
Peter:	If you speak slowly	**Se lei parla lentamente**
	I understand almost everything.	**capisco quasi tutto.**
	But I still have a lot to learn!	**Però ho ancora molto da imparare!**
	Scene 3	**Scena 3**
	After breakfast Peter meets	**Dopo colazione Peter incontra**
	Signora Alberti.	**la Signora Alberti.**
S.A.:	Good morning, Mr. West,	**Buongiorno Signor West,**
	did you sleep well?	**ha dormito bene?**
Peter:	Very well, thank you.	**Benissimo, grazie.**
	The bed is very comfortable.	**Il letto è molto comodo.**
S.A.:	I'm so glad.	**Sono contenta.**
	Oh look, the sun's out now.	**Guardi, ora c'è il sole.**
	It's a beautiful Spring day.	**È una bella giornata di primavera.**
	But last month	**Ma il mese scorso**
	the weather was awful.	**ha fatto brutto tempo.**
	It was very cold.	**Ha fatto molto freddo.**
	Later Peter leaves the hotel	**Più tardi Peter esce dall'albergo**
	and goes for his appointment	**e va all'appuntamento**
	with Bella.	**con Bella.**

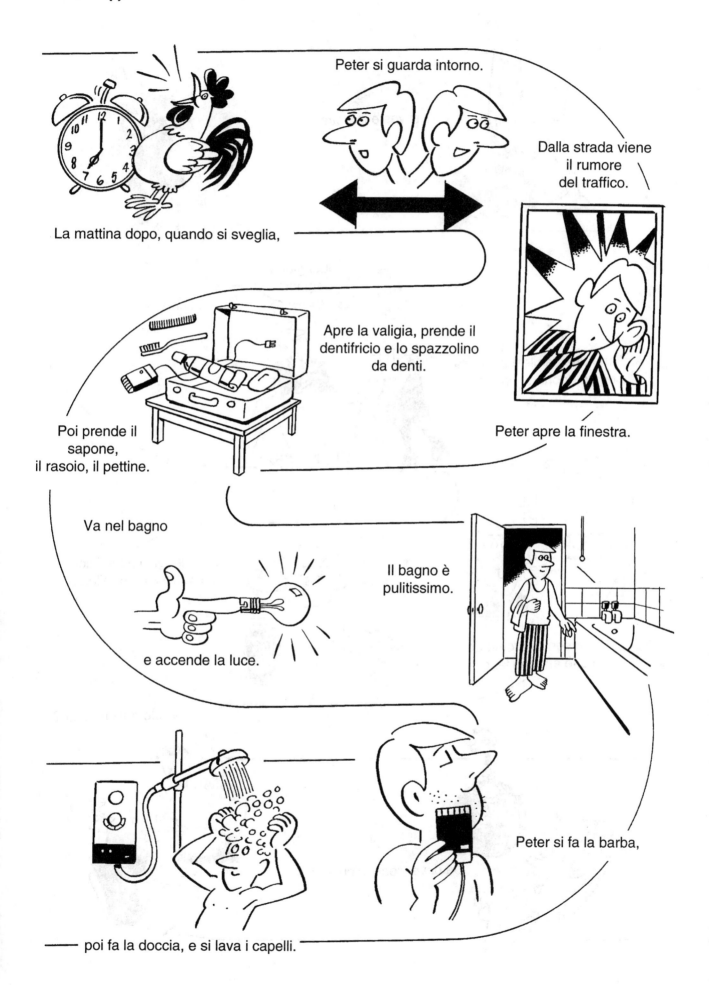

La mattina dopo, quando si sveglia,

Peter si guarda intorno.

Dalla strada viene il rumore del traffico.

Peter apre la finestra.

Apre la valigia, prende il dentifricio e lo spazzolino da denti.

Poi prende il sapone, il rasoio, il pettine.

Va nel bagno

e accende la luce.

Il bagno è pulitissimo.

Peter si fa la barba,

poi fa la doccia, e si lava i capelli.

Peter si veste in fretta,

e scende a fare colazione.

Buongiorno, signore

Porta una camicetta bianca con una gonna nera corta.

Peter mangia i panini coldi con burro e marmellata.

Peter sente l'aroma del caffè appena fatto.

Vuole ancore caffè?

Da dove viene, signore?

Intonation and Pronunciation

a) **G** in Italian may have a hard or a soft sound.
It has a hard sound like 'G' in 'Go', when followed by **a, o, u,** or most consonants:

> 1. **Una gonna corta nera.**
> 2. **È una vacanza gratuita.**
> 3. **È una ragazza grassoccia.**

b) **G** has a soft sound, as in 'Ginger', 'Joy', or 'Gentle', when followed by **e** or **i:**

> 1. **Apre la valigia.**
> 2. **Buongiorno.**
> 3. **Peter mangia i panini.**

c) **'Gli'** is pronounced rather like 'lli' in 'Million':

> 1. **Quando si sveglia.**
> 2. **Gli asciugamani sono grandi.**
> 3. **Con gli occhi marroni.**

d) **'Gn'** has a sound similar to 'ni' in 'Onion' or 'Union', or 'gn' in 'Champignon':

> 1. **La strada è bagnata di pioggia.**
> 2. **Peter va nel bagno.**
> 3. **La signora Alberti.**

e) Double consonants are pronounced with greater energy and deliberation than single ones:

> 1. **I mobili della camera sono vecchi e belli.**
> 2. **Un tappeto rosso scuro.**
> 3. **Il rumore del traffico.**
> 4. **Una bella avventura.**

f) Double **'gg'** is pronounced as in 'edge' or 'wedge':

> 1. **Oggi.**
> 2. **La strada è bagnata di pioggia.**

g) **'Z'** and **'zz'** are pronounced rather like 'ts' in bits':

> 1. **La colazione.**
> 2. **Lo spazzolino da denti.**
> 3. **È una ragazza grassoccia.**

h) **'r'** or double **'r'** is always rolled as in the Scottish pronunciation:

> 1. **La cameriera porta la colazione.**
> 2. **Con burro e marmellata.**
> 3. **Con un sorriso.**

i) Finally, note that in Italian the 'h' is always silent:

> 1. **Ha dormito bene?**
> 2. **Ho ancora molto da imparare.**

RHYMES AND PROVERBS

The following Italian sayings are a useful reminder of these sounds:

1. **Ciò che è fatto è fatto.**
   (What's done is done).

2. **Chi dorme non piglia pesci.**
   (It's the early bird that catches the worm
   – see also Lesson 1.)

3. **Occhio per occhio, dente per dente.**
   (An eye for an eye, a tooth for a tooth.)

4. **Paese che vai, usanze che trovi.**
   (When in Rome, do as the Romans do.)

5. **Meglio tardi che mai.**
   (Better late than never.)

6. **Rosso di sera, bel tempo si spera.**
   (Red sky at night, shepherd's delight.)

The English renderings are rough equivalents, not translations.

Functional Dialogues

1. Peter wakes up in the hotel. **Peter si sveglia all'hotel.**

Bella phones. **Bella telefona.**

Peter:	Hello!	**Pronto!**
Bella:	Good morning Peter, it's Bella.	**Buongiorno, Peter, sono Bella.**
Peter:	Ah, good morning.	**Ah, buongiorno.**
Bella:	What's the hotel like?	**Com'è l'albergo?**
Peter:	It's comfortable and quiet.	**È comodo, e tranquillo.**
Bella:	How's the room?	**Com'è la camera?**
Peter:	It's small, but quiet.	**È piccola, ma tranquilla.**
Bella:	What's the furniture like?	**Come sono i mobili?**
Peter:	The furniture is old and beautiful.	**I mobili sono vecchi e belli.**
Bella:	Is there a carpet?	**C'è un tappeto?**
Peter:	Yes, there's a dark red carpet.	**Sì, c'è un tappeto rosso scuro.**
Bella:	Is there a bathroom?	**C'è il bagno?**
Peter:	Yes, it's very clean.	**Sì, è pulitissimo.**
Bella:	Are there towels?	**Ci sono asciugamani?**
Peter:	Yes, they're big and soft.	**Sì, sono grandi e morbidi.**
Bella:	OK, 'bye Peter!	**Va bene, ciao Peter!**
Peter:	Goodbye.	**Arrivederci.**

2. Peter has breakfast. **Peter fa colazione.**

The Waitress **Cameriera = Cam:**

Cam:	Good morning, sir.	**Buongiorno, signore.**
Peter:	Good morning.	**Buongiorno.**
	What's for breakfast?	**Che cosa c'è per colazione?**
Cam:	Rolls, croissants and coffee.	**Ci sono panini, brioches, e caffè.**
Peter:	Butter and jam?	**C'è burro e marmellata?**
Cam:	Yes, of course.	**Sì, certo.**
Peter:	Fine.	**Va bene.**
Cam:	Where do you come from, sir?	**Da dove viene, signore?**
Peter:	I come from London, I'm English.	**Vengo da Londra, sono inglese.**
Cam:	Is it a beautiful city?	**È una bella città?**
Peter:	Yes, it's beautiful, and very big.	**Sì, è bella, e molto grande.**
Cam:	I'd love to visit London!	**Vorrei tanto visitare Londra!**

Vorrei tanto visitare Londra.

3.   What does Peter do for a living?   **Che cosa fa Peter di professione?**

Cam:	What do you do for a living?	**Che cosa fa di professione?**
Peter:	I'm a student.	**Sono studente.**
Cam:	Is it your first time in Rome?	**È la prima volta che viene a Roma?**
Peter:	Yes, I arrived yesterday by plane.	**Sì, sono arrivato ieri in aereo.**
Cam:	You speak very good Italian.	**Parla italiano molto bene.**
Peter:	I've still got a lot to learn!	**Ho ancora molto da imparare!**

4.   Peter meets Signora Alberti.   **Peter incontra la Signora Alberti.**

S.A.:	Good morning, Mr. West.	**Buongiorno, signor West.**
	Did you sleep well?	**Ha dormito bene?**
Peter:	Very well, thanks.	**Benissimo, grazie.**
	The bed's very comfortable.	**Il letto è molto comodo.**
S.A.:	I'm glad.	**Sono contenta.**
	Look, the sun's shining now.	**Guardi, ora c'è il sole.**
	It's a beautiful Spring day.	**È una bella giornata di primavera.**
Peter:	Yes, very beautiful.	**Sì, molto bella.**
	In London it's very cold.	**A Londra fa molto freddo.**
	It's raining.	**C'è la pioggia.**

Peter incontra la signora Alberti.

Personalised Dialogues

1. You're in a hotel room. The phone rings. It's your friend Sandra, making sure everything's OK.

Lei:	(Say Hello ...)
Sandra:	**Buongiorno, sono Sandra.**
Lei:	(Say good morning to her.)
Sandra:	**Com'è l'albergo?**
Lei:	(Say it's comfortable and quiet.)
Sandra:	**E com'è la camera?**
Lei:	(Say it's small, but quiet.)
Sandra:	**Come sono i mobili?**
Lei:	(Say they're old and beautiful.)
Sandra:	**C'è il bagno?**
Lei:	(Say yes, it's very clean.)
Sandra:	**Ci sono asciugamani?**
Lei:	(Say yes, they're big and soft.)
Sandra:	**Va bene. Ciao!**
Lei:	(Say goodbye.)

2. You're having breakfast in a hotel. The waitress is very friendly.

(**Cameriera**/Waitress)

Cameriera:	**Buongiorno, signore.**
Lei:	(Say Good morning and ask what's for breakfast.)
Cameriera:	**Ci sono panini, brioches e caffè.**
Lei:	(Ask if there's butter and jam.)
Cameriera:	**Sì, certo.**

Later ...

Cameriera:	**Vuole ancora caffè?**
Lei:	(Yes, please.)
Cameriera:	**Da dove viene, signore?**
Lei:	(You come from London, you're English.)
Cameriera:	**È una bella città?**
Lei:	(Yes, it's beautiful, and very big.)
Cameriera:	**Vorrei tanto visitare Londra!**

Il letto è molto comodo.

3. Talking about yourself. You're being chatted up and enjoying it.

(Ragazza/ragazzo/Girl/Boy)

Ragazza/o: **Che cosa fa di professione?**
Lei: (Say what job you do.)

Ragazza/o: **È interessante?**
Lei: (Say it's very interesting.)

Ragazza/o: **È la prima volta che viene a Roma?**
Lei: (Say yes, you arrived yesterday by plane.)

Ragazza/o: **Parla italiano molto bene.**
Lei: (Say thank you, but you've still got a lot to learn.)

4. Passing the time of day. Your landlady likes talking about the weather.

(Proprietaria/Landlady)

Proprietaria: Buongiorno, signore, ha dormito bene?
Lei: (Very well, thanks. The bed's very comfortable.)
Proprietaria: Sono contenta. Guardi, ora c'è il sole.
È una bella giornata di primavera.
Lei: (Say it's cold in London. And rainy.)

Ha fatto molto freddo.

Grammar

1. PLURALS

Forming the plural in Italian is quite straightforward.
Masculine nouns ending in **-o** change to **-i**:

il letto	**i letti**
il panino	**i panini**

Feminine nouns ending in **a** change to **e**:

la strada	**le strade**
la valigia	**le valigie**

Adjectives agree in the plural:

Masc:
I mobili sono vecchi e belli.
Gli occhi marroni e i capelli castani.
Gli asciugamani sono grandi e morbidi.

Fem:
Le strade sono bagnate.   (Sing: **la strada è bagnata.**)
Le camere sono piccole.   (Sing: **la camera è piccola.**)

Note the following exception to the rule:

il lenzuolo   (Sing.)
but
le lenzuola   (Plur.)

2. C'È ... CI SONO

The plural of **c'è** (there is) is **ci sono** (there are):

c'è un tappetto rosso scuro.
ci sono la doccia e il gabinetto.

3. VERBS

3.1 Note the following examples of **-are, – ere, – ire,** verbs:

-ARE	3rd person Sing.	Example
ritornare	**ritorna**	**Peter ritorna a letto.**
portare	**porta**	**La cameriera porta la colazione.**
incontrare	**incontra**	**Peter incontra la Signora Alberti.**
-ERE		
prendere	**prende**	**Peter prende il sapone.**
accendere	**accende**	**Peter accende la luce.**
scendere	**scende**	**Peter scende a fare colazione.**
-IRE		
venire	**viene**	**dalla strada viene il rumore del traffico.**
aprire	**apre**	**Peter apre la finestra.**
uscire	**esce**	**Peter esce dall'albergo.**

3.2 REFLEXIVE VERBS

This form is used when the subject does something to him or herself.
In Italian this idea is always shown by a pronoun – in the 3rd person, **si**:

Peter si lava i capelli.

Peter si veste in fretta.

Peter si alza.

3.3 AVERE: 'to have'

ho ...	I have
ha ...	he, she, you ...
hanno ...	they have

3.4 FARE: 'to make', 'to do'

fa ...	he, she, you ...

Used idiomatically:

fa freddo	it's cold
fare colazione	to have breakfast

3.5 Note these special forms (they will be explained later in the course):

Sono arrivato.	I arrived.
Ha fatto molto freddo.	It was very cold.
Ha dormito bene?	Did you sleep well?

4. SUL, DEL, NEL, DEI

sul pavimento	**su + il = sul**
il rumore del traffico	**di + il = del**
va nel bagno	**in + il = nel**
l'odore dei panini	**di + i = dei**

5. -ISSIMO

If you want to express your enthusiasm about something in Italian use **-issimo:**

buono	**buonissimo**
good	very good
bene	**benissimo**
well	very well
pulito	**pulitissimo**
clean	very clean

Games

1. WORD CARDS

Using the word cards, make up the Italian version of the following sentences. Write each sentence down, then check the correct answer.

1. 1   Peter wakes up and looks around him.
1. 2   The furniture in the room is old and beautiful.
1. 3   Peter gets up and opens the window.
1. 4   Peter opens his suitcase and takes out his toothpaste and toothbrush.
1. 5   The bathroom is very clean.
1. 6   Peter gets dressed quickly.
1. 7   What's for breakfast?
1. 8   I come from London, I'm English.
1. 9   What do you do for a living?
1.10   Peter leaves the hotel.

2. COLOURS: (**I colori**)

Match the following objects to their colour, as in the story:

2. 1   **un tappeto**   **nera**
2. 2   **gli occhi**   **bianca**
2. 3   **i capelli**   **rosso scuro**
2. 4   **una camicetta**   **marroni**
2. 5   **una gonna**   **biondi**

3. WHAT'S THE OPPOSITE?

Find the opposites for the words underlined.
Use a dictionary when necessary, and pay attention to word endings:

3.1   **I mobili sono <u>vecchi</u> e <u>belli</u>.**
3.2   **Peter <u>apre</u> la finestra.**
3.3   **Poi <u>apre</u> le persiane.**
3.4   **<u>Accende</u> la luce.**
3.5   **Gli asciugamani sono <u>grandi</u>.**
3.6   **Una <u>bella</u> avventura.**

4. WORD CLUSTERS

On the Word Cluster Card you will find clusters of letters which allow you to make up words or phrases from the story.

See how many you can make up from each circle.

Use each letter in the circle as many times as you like. Re-write the letters, using colour. Cut them out if you wish.

Then put them together like a jig-saw puzzle.

What if...? **Se invece...**

Continue creating your own story, step by step. Remember to build on the structures, phrases and vocabulary you already know, adding new vocabulary and place names as you go. Use a dictionary for this purpose. Check the accuracy of new forms, especially plurals, agreements, verb forms, but don't let this inhibit you. The main aim is to develop your own Italian fantasy world. **Buona fortuna!**

A few clues:

What's the hotel room/suite like?

What's the weather like?

What's for breakfast?

What's the waiter/waitress like?

Who's the appointment with?

Act 3 **Atto 3**

<table>
<tr><td></td><td>Scene 1</td><td>**Scena 1**</td></tr>
<tr><td></td><td>Peter goes to Bella's house, and together they go shopping for lunch.</td><td>**Peter va a casa di Bella, e insieme vanno a fare la spesa per il pranzo.**</td></tr>
<tr><td></td><td>Peter walks slowly along the via Veneto. From time to time he stops to admire the old Roman palaces, or to look in the shop windows. In a square there's a beautiful seventeenth century church.</td><td>**Peter cammina lentamente lungo via Veneto. Di tanto in tanto si ferma ad ammirare i vecchi palazzi romani, o a guardare le vetrine dei negozi. In una piazza c'è una bella chiesa del diciassettesimo secolo.**</td></tr>
<tr><td></td><td>At ten o'clock exactly Peter rings the bell of the Bruni home. Bella opens the door.</td><td>**Alle dieci in punto, Peter suona il campanello di casa Bruni. Bella apre la porta.**</td></tr>
<tr><td>**Bella:**</td><td>Good morning. How are you?</td><td>**Buongiorno, come sta?**</td></tr>
<tr><td>**Peter:**</td><td>Fine, thanks.</td><td>**Bene, grazie.**</td></tr>
<tr><td>**Bella:**</td><td>My uncle phoned this morning. He asks if you can stay in Rome for another day or two.</td><td>**Mio zio ha telefonato questa mattina. Domanda se lei può rimanere a Roma ancora un giorno o due.**</td></tr>
<tr><td>**Peter:**</td><td>Yes, of course.</td><td>**Sì, certo.**</td></tr>
<tr><td>**Bella:**</td><td>Very good, so today we'll have lunch together. But first we have to go shopping. Will you come with me?</td><td>**Benissimo, allora oggi pranziamo insieme. Ma prima bisogna andare a fare la spesa. Viene con me?**</td></tr>
<tr><td>**Peter:**</td><td>With pleasure.</td><td>**Con piacere.**</td></tr>
<tr><td></td><td>Peter is happy to go out with Bella. She's an attractive girl, and today looks very smart.</td><td>**Peter è felice di uscire con Bella. È una ragazza attraente, e oggi è molto elegante.**</td></tr>
<tr><td></td><td>She's wearing a very simple yellow dress. Bella too is happy to go out with Peter.</td><td>**Ha un vestito giallo, semplicissimo. Anche Bella è felice di uscire con Peter.**</td></tr>
<tr><td></td><td>He 's very good looking, tall and slim, with blue eyes and blonde hair. He seems a bit shy, but Bella likes shy people ...</td><td>**E un bel ragazzo, alto e magro, con gli occhi azzurri e i capelli biondi. Sembra un po' timido, ma a Bella piacciono le persone timide ...**</td></tr>
</table>

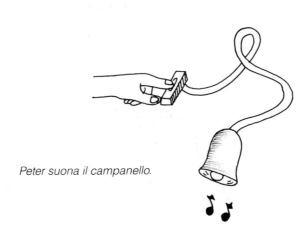

Peter suona il campanello.

43

	Scene 2	**Scena 2**
	They go shopping.	**Vanno a fare la spesa.**
	Bella says she doesn't like	**Bella dice che non le piace**
	shopping in big supermarkets.	**fare la spesa nei grandi supermercati.**
	She prefers going to the market,	**Preferisce andare al mercato,**
	or to the smaller shops.	**o nei negozi più piccoli.**
Bella:	Do you like pasta?	**Le piace la pastasciutta?**
Peter:	I love it.	**Mi piace moltissimo.**
Bella:	Good, then today	**Bene, allora oggi**
	we'll make pasta for lunch.	**facciamo la pasta per pranzo.**

At the baker's there's a delicious smell
of fresh bread just out of the oven.
There's also the smell of fresh cakes,
still warm,
and there's home-made pasta.
Bella buys a kilo of bread,
and half a kilo of egg noodles.

**Dal fornaio c'è un delizioso profumo
di pane fresco, appena uscito dal forno.
C'è anche il profumo delle torte fresche,
ancora calde,
e c'è la pasta fatta in casa.
Bella compra un chilo di pane,
e mezzo chilo di tagliatelle all'uovo.**

Bella:	How much is that pie?	**Quanto costa quella torta?**
Baker:	The apple pie, signorina?	**La torta di mele, signorina?**
	It's 10.000 (ten thousand) lire.	**Costa 10,000 (dieci mila) lire**
	But this one's smaller,	**Ma questa è più piccola,**
	it's only 8.000 (eight thousand) lire.	**costa solo 8,000 (otto mila) lire.**

Next to the baker's
there's a grocery shop.
Bella buys 100 grams of butter,
a jar of cream,
and 200 grams of local cheese.

**Di fianco al fornaio
c'è un negozio di alimentari.
Bella compra un etto di burro,
un vasetto di panna,
e due etti di formaggio locale.**

Bella:	How much is the ham?	**Quanto costa il prosciutto?**
Grocer:	3.000 (three thousand) lire	**3,000 (tremila) lire all'etto**
	the smoked ham, and	**il prosciutto crudo e**
	2.500 (two thousand five hundred)	**2,500 (duemila cinquecento)**
	the cooked ham, signorina.	**il cotto, signorina.**
Bella:	So, give me 100 grams smoked,	**Allora mi dia un etto di crudo,**
	and 100 cooked, please.	**e uno di cotto per favore.**
Grocer:	Anything else?	**Desidera altro?**
Bella:	Yes, I'd like 300 grams	**Sì, vorrei tre etti**
	of local cheese,	**di formaggio locale,**
	and a mozzarella cheese.	**e una mozzarella.**
Grocer:	Anything else, signorina?	**Altro, signorina?**
Bella:	No, thanks, that's all.	**No, grazie, basta così.**
	How much is it altogether?	**Quant'è in tutto?**

Un chilo di pane.　　　*Mezzo chilo di tagliatelle.*

Opposite the grocer's there's a butcher's.	**Di fronte al negozio di alimentari c'è una macelleria.**
Bella: How much are the veal escalopes?	**Quanto costano le scaloppine di vitello?**
Butcher: 18.000 (eighteen thousand) lire a kilo, signorina.	**18,000 (diciotto mila) lire al chilo, signorina.**
Bella thinks they're very expensive, but takes four of them, and goes to pay at the cash desk.	**Bella pensa che sono molto care, ma ne prende quattro, e va a pagare alla cassa.**
At the end of the street there's a fruit and vegetable market. The lettuce is lovely and fresh. On the green leaves drops of water gleam in the sunshine like tiny diamonds. There are green, yellow and red peppers. Enormous tomatoes, giant mushrooms. Cucumbers, asparagus, spinach ... There's a smell of fresh basil, fruit, and all kinds of aromatic herbs ...	**In fondo alla strada c'è un mercato di frutta e verdura. L'insalata è bella e fresca. Sulle foglie verdi, gocce d'acqua brillano al sole come piccoli diamanti. Ci sono peperoni verdi, gialli e rossi. Pomodori enormi, funghi grandissimi. Cetrioli, aspàragi, spinaci ... C'è il profumo del basilico fresco, della frutta, e di tutti i tipi di erbe aromatiche ...**
Bella: Today we'll make a nice mixed salad. Do you like salad?	**Oggi facciamo una buona insalata mista. Le piace?**
Peter: I love it, I really love vegetables. I don't eat meat, I'm a vegetarian.	**Mi piace moltissimo, Amo molto i legumi. Io non mangio carne, sono vegetariano.**
Bella: Really? OK, then today we'll both eat vegetarian: noodles with mushroom and cream, mixed salad, cheese and fruit. Then apple pie and coffee. What do you say?	**Davvero? Bene, allora oggi mangiamo vegetariano tutti e due: tagliatelle al funghi e panna, insalata mista, formaggio e frutta. Poi torta di mele e caffè. Che ne dice?**
Peter: Excellent, my mouth's watering already!	**Ottimo, ho già l'acquolina in bocca!**

*Di fronte al negozio di alimentari
c'è una macelleria.*

	They laugh happily, listening to the cries of the fruit and vegetable sellers. They all seem like opera singers or poets.	**Ridono felici mentre ascoltano le grida dei venditori di frutta e verdura. Sembrano tutti cantanti d'opera o poeti.**
Seller:	Onions, artichokes ...!	**Cipolle. Carciofi ...!**
Seller:	Lovely juicy peaches!	**Le belle pesche sugose!**
Seller:	Grapefruits, pineapples, lemons, watermelons!	**Pompelmi, ananas, limoni, angurie!**
Seller:	Only 3.000 (three thousand) lire a kilo, lovely strawberries!	**Solo 3,000 (tremila) lire al chilo le fragole buone!**
Seller:	Nice plums, sweet as honey! Cherries, apples, pears, grapes ...	**Susine belle, dolci come il miele! Ciliege, mele, pere, uva ...!**
Seller:	Lovely melons, over here ... Like to taste, miss?	**I buoni meloni, signori, da questa parte ... Vuole assaggiare, signorina?**
	The seller cuts up a melon and offers some to Bella and Peter.	**Il venditore taglia un melone e ne offre a Bella e a Peter.**
Seller:	Just taste this, signorina. And you, sir, come on, have a taste!	**Senta che buono signorina. Anche lei, signore, prego, vuole assaggiare?**
Peter:	It's delicious	**E buonissimo.**
Bella:	Yes, it's a nice one.	**Sì, è buono.**
	Bella chooses a large ripe melon, scented, like flowers.	**Bella sceglie un melone grande e maturo, ha profumo di fiori.**
Bella:	I'll take this one. How much is it?	**Prendo questo. Quanto viene?**
	The seller weighs it.	**Il venditore lo pesa.**
Seller:	4.000 (four thousand) lire, signorina. Anything else? We've got some nice watermelons too, going cheap.	**4,000 (quattromila) lire, signorina. Desidera altro? Abbiamo anche le angurie buone, a buon mercato.**
Bella:	No, that's all, thank you.	**No, basta così, grazie.**
	They stop here and there to buy peppers, lettuce, tomatoes, cucumbers, mushrooms, celery, cherries, strawberries, peaches, and a large bunch of fresh basil.	**Si fermano qua e là a comprare peperoni, insalata, pomodori, cetrioli, funghi, sedano, ciliege, fragole, pesche, e un grande mazzo di basilico fresco.**
	Then, the shopping finished, they go back home, tired and starving.	**Poi, terminate le spese, ritornano a casa, stanchi e affamati.**

		Scena 3
	Scene 3	**Scena 3**
	Bella offers Peter an aperitif, and she also has one. They go straight into the kitchen to get lunch ready.	**Bella offre a Peter un aperitivo, e anche lei ne prende uno. Vanno subito in cucina a preparare il pranzo.**
	Bella cooks the pasta, while Peter washes the greens and prepares the mixed salad.	**Bella cuoce la pasta, mentre Peter lava la verdura e prepara l'insalata mista.**
Bella:	Are your parents vegetarian too, Peter?	**Sono vegetariani anche i suoi genitori, Peter?**
Peter:	No, just me. I haven't eaten meat for five years. But sometimes I eat fish.	**No, solo io. Non mangio carne da cinque anni. Però qualche volta mangio pesce.**
	While the pasta is cooking Bella prepares a sauce with mushrooms, butter, cream, and parmesan.	**Mentre la pasta cuoce, Bella prepara la salsa con funghi, burro, panna e parmigiano.**
Bella:	What wine do you prefer Peter – white or red?	**Che vino preferisce, Peter — bianco o rosso?**
Peter:	White, please.	**Bianco, per favore.**
	Bella opens the fridge, takes out a bottle of white wine, and puts it on the table.	**Bella apre il frigorifero, prende una bottiglia di vino bianco, e lo mette sulla tavola.**
	At last lunch is ready, and they sit at the table. Peter opens the bottle and pours the wine into the glasses. Bella raises her glass and smiles.	**Finalmente il pranzo è pronto, e si siedono a tavola. Peter apre la bottiglia e versa il vino nei bicchieri. Bella alza il bicchiere e sorride.**
Bella:	*Bon appétit*, Peter.	**Buon appetito, Peter.**
Peter:	Thanks, same to you.	**Grazie, altrettanto.**

Peter apre la bottiglia

ATTO 3 (i)

VIA VENETO

In una piazza c'è una bella chiesa del diciasettesimo secolo.

Peter cammina lentamente lungo via Vento.

Alle dieci in punto,

Buongiorno, come sta?

Peter suona il campanello di casa Bruni.

Bella apre la porta.

ancora un giorno o due.

Domanda se lei può rimanere a Roma

Viene con me?

Ma prima bisogna andare a fare la spesa.

E un bel ragazzo, alto e magro, con gli occhi azzurri e i capelli biondi.

È una ragazza attraente, e oggi è molto elegante.

Preferisce andare al mercato, o nei negozi più piccoli.

Dal fornaio c'è un delizioso profumo di pane fresco, appena uscito dal forno.

Quanto costa il prosciutto?

?

Allora mi dia uno di cotto, per favore.

MACELLERIA

?

Vorrei tre etti di formaggio locale.

Quant'è in tutto?

Di fronte al negozio di alimentari c'è una macelleria.

ATTO 3 (iii)

C'è un mercato di frutta e verdura.

Mangiamo vegetariano tutti e due.

Poi torta di mele e caffè.

Le belle pesche sugose!

Vanno subito in cucina a preparare il pranzo.

Bella apre il frigorifero,

Buon appetito, Peter.

Grazie, altrettanto.

e prende una bottiglia di vino bianco.

Intonation and Pronunciation

Vowels

Now brush up your vowel sounds.

Listen to the following sentences and repeat them, imitating as closely as possible the music of the Italian language, and the purity of the vowel sounds:

1. **Ha un vestito giallo semplicissimo.**
2. **È un bel ragazzo alto e magro.**
3. **Dal fornaio c'è un delizioso profumo di pane fresco, appena uscito dal forno.**
4. **Sulle foglie verdi, gocce d'acqua brillano al sole come piccoli diamanti.**
5. **Ci sono peperoni verdi, gialli, rossi. Pomodori enormi, funghi grandissimi.**

Functional Dialogues

1.

	Peter goes to Bella's house.	**Peter va a casa di Bella.**
	Bella opens the door.	**Bella apre la porta.**

Bella:	Good morning. How arè you?	**Buongiorno, come sta?**
Peter:	Fine thanks. And you?	**Bene grazie. E lei?**
Bella:	Very well.	**Benissimo.**
	My uncle phoned this morning.	**Ha telefonato mio zio questa mattina.**
	Can you stay in Rome	**Può rimanere a Roma**
	another day or two?	**ancora un giorno o due?**
Peter:	Yes, of course.	**Sì, certo.**
Bella:	Very good; so today	**Benissimo, allora oggi**
	we'll have lunch together.	**pranziamo insieme.**
	But first we have to go shopping.	**Ma prima bisogna andare a fare la spesa.**
Peter:	OK, let's go!	**Va bene, andiamo!**

2.

	Bella and Peter go shopping.	**Bella e Peter vanno a fare la spesa**

Bella:	I don't like shopping	**Non mi piace fare la spesa**
	in big supermarkets.	**nei grandi supermercati.**
	I prefer to go to the market,	**Preferisco andare al mercato,**
	or to the smaller shops.	**o nei negozi più piccoli.**
Peter:	Me too.	**Anch'io.**
Bella:	Do you like pasta?	**Le piace la pastasciutta?**
Peter:	I love it.	**Mi piace moltissimo.**
Bella:	Fine, so today	**Bene, allora oggi**
	we'll make pasta for lunch.	**facciamo la pasta per pranzo.**

	At the baker's.	**Dal fornaio.**
	Baker	**Fornaio = For:**

Bella:	How much is that pie?	**Quanto costa quella torta?**
For:	The apple pie, signorina?	**La torta di mele, signorina?**
	It's 10,000 lire.	**Costa 10,000 lire.**
	But this one's smaller.	**Ma questa è più piccola.**
	It's only 8,000 lire.	**Costa solo 8,000 lire.**

Mi piace moltissimo.

	At the grocer's.	**Nel negozio di alimentari.**
	Shopkeeper	**Negoziante = Negoz:**
Bella:	How much is the ham?	**Quanto costa il prosciutto?**
Negoz:	3,000 lire the smoked ham and 2,500 the cooked ham signorina.	**3,000 lire all'etto il prosciutto crudo, e 2,500 il cotto, signorina.**
Bella:	So give me 100 grams smoked, and 100 cooked, please.	**Allora, mi dia un etto di crudo, e uno di cotto, per favore.**
Negoz:	Anything else?	**Desidera altro?**
Bella:	Yes, I'd like 300 grams of local cheese, and a mozzarella cheese.	**Sì, vorrei 3 etti di formaggio locale, e una mozzarella.**
Negoz:	Anything else, signorina?	**Altro, signorina?**
Bella:	No thanks, that's all.	**No grazie, basta così.**

	At the butcher's.	**Dal macellaio.**
	Butcher	**Macellaio = Mac:**
Bella:	How much are the veal escalopes?	**Quanto costano le scaloppine di vitello?**
Mac:	18,000 lire a kilo, signorina.	**18,000 lire al chilo, signorina.**
Bella:	Hmm, I'll take four... How much is it altogether?	**Mmm, ne prendo quattro. Quant'è in tutto?**

3.	At the market.	**Al mercato**
	Vendor	**Venditore = Vend:**
Bella:	Today we'll make a nice mixed salad. Do you like salad?	**Oggi facciamo una buona insalata mista. Le piace?**
Peter:	I love it. I love vegetables. I don't eat meat, I'm a vegetarian.	**Mi piace moltissimo. Amo i legumi. Io non mangio carne, sono vegetariano.**
Vend:	Lovely melons, over here, like to taste, Miss?	**I buoni meloni signore, da questa parte, vuole assaggiare, signorina?**
Bella:	Yes, please.	**Sì. grazie.**
Vend:	And you sir, come on, have a taste!	**Anche lei, signore, prego, vuole assaggiare?**

Io non mangio carne, sono vegetariano.

Peter:	It's delicious!	**È buonissimo!**
Bella:	Yes, it's a nice one.	**Sì, è buono.**
	I'll take this one.	**Prendo questo.**
	How much is it?	**Quanto viene?**
Vend:	4,000 lire, signorina…	**4,000 lire, signorina…**
	Anything else?	**Desidera altro?**
Bella:	No, that's all, thanks.	**No, basta così, grazie.**

4. Lunch. **Il pranzo.**

Bella:	Shall we have an aperitif?	**Prendiamo l'aperitivo?**
Peter:	Yes, Campari Soda for me.	**Sì, per me un Camparisoda.**
Bella:	Me too.	**Anche per me.**
	What wine do you prefer?	**Che vino preferisce?**
	White or red?	**Bianco o rosso?**
Peter:	White please.	**Bianco, per favore.**
Bella:	Fine, there's a bottle of	**Bene. C'è una bottiglia di**
	white wine in the fridge.	**vino bianco nel frigorifero.**
Bella:	The pasta's ready.	**La pasta è pronta.**
Peter:	So's the salad.	**Anche l'insalata è pronta!**
Bella:	*Bon appetit*, Peter.	**Buon appetito, Peter.**
Peter:	Thanks, same to you.	**Grazie, altrettanto.**

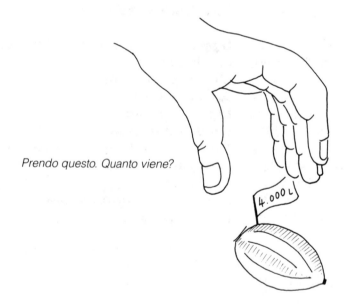

Prendo questo. Quanto viene?

Personalised Dialogues

1. You are visiting **Signora Visentini** again. This time she answers the door herself.

Sa.Visentini:	**Buongiorno, come sta?**
Lei:	(Say you're fine, thanks. Ask her how she is.)
Sa.Visentini	**Bene, grazie. Prego, s'accomodi.**
Lei:	(Say thank you.)

2. A market researcher asks you about your likes and dislikes in food and drink. She clearly has a liking for you...
   (The English term Market Researcher is used in Italy)

Market Res.:	**Le piace la pastasciutta?**
Lei:	(Say you like it a lot.)
Market Res.:	**Le piace l'insalata mista?**
Lei:	(Yes, you like it a lot, you love vegetables.)
Market Res.:	**Le piace il vitello?**
Lei:	(No, you don't like it. You don't eat meat. You're a vegetarian.)
Market Res.:	**Che vino preferisce, bianco o rosso?**
Lei:	(You prefer white wine.)
Market Res.:	**Anch'io, prendiamo l'aperitivo insieme? Che ne dice?**
Lei:	(Excellent, your mouth's watering already!)

3. You've decided to cook lunch for a guest. Unfortunately, he's not a vegetarian so you have to go to the grocer's and butcher's, as well as the baker's.

Dal Fornaio

(Fornaio/Baker)

Lei:	(Ask for a kilo of fresh bread, please.)
Fornaio:	**Desidera altro?**
Lei:	(Half a kilo of egg noodles.)
Fornaio:	**Altro, signora?**
Lei:	(Ask him how much that pie is.)
Fornaio:	**La torta di mele, signora? Costa 10,000 lire.**
Lei:	(OK, you'll take one.)

Nel negozio di alimentari

(Negoziante/Shopkeeper)

Lei:	(Ask how much the ham is.)
Negoziante:	**3,000 lire all'etto il prosciutto crudo, e 2,500 il cotto, signora.**
Lei:	(Ask him to give you 100 grams of smoked and 100 grams of cooked, please.)
Negoziante:	**Desidera altro?**
Lei:	(Yes, you'd like 300 grams of local cheese and a mozzarella cheese.)
Negoziante:	**Altro, signora?**
Lei:	(No thanks, that's enough.)

Dal macellaio

(Macellaio/Butcher)
Lei: (Ask how much the veal escalopes are.)
Macellaio: **18,000 lire al chilo.**
Lei: (To yourself: They're very expensive.
             To the butcher: You'll take four of them.)

4. Now you can indulge your vegetarianism at the fruit and vegetable market. (**Venditore**/Vendor)

Lei: (Ask how much the tomatoes are.)
Venditore: **2,000 al chilo, signora.**
Lei: (A kilo please.)
             (Ask how much the mushrooms are.)
Venditore: **5,000 lire al chilo. Sono buonissimi.**
Lei: (OK, you'll take 300 grams of them.)
Venditore: **Altro, signora?**
Lei: (Yes, how much is a melon?)
Venditore: **4,000 lire, signora.**
Lei: (You'll take this one.)
Venditore: **Desidera altro?**
Lei: (No, that's enough, thanks.)
             (How much altogether?)

5. Meanwhile, back in the kitchen, lunch with a market researcher is going well.

Lei: (Would he like an aperitive?)
Market Res.:   **Sì, grazie, un Camparisoda.**
Lei: (You'll have one too.)
Market Res.:   **La pasta è pronta.**
Lei: (So's the salad!)
             (What wine does he prefer, white or red?)
Market Res.:   **Preferisco vino bianco.**
Lei: (There's a bottle of white wine in the 'fridge.)
Market Res.:   **Buon appetito!**
Lei: (Thanks, the same to him.)

*Che vino preferisce:
bianco o rosso?*

56

Grammar

1. VERBS

This Act contains various new forms and uses of the verb:

1.1 1st person plural ('we'...): ends in **-iamo**

Infinitive	1st person plural	Story example
pranzare	**pranziamo**	**oggi pranziamo insieme**
fare	**facciamo** (irreg.)	**oggi facciamo la pasta**
mangiare	**mangiamo**	**oggi mangiamo vegetariano**
avere	**abbiamo** (irreg.)	**abbiamo anche le angurie buone**

This form also has the meaning of 'Let's'...:

	andiamo	let's go
	pranziamo	let's have lunch

1.2 3rd person plural ('they'...): ends in **-ano** (for **-are** verbs)

or **-ono** (for **-ere, –ire** verbs)

Infinitive	3rd person plural	Story example
costare	**costano**	**quanto costano le scaloppine?**
comprare	**comprano**	**comprano frutta e verdura**
ritornare	**ritornano**	**ritornano a casa**
sedersi	**si siedono**	**si siedono a tavola**
andare	**vanno** (irreg.)	**vanno subito in cucina**

1.3 Infinitives ('to'...)

Note the following uses of the infinitive:

After **'a':**

> **Bisogna andare a fare la spesa**

(**'bisogna'**, expressing need or necessity is also followed by the infinitive)

> **Bella va a pagare alla cassa.**

After **'di':**

> **Peter è felice di uscire con Bella**

After verbs like **vuole, può, preferisce...**

Vuole assaggiare, signorina?	Do you want to...?
Può rimanere a Roma?	Can you...?
Bella preferisce andare al mercato.	Prefers to...

2. ADJECTIVES

Not all adjectives end in −**o**, or −**a** in the singular. Some end in −**e**:

felice	**Peter è felice.**
attraente	**Bella è una ragazza attraente.**
elegante	**Bella è molto elegante.**
dolce	**Il melone è dolce.**

The plural of such adjectives ends in −**i** for both masculine and feminine:

Masc:	**I meloni sono dolci**.
Fem:	**Susine belle, dolci come il miele!**

3. NEGATIVES

Forming the negative in Italian is very simple: just add **non** before the verb:

mangio	**non mangio**	**non mangio carne**
è	**non è**	**non è caro**
mi piace	**non mi piace**	**non mi piace la carne**

4. PIACE...PIACCIONO

A common way of saying you like something is to use the impersonal form: **mi piace**...

The subject/object comes after:

Mi piace la pasta.   I like pasta.

In the plural it is: **mi piacciono**:

Mi piacciono le ragazze.   I like girls.

A Bella piacciono le persone un po' timide...

Do you like...? is: **Le piace...?**

Le piace la pastasciutta?

or: **Le piacciono...?**

Le piacciono i diamanti?   Do you like diamonds?

He likes: **gli piace...**   **gli piacciono...**

She likes: **le piace...**   **le piacciono...**

5. NE

A useful word meaning 'of it', 'of them', 'about it' etc., **ne** is not usually translated in English.

Ne prendo quattro   I'll take four (of them.)

**Bella offre a Peter un aperitivo
e anche lei ne prende uno**   ...she has one (of them) too.

*Sembra un po' timido, ma a Bella
piacciono le persone timide*

Games

1. I PREZZI

Quanto costa?   How much is it?
Quanto costano?   How much are they?

Price each of the items as in the text.
Speak the numbers aloud as you write them on each price tag.

Quanto costa?

**La torta di mele
(grande)**

**La torta di mele
(piccola)**

**Il prosciutto
(cotto)**

Il melone

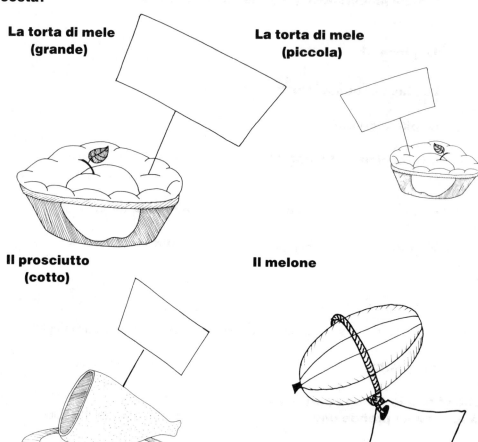

Quanto costano?

Le scaloppine di vitello

Le fragole

2. A Puzzle

Re-write and complete the following sentences.
Cut them out adding colour and drawings, then put them in their chronological order as in the text:

1. _ _ _ _ _ _
   **SUBITO
   IN CUCINA
   A** _ _ _ _ _ _ _ _ _
   IL PRANZO

2. **IN FONDO
   ALLA STRADA**
   _ _ _
   **UN MERCATO
   DI FRUTTA
   E** _ _ _ _ _ _ _

3. **QUANTO** _ _ _ _ _
   **IL
   PROSCIUTTO**

4. **VANNO A** _ _ _ _ _
   LA SPESA

5. **OGGI** _ _ _ _ _ _ _ _
   **UNA BUONA
   INSALATA
   MISTA**

6. **RITORNANO
   A CASA**
   _ _ _ _ _ _ _
   E AFFAMATI

7. **OTTIMO** _ _
   **GIÀ
   L'ACQUOLINA IN BOCCA!**

8. **NON** _ _ _ _ _ _ **CARNE
   PERÒ QUALCHE VOLTA**
   _ _ _ _ _ _ **PESCE**

9. **BELLA** _ _ _ _ _
   **LA PASTA
   MENTRE PETER**
   _ _ _ _ **LA VERDURA**
   E _ _ _ _ _ _ _
   L'INSALATA MISTA

10. **BELLA PENSA
    CHE** _ _ _ _
    **MOLTO CARE
    MA NE PRENDE 4
    E VA A** _ _ _ _ _
    ALLA CASSA

11. **BELLA OFFRE
    A PETER UN
    APERITIVO
    E ANCHE LEI
    NE** _ _ _ _ _ _ **UNO**

3. LET'S DO IT

   3.1   Let's eat!
   3.2   Let's make pasta!
   3.3   Let's have lunch!
   3.4   Let's buy fruit!
   3.5   Let's go!

4. LIKE IT OR NOT?

Under interrogation, admit you like the following:

   4.1   pasta
   4.2   girls
   4.3   boys
   4.4   meat
   4.5   fruit
   4.6   vegetables
   4.7   diamonds
   4.8   ham
   4.9   strawberries
   4.10 white wine

5. Now it's your turn to ask the questions.
   Ask your suspect if he likes the following:

   5.1   red wine
   5.2   bread
   5.3   egg noodles
   5.4   local cheese
   5.5   mushrooms

What if...? **Se invece...**

Your own Italian fantasy continues. You too have to stay on in Rome (Venice? Palermo? Rio?) for a few more days. An opportunity to get to know your market researcher? The chance to indulge yourself with hitherto undiscovered delights – food, drink etc. Develop your likes and dislikes, and, while accentuating the positive, don't forget to use the negative too! Use the new verb forms at your disposal, adding new verbs with the help of the dictionary.

Act 4 **Atto 4**

Scene 1 — **Scena 1**

Peter and Bella go to the bank, then go shopping. — **Bella e Peter vanno alla banca, poi vanno a fare le compere.**

Peter: It was an excellent lunch, I was very hungry. You're a very good cook, you know! — **È stato un ottimo pranzo, avevo molta fame. Sa che lei è una bravissima cuoca?**

Bella: Thank you, so are you. You prepared an excellent salad. — **Grazie, anche lei. Ha preparato un'ottima insalata.**

Peter: But now I must phone home. I have to tell my parents that I'm staying in Rome for another couple of days. — **Ora però devo telefonare a casa. Devo dire ai miei genitori che rimango a Roma ancora un paio di giorni.**

Bella: You can phone from here, if you like. — **Può telefonare da qui, se vuole.**

The code for London is 00441, (zero, zero, four, four, one) plus your home number. — **Il prefisso per Londra è 00441,* (zero, zero, quattro, quattro, uno) più il suo numero di casa.**

Peter phoned home and spoke with his mother. He told her he has to stay in Rome for another couple of days. — **Peter ha telefonato a casa e ha parlato con sua madre. Le ha detto che deve rimanere a Roma ancora un paio di giorni.**

Peter: I've got to go and buy a pair of lightweight trousers and a couple of shirts. But first I have to go to the bank and change some money. — **Devo andare a comprare un paio di pantaloni leggeri e due camicie. Ma prima devo andare in banca a cambiare dei soldi.**

Bella: OK, let's have a coffee, then I'll come with you. — **Va bene, prendiamo il caffè, poi l'accompagno.**

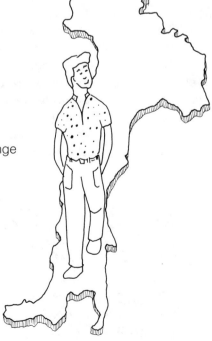

*Dialogue published before the change of London telephone codes.

	Scene 2	**Scena 2**
	At the bank Peter went	**Alla banca Peter è andato**
	straight up to the exchange counter.	**subito allo sportello del cambio.**
Peter:	I'd like to change some	**Vorrei cambiare dei**
	English money into Italian lire.	**soldi inglesi in lire italiane.**
	What is the exchange rate today?	**Quant'è il cambio oggi?**
Clerk:	2.400 (two thousand four hundred)	**2,400 (duemila quattro cento)**
	lire for cash,	**lire per denari contanti,**
	and 2.350	**e 2,350**
	(two thousand three hundred and fifty)	**(duemila tre cento cinquanta)**
	for Traveller's Cheques.	**per Traveller's Cheques.**
Peter:	I'd like to change £200	**Vorrei cambiare 200 (duecento)**
	Traveller's Cheques, please.	**sterline di Traveller's Cheques, per favore.**
	Peter signed the Traveller's Cheques.	**Peter <u>ha firmato</u> i Traveller's Cheques.**
Clerk:	Will you give me your passport,	**Mi dà il passaporto,**
	please?	**per piacere?**
	At the cash desk the clerk gave Peter	**Alla cassa l'impiegata ha dato a Peter**
	50.000 (fifty thousand)	**biglietti da 50,000 (cinquantamila)**
	and 10.000 (ten thousand) lire notes.	**e da 10,000 (diecimila) lire.**
Clerk:	There you are Mr. West, 470.000	**Ecco, Signor West, 470,000**
	(four hundred and seventy thousand)	**(quattrocento settanta milla)**
	lire in all.	**lire in tutto.**
	When Bella and Peter left the bank	**Quando Bella e Peter <u>sono usciti</u> dalla banca,**
	the sun outside	**fuori il sole**
	was very hot.	**<u>era</u> caldissimo.**
	Scene 3	**Scena 3**
Bella:	There's a men's clothes shop	**C'è un negozio di abiti da uomo**
	near here.	**qui vicino.**
	Let's go and see if we can find	**Andiamo a vedere se troviamo**
	something for you, shall we?	**qualcosa per lei?**
Peter:	Yes, let's.	**Sì, andiamo.**
	These trousers are too heavy,	**Questi pantaloni sono troppo pesanti,**
	I'm very hot.	**ho molto caldo.**
	The shop assistant	**Il commesso del negozio**
	was a middle-aged gentleman.	**era un signore di mezza età.**
	He was wearing a very smart	**<u>Portava</u> un abito grigio**
	grey suit.	**molto elegante.**
	He was an excellent advertisement	**<u>Faceva</u> ottima pubblicità**
	for the shop.	**al negozio.**

Peter ha firmato i Traveller's Cheques.

£200

64

Assist:	Good evening. Can I help you?	**Buona sera signori, desiderano?**
Peter:	Can you show me some sports shirts, please?	**Può mostrarmi qualche camicia sportiva, per piacere?**
Assist:	Of course. What size are you?	**Certamente, che taglia porta?**
Peter:	I take medium size: 40 (forty) or 42 (forty two.)	**Porto una taglia media: 40 (quaranta) o 42 (quarantadue).**
Assist:	Here you are, have a look at these sports shirts. They're the latest fashion, just in today.	**Ecco, guardi, di tipo sportivo abbiamo questi modelli. Ultima moda, arrivati oggi.**
Peter:	I like this one. Have you any other colours?	**Mi piace questo modello. Ha altri colori?**
Assist:	We have that one in white, red, pink, yellow or blue.	**L'abbiamo in bianco, rosso, rosa, giallo o azzurro.**
Peter:	How much is it?	**Quanto viene?**
Assist:	It's 40.000 (forty thousand) lire. It's pure cotton. We have the same design in pure silk as well. You can wear this shirt with or without a tie.	**Viene 40,000 (quaranta mila) lire. È cotone puro. Abbiamo lo stesso modello anche in seta pura. Può portare questa camicia con o senza cravatta.**
Peter:	It's very beautiful, but pure silk is too expensive.	**È molto bella, ma la seta pura costa troppo cara.**
Assist:	No, it's not too expensive. It's only 62.000 (sixty two thousand) lire.	**No, non costa molto. Viene solo 62,000 (sessanta due mila) lire.**
Peter:	What do you think, Bella, do you like it?	**Che ne pensa, Bella, le piace?**
Assist:	You can feel it, signorina. Please, feel what soft silk it is. A shirt like this is always smart, for every occasion.	**La può toccare, signorina. Prego, senta che seta morbida. Una camicia come questa è sempre elegante, per tutte le occasioni.**
Bella:	It's really very beautiful. I like it very much.	**È veramente molto bella. Mi piace molto.**
Peter:	Fine, so I'll take the blue one in cotton, and the white one in silk.	**Bene, allora prendo l'azzurra di cotone, e la bianca di seta.**
Bella:	Do you like this tie, Peter? Look, it goes well with the silk shirt. I'd like to give you a little present. A souvenir of Rome.	**Le piace questa cravatta, Peter? Guardi, sta bene con la camicia di seta. Vorrei farle un piccolo regalo. Un ricordo di Roma.**
Peter:	Really? Thank you Bella, you're very kind.	**Davvero? Grazie, Bella, è molto gentile.**

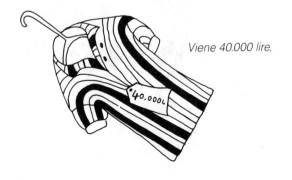

Viene 40.000 lire,

65

	Scene 4	**Scena 4**

	The assistant showed Peter a pair of white trousers.	**Il commesso <u>ha mostrato</u> a Peter un paio di pantaloni bianchi.**
Assist:	This year white is very fashionable. We have other designs as well. There are these striped ones, if you prefer.	**Quest'anno il bianco è molto di moda. Abbiamo anche altri modelli. Ci sono questi a righe, se preferisce.**
Peter:	No, I don't like the striped ones. I'd like to try the white ones on.	**No quelli a righe non mi piacciono. Vorrei provare i bianchi.**
	Peter went to try on the white trousers with the white silk shirt.	**Peter <u>è andato</u> a provare i pantaloni bianchi con la camicia bianca di seta.**
Bella:	They suit you very well, Peter. The shirt suits you as well.	**Le stanno molto bene, Peter. Anche la camicia le sta bene.**
Peter:	OK, I'll take them. How much is that, altogether?	**Bene, li prendo. Quant'è in tutto?**
Assist:	The two shirts come to 102.000 (one hundred and two thousand) lire, plus 60.000 (sixty thousand) the trousers ... a total of 162.000 (one hundred and sixty two thousand) lire. Let's make it 160.000 (one hundred and sixty thousand), I'll give you a little discount. Anything else? Socks, briefs, pullovers, a jacket ...	**Le due camicie vengono 102,000 (centoduemila) lire più 60,000 (sessantamila) i pantaloni ... totale 162,000 (centosessanta duemila) lire. Facciamo 160,000 (centosessanta mila), le faccio un piccolo sconto. Desidera altro? Calzini, slip, pullover, una giacca ...?**
Peter:	No, no, that's all. I haven't got much money ...	**No, no, basta così. Non ho molti soldi ...**
	Bella paid for the tie separately, and gave it to Peter.	**Bella <u>ha pagato</u> la cravatta a parte, e <u>l'ha data</u> a Peter.**
Bella:	You can wear it this evening. Shall we go for a drink? And we can decide what to do this evening.	**La può mettere questa sera. Andiamo a bere qualcosa? Così possiamo decidere che cosa fare questa sera.**
Peter:	What an excellent idea, I'm very thirsty.	**Che ottima idea, ho molta sete.**

Vorrei farle un piccolo regalo.

ATTO 4 (i)

È stato un ottimo pranzo.

Ora però devo telefonare a casa.

Devo dire ai miei genitori che rimango a Roma ancora un paio di giorni.

Il prefisso per Londra è 00441.

Devo andare a comprare un paio di pantaloni leggeri e due camicie.

Ma prima devo andare in banca a cambiare dei soldi.

Alla banca Peter è
andato subito
allo sportello del cambio.

Quant'è il cambio oggi?
2,400 (duemila quattro cento)

Peter ha firmato i
Traveller's Cheques.

Mi dà il passporto,
per piacere?

L'impiegata ha dato a Peter biglietti
da 50,000 e da 10,000 lire.

ATTO 4 (iii)

NEGOZIO

C'è un negozio di abiti da uomo qui vicino.

Il commesso del negozio era un signore di mezza età.

Portava un abito grigio molto elegante.

Può mostrami qualche camicia sportiva, per piacere?

Porto una taglia media: 40 (quaranta) o 42 (quarantadue).

Che ne pensa, Bella, le piace?

No, non costa molto.

62,000 lire

Viene solo sessante due mila lire.

Le piace questa cravatta, Peter?

69

ATTO 4 (iv)

70

Intonation and Pronunciation

Question and answer pattern

a) In general questions that can be answered with "yes" or "no" keep the same form and word order in the answer as in the question. The only difference is that in the question the intonation changes. Listen carefully to the following questions and answers:

1. **Ha altri colori?**
   Si, ho altri colori.

2. **Porta una taglia media?**
   No, porto una taglia grande.

3. **Andiamo in banca?**
   Si, andiamo in banca.

4. **Viene da Roma?**
   No, vengo da Londra.

5. **È una bella città?**
   Si, è una bella città.

6. **È una città piccola?**
   No, è una città grande.

b) Italian Numbers

1 **uno**	11 **undici**	21 **ventuno**	40 **quaranta**
2 **due**	12 **dodici**	22 **ventidue**	50 **cinquanta**
3 **tre**	13 **tredici**	23 **ventitre**	60 **sessanta**
4 **quattro**	14 **quattordici**	24 **ventiquattro**	70 **settanta**
5 **cinque**	15 **quindici**	25 **venticinque**	80 **ottanta**
6 **sei**	16 **sedici**	26 **ventisei**	90 **novanta**
7 **sette**	17 **diciasette**	27 **ventisette**	100 **cento**
8 **otto**	18 **diciotto**	28 **ventotto**	200 **duecento**
9 **nove**	19 **diciannove**	29 **ventinove**	300 **trecento**
10 **dieci**	20 **venti**	30 **trenta**	400 **quattrocento**
0 **zero**	1,000 **mille**	1,000,000 **un milione**	

A REMINDER

Are you still doing the 'extra exercises' we described on page xxvii :

1. Making up post cards to revise with.

2. Acting out the Dialogues expressively.

3. Putting up post-it notes around the house or office or even in the car!

4. Representing at least 10 words visually.

5. Selecting the 10 most useful words per Act. (That gets you reviewing them all!)

6. Underlining, highlighting and <u>writing down</u> key words and sentences.

7. Describing the scenes out loud in your new language.

Functional Dialogues

1. Peter has to phone home. **Peter deve telefonare a casa.**

Peter: But now I must phone home. I have to tell my parents that I'm staying in Rome for another couple of days. **Ora però devo telefonare a casa. Devo dire ai miei genitori che rimango a Roma ancora un paio di giorni.**

Bella: You can phone from here if you like. The code for London is: 00-44-1 plus your home number. **Può telefonare da qui, se vuole. Il prefisso per Londra è 00-44-1, più il suo numero di casa.**

Peter: Hello, Mother! How are you...? Fine, thanks... But I have to stay in Rome for another couple of days. **Ciao, mamma! Come stai? ...Bene, grazie... Ma devo rimanere a Roma ancora un paio di giorni.**

Bella: Now what do you have to do? **Ora che cosa deve fare?**

Peter: I've got to go and buy a pair of lightweight trousers and a couple of shirts. **Devo andare a comprare un paio di pantaloni leggeri e due camicie.**

Bella: OK. **Va bene.**

Peter: But first I have to go to the bank to change some money. **Ma prima devo andare in banca a cambiare dei soldi.**

Bella: OK. Let's have some coffee, then I'll come with you. **Va bene. Prendiamo il caffè poi l'accompagno.**

2. At the bank. **Alla banca.**

Clerk **Impiegato = Imp:**

Peter: I'd like to change English money into Italian lire. What's the exchange rate today? **Vorrei cambiare dei soldi inglesi in lire italiane. Quant'e il cambio oggi?**

Imp: 2,400 lire for cash, and 2,350 for travellers cheques. **2,400 lire per denari contanti, e 2,350 per travellers cheques.**

Peter: I'd like to change £200 in travellers cheques, please. **Vorrei cambiare 200 sterline di travellers cheques, per favore.**

Imp: Will you give me your passport, please. There you are, Mr.West – 470,000 lire in all. **Mi dà il passaporto, per piacere? Ecco, Signor West, 470,000 lire in tutto.**

Peter: Thank you. Good day. **Grazie, buongiorno.**

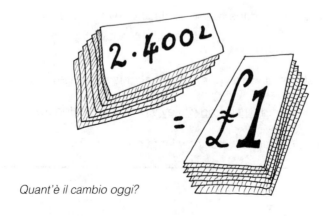

Quant'è il cambio oggi?

72

3.

At the clothes shop
Peter buys a shirt.

Nel negozio di abiti.
Peter compra una camicia

Salesman

Commesso = Com:

Com: Good evening.
Can I help you?

Buona sera, signori,
desiderano?

Peter: Can you show me some sports shirts please?

Può mostrarmi qualche camicia sportiva,
per piacere?

Com: Of course. What size are you?

Certamente, che taglia porta?

Peter: I take medium size: 40 or 42.

Porto una taglia media: 40 o 42.

Com: Here you are, have a look at these sports shirts.
They're the latest fashion, just in today.

Ecco, guardi, di tipo sportivo
abbiamo questi modelli.
Ultima moda,
arrivati oggi.

Peter: I like this one. Have you got any other colours?

Mi piace questo modello. Ha
altri colori?

Com: We have it in white, red, pink, yellow and blue.

L'abbiamo in bianco, rosso,
rosa, giallo e azzurro.

Peter: How much is it?

Quanto viene?

Com: It's 40,000 lire.
It's pure cotton.

Viene 40,000 lire.
È cotone puro.

Peter: OK, I'll take this one.

Va bene, prendo questo.

4.

At the clothes shop
Peter buys a pair of trousers.

Nel negozio di abiti
Peter compra un paio di pantaloni.

Com: This year white is very fashionable.
We also have other designs.
There are these striped ones, if you prefer.

Quest'anno il bianco
è molto di moda.
Abbiamo anche altri modelli.
Ci sono questi a righe,
se preferisce.

Peter: No, I don't like the striped ones.
I'd like to try the white ones on.

No, quelli a righe non mi piacciono.
Vorrei provare i bianchi.

Bella: They suit you very well, Peter.

Le stanno molto bene, Peter.

Peter: OK, I'll take them.
How much is that altogether?

Bene, li prendo.
Quant'è in tutto?

Com: The shirt is 40,000 lire, plus 40,000 the trousers.
Total 80,000 lire.

La camicia viene 40,000 lire,
più 40,000 i pantaloni.
Totale: 80,000 lire.

Com: Anything else?

Desidera altro?

Peter: No, that's enough.
I haven't got much money.

No, basta così.
Non ho molto denaro.

Personalised Dialogues

1. You're stopped by another market researcher. This time you're too busy to answer the questions, but the researcher is persistent...

Market Res.: Le piace la...?
Lei: (Tell her you must phone home.)
Market Res.: Perchè?
Lei: (You've got to tell your parents you're staying in Rome for a couple more days.)
Market Res.: Le piaccione le...?
Lei: (You've got to go and buy a pair of trousers.)
Market Res.: Sì, ma...
Lei: (and a couple of shirts.)
Market Res.: Ah, le piacciono le camicie di seta?
Lei: (Yes, but first you must go to the bank. You must change some money.)
Market Res.: Ma...
Lei: (Say goodbye.)

2. You've made it to the bank with a few minutes to spare before closing time. You're in a hurry, but the bank clerk isn't.

(**Impiegata**/Clerk)

Lei: (Say hello.)
(You'd like to change some English money...)
Impiegata: Sì, signore.
Lei: (...into Italian lire.)
Impiegata: Sì, signore.
Lei: (Ask her what the exchange rate is today.)
Impiegata: Per denari contanti, o per travellers cheques?
Lei: (For travellers cheques.)
Impiegata: 2,350.
Lei: (You would like to change £200 worth please.)
Impiegata: Va bene. Mi dà il passaporto, per piacere?
Lei: (Oh no, it's in the hotel!)

3. You're in a clothes shop. The assistant is anxious to sell you as much as possible, but unfortunately you haven't got much money.

(**Commessa**/Saleswoman)

Commessa: Buona sera, signore, desidera?
Lei: (Say good evening. Ask her to show you a few sports shirts, please.)
Commessa: Certamente. Che taglia porta?
Lei: (You take a medium size: 40 or 42)
Commessa: Ecco, guardi, di tipo sportivo abbiamo questi modelli. Ultima moda, arrivati oggi.
Lei: (Say you like this one. Has she got any other colours?)
Commessa: L'abbiamo in bianco, rosso, rosa, giallo e azzurro.
Lei: (Ask her how much it is.)
Commessa: Viene 40,000 lire. È cotone puro.
Lei: (OK, you'll take the yellow shirt.)
Commessa: Altro, signore? Una cravatta, calzini, slip, pullover, una giacca?
Lei: (No, no, that's enough. You haven't got much money.)

4. The assistant is very persuasive. She insists on showing you a pair of white trousers.

Commessa: **Quest'anno il bianco è molto di moda.**
Lei: (You don't like them.)
Commessa: **Abbiamo anche altri modelli. Ci sono questi a righe, se preferisce.**
Lei: (You don't like striped ones.)
Commessa: **Li abbiamo anche in giallo.**
Lei: (You don't like them.) (Has she got any other colours?)
Commessa: **Li abbiamo anche in rosso, azzurro, e nero.**
Lei: (You'd like to try the black ones.)
Commessa: **Le stanno molto bene, signore. Anche la camicia le sta molto bene.**
Lei: (OK, you'll take them. How much is that altogether?)
Commessa: **102,000 lire, signore.**
Lei: (Ah, first you must go to the bank!)

No, quelli a righe non mi piacciono.

Grammar

1. VERBS – PERFECT TENSE

Until now the story has taken place in the present tense. From this Act on the narrative is in the perfect tense, describing <u>what happened</u>, rather than what is happening.

The past tenses are underlined in the text.

In this Act the perfect tense in Italian is used to refer to an action or process which has been completed. It is formed by using the present tense of the verb **avere**, or **essere**, with the past participle.

In general, verbs which take an object use **avere**; verbs not taking an object (e.g. verbs of movement) use **essere**.

The regular past participle is formed by replacing the endings of the infinitive as follows:

-ARE verbs : **-ato**

    preparare – preparato
    andare – andato

-IRE verbs : **– ito**

    finire – finito
    uscire – uscito

Some verbs ending in **-ERE** form their past participle in **-uto**

vendere – to sell

    venduto.

But most are unpredictable and should be learned along with irregular forms of other verbs. Here are some examples from the story:

1.1 With **AVERE**

telefonare	**telefonato**	**Peter ha telefonato a casa.**
parlare	**parlato**	**Peter ha parlato con sua madre.**
dare	**dato**	**L'impiegato ha dato a Peter biglietti 50,000 lire.**
mostrare	**mostrato**	**Il commesso ha mostrato a Peter un paio di pantaloni.**
preparare	**preparato**	**Ha preparato un' ottima insalata.**

Peter ha telefonato a casa

1.2 With **ESSERE**

andare	**andato**	**Peter è andato subito allo sportello del cambio.**
uscire	**uscito**	**Peter e Bella sono usciti dalla banca.**

Note that with **essere** the past participle agrees, like an adjective:

Peter è uscito	(Masc.)
Bella è uscita	(Fem.)
Sono usciti	(Plur.)

1.3 IRREGULAR FORMS

essere	**stato**	**È stato un ottimo pranzo.**
dire	**detto**	**Ha detto che deve rimanere a Roma.**

2. VERBS – IMPERFECT TENSE

The imperfect tense is used to describe past actions or states which are incomplete. The formation of this tense will be dealt with later.

Note the following examples from the story:

Avevo molta fame.	I was very hungry.
Il sole era caldissimo.	The sun was very hot.
Il commesso del negozio era un signore di mezza età.	The shop assistant was a middle-aged gentleman.
Portava un abito grigio.	He was wearing a grey suit.
Faceva ottima publicità al negozio.	He was an excellent advertisement for the shop.

3. **DOVERE** – 'to have to'   **POTERE** – 'to be able to'

devo   I must, have to

deve   He, she, you must/have to

This verb is always followed by the infinitive:

devo	**devo dire**	**devo dire ai miei genitori.**
	devo andare	**devo andare in banca.**
deve	**deve rimanere**	**deve rimanere a Roma.**

Potere – 'to be able to' is used in the same way:

può	**può telefonare**	**può telefonare da qui**
	può mostrare	**può mostrarmi qualche camicia sportiva?**

Note: **Qualche** ('some') is followed by the singular, not plural, as you might expect.

Vorrei – 'I'd like to' is also followed by the infinitive:

vorrei	**vorrei cambiare**	**vorrei cambiare dei soldi inglesi**
	vorrei provare	**vorrei provare i pantaloni bianchi**

4. EXPRESSIONS with **AVERE**

Ho fame	I'm hungry
Ho caldo	I'm hot
Ho sete	I'm thirsty
Ho freddo	I'm cold

5. **'LO'**

The article **il** becomes **lo** before 'st', 'sp' etc., :

il modello	**lo stesso modello**
il tennis	**lo sport**

The reason for this is phonetic.

6. **QUESTO/QUELLO** – 'this', 'that', 'these', 'those'

These agree like an adjective:

questo modello
questa cravatta
quelli a righe
quelli bianchi

mi   to me

gli   to him

le   to her, to you

Può mostrar<u>mi</u> qualche camicia sportiva?

<u>Le</u> ha detto.
He told her.

Vorrei far<u>le</u> un piccolo regalo.
I'd like to make you a small present.

Games

1. NUMBERS

Unscramble the following list of numbers, matching them with the correct numeral:

1	**tre**	6	**otto**
2	**quattro**	7	**dieci**
3	**due**	8	**sette**
4	**nove**	9	**cinque**
5	**uno**	10	**sei**

2. COLOURS

Pick out all the colours in the text of Act 4, and highlight them appropriately with your marker pen, e.g. **azzurro**...

3. OPERATOR

Your working for Italian Directory Enquiries. Spell out the following telephone numbers in full, digit by digit.

3.1   00-44-1-734-8001

3.2   99457

3.3   756626

3.4   23480

3.5   69251

4. IF THE PRICE IS RIGHT...

Fill in the missing numbers, and write them out in full:

4.1   **L'impiegato ha dato a Peter biglietti da _ _ _ _ _ _ e da _ _ _ _ _ _ lire.**

4.2   **_ _ _ _ lire per denari contanti e _ _ _ _ lire per travellers cheques.**

4.3   **Ecco, signor West, _ _ _ _ _ _ _ lire in tutto.**

4.4   **Porto una taglia media: _ _ o _ _.**

4.5   **Non costa molto. Viene solo _ _ _ _ _ lire.**

4.6   **Le due camicie vengono _ _ _ _ _ _ _.**

5. INVENTORY

You are in charge of a mens' clothes shop. Make an inventory of all the items you sell. They are all in the text, and all in the plural. Use a dictionary if you wish to expand your stock.

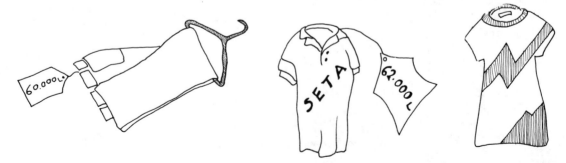

What if...? **Se invece...**

Continue your version of the story, using the perfect tense in the narrative. Dress as wildly as you wish...!

Act 5 **Atto 5**

Scene 1 **Scena 1**

Bella and Peter make plans **Bella e Peter fanno i piani**
for the evening. **per la serata.**

Bella took Peter **Bella ha portato Peter**
to the **Caffé degli Artisti**. **al Caffè degli Artisti.**
It's a well-known old café **È un vecchio caffè famoso,**
once frequented by **dove un tempo si incontravano**
artists, writers and poets **artisti, scrittori e poeti**
– local and foreign. **romani e stranieri.**
In front of the café, **Davanti al caffè,**
on the pavement, **sul marciapiede,**
surrounding the tables, **attorno ai tavolini,**
were huge terra-cotta vases **c'erano grandi vasi di terracotta**
of azaleas, geraniums and acacias **con azalee, gerani e acacie**
in bloom. **in fiore.**

The scent of the flowers mingled **Il profumo dei fiori si mescolava**
with the smell of ice-cream **con l'aroma dei gelati**
and of the traffic. **e gli odori del traffico.**
By the side of the café **Di fianco al caffè**
was an enormous **c'era un'enorme**
bright green palm tree. **palma verdissima.**
There were lots of people **C'era molta gente**
sitting at the tables. **seduta ai tavolini.**
Smart people, and people **C'era gente elegante, e gente**
in strange clothes. **vestita in modo strano.**

Bella and Peter sat down **Bella e Peter si sono seduti**
at the one free table. **all'unico tavolino libero.**
The waiters were very busy, **I camerieri erano molto occupati,**
running backwards and forwards. **e correvano di qua e di là.**
Peter thought it very amusing **Peter pensava che era molto divertente**
just sitting and **rimanere qui, seduto,**
looking at the people. **a guardare la gente.**

In front of the café **Davanti al caffè,**
an elderly painter **un anziano pittore**
with a white beard **con la barba bianca**
was painting the people **dipingeva la gente**
sitting at the tables. **seduta ai tavolini.**

From a nearby window **Da una finestra vicina,**
a beautiful tenor voice **una bella voce di tenore**
was singing **cantava**
a well-known aria from Rigoletto. **una famosa aria dal Rigoletto.**

At last the waiter **Finalmente il cameriere**
came to serve them. **è venuto a servirli.**

81

Bella:	What will you have, Peter, tea or coffee?	**Che cosa prende, Peter, tè o caffè?**
Peter:	I'll have tea.	**Io prendo un tè.**
Waiter:	With milk or lemon?	**Al latte o al limone?**
Peter:	Milk, please.	**Al latte, per favore.**
Bella:	For me a lemon tea. Bring us some cakes as well, please.	**Per me un tè al limone. Ci porti anche qualche pasta, per favore.**

The waiter came back a little later, with a plate full of cakes — chocolate, cream and liqueur. When Bella saw the look of surprise on Peter's face, she burst out laughing.

Il cameriere è tornato poco dopo, con un piatto pieno di paste al cioccolato, alla panna, e al liquore. Quando Bella ha visto l'espressione sorpresa sul viso di Peter, è scoppiata a ridere.

Bella: Don't worry, Peter, we don't have to eat them all! Go on, try one. They're the house speciality. Just smell them!

Non si preoccupi, Peter, non siamo obbligati a mangiarle tutte! Prego, ne assaggi una. Sono la specialità della casa. Senta che profumo!

Peter tried a liqueur cake.

Peter ha assaggiato una pasta al liquore.

Peter: Mmmm, delicious!

Mmmm, che squisita!

Peter gave Bella a serious look.

Peter ha guardato Bella molto serio.

Peter: Tell me, Bella. What was in the package?

Mi dica, Bella, che cosa c'era nel pacchetto?

After a moment's hesitation, Bella too gave him a serious look.

Dopo un momento di esitazione, Bella lo ha guardato seria anche lei.

Bella: Nothing. Only papers.

Niente. Solo documenti.

Then she smiled again.

Poi ha sorriso di nuovo.

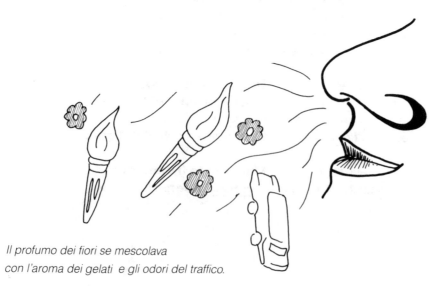

Il profumo dei fiori se mescolava con l'aroma dei gelati e gli odori del traffico.

	Scene 2	**Scena 2**
Peter:	What shall we do this evening?	**Che cosa facciamo questa sera?**
	Shall we go to the cinema,	**Andiamo al cinema,**
	or the theatre?	**o a teatro?**
	Maybe we can still buy tickets.	**Forse possiamo ancora comprare i biglietti.**
	Or would you prefer to go dancing?	**O preferisce andare a ballare?**
Bella:	I like everything: cinema,	**Mi piace tutto: il cinema,**
	theatre, dancing ...	**il teatro, il ballo ...**
	You're the guest. You choose.	**Lei è l'ospite. Scelga lei.**
Peter:	I'd like to go out.	**Vorrei uscire.**
	I don't fancy staying at home	**Non vorrei rimanere in casa**
	and watching television!	**a guardare la televisione!**
Bella:	I'd rather go out too.	**Anch'io preferisco uscire.**

They looked
at the listings in the newspaper,
but there was nothing interesting.
So they decided to go out to dinner
in a trattoria Bella knew.

Hanno guardato
l'elenco degli spettacoli sul giornale,
ma non c'era niente d'interessante,
così hanno deciso di andare fuori a cena
in una trattoria che Bella conosceva.

Bella:	It's a small trattoria,	**È una trattoria piccola,**
	but very intimate and friendly,	**ma molto intima e simpatica,**
	in Trastevere.	**a Trastevere.**
	They have excellent home-cooking.	**Fanno ottima cucina casalinga.**
	Sometimes they have music too.	**Qualche volta c'è anche la musica.**
	And it's not very expensive either.	**E poi non è cara.**
Peter:	What an excellent idea!	**Che ottima idea!**
	That way I can wear the silk shirt	**Così posso mettere la camicia di seta**
	with the tie you bought me.	**con la cravatta che mi ha comprato lei.**

Bella put a hand
on Peter's arm.

Bella ha messo la mano
sul braccio di Peter.

Bella:	Listen, Peter,	**Senta, Peter,**
	why don't we say	**perchè non ci diamo**
	tu to each other?	**del 'tu'?**
	After all we're friends now,	**Ormai siamo amici,**
	aren't we?	**no?**
Peter:	Fine by me,	**Con piacere**
	but it'll be	**però per me sarà**
	a bit difficult for me,	**un po' difficile,**
	because Italian verbs	**perchè i verbi italiani**
	are pretty hard going.	**sono un osso duro!**
Bella:	We must go now,	**Ora dobbiamo andare,**
	it's already 6 o'clock.	**sono già le sei.**
	I've still got to do some shopping.	**Devo ancora fare qualche compera.**
	And we've got to change	**E poi dobbiamo cambiarci**
	before dinner.	**prima di cena.**
	Peter called the waiter	**Peter ha chiamato il cameriere**
	and asked for the bill.	**e ha domandato il conto.**
Waiter:	10.400 (ten thousand	**10,400 (dieci mila**
	four hundred) lire, sir.	**quattrocento) lire, signore.**
	Peter paid.	**Peter ha pagato.**
Peter:	Do I have to leave a tip?	**Devo lasciare la mancia?**
Bella:	No, it's not necessary.	**No, non è necessario.**
	The service is already included.	**Il servizio è già incluso.**

Scene 3	**Scena 3**
Before going home	**Prima di ritornare a casa**
Bella and Peter	**Bella e Peter**
went into a big store,	**sono entrati in un grande magazzino,**
where Bella saw a dress	**dove Bella ha visto un vestito**
she wanted to buy.	**che voleva comprare.**
It was a pale pink dress,	**Era un vestito rosa pallido,**
very simple and very smart.	**molto semplice e molto elegante.**
Bella tried it on.	**Bella lo ha provato.**
It suited her,	**Le stava bene,**
so she decided to buy it.	**così ha deciso di comprarlo.**
She also bought a pair of tights	**Ha comprato anche un collant,**
with little silver stars	**con piccole stelle d'argento**
on the legs.	**sulle gambe.**
As they came out of the store	**Quando sono usciti dal grande magazzino**
the sun was beginning to set,	**il sole cominciava a tramontare,**
and the sky was bright red.	**e il cielo era rosso vivo.**
In the trees the birds	**Sugli alberi gli uccelli**
seemed very excited.	**sembravano molto eccitati.**
It was warm.	**L'aria era tiepida.**
It was nice to be out.	**Si stava molto bene.**
Bella decided	**Bella ha deciso**
to go back home straight away,	**di andare subito a casa,**
and Peter decided	**e Peter ha deciso**
to return to the hotel	**di ritornare all'albergo**
to change and have a shower.	**a cambiarsi, e a fare la doccia.**
They arranged to meet	**Si sono dati appuntamento**
at Bella's house at eight.	**a casa di Bella alle otto.**

*Si sono dati appuntamento
a casa di Bella alle otto.*

	Scene 4	**Scena 4**
	On the way	**Per la strada**
	Peter stopped at a chemist's.	**Peter si è fermato in una farmacia.**
Chemist:	Good evening.	**Buonasera.**
	What can I do for you?	**Desidera?**
Peter:	I'd like some pills	**Vorrei qualche pastiglia**
	for a headache.	**per il mal di testa.**
	I don't feel too bad,	**Non sto molto male,**
	but I'd sooner take something	**ma preferisco prendere qualcosa**
	straight away.	**subito.**
Chemist:	Yes, I agree,	**Sì, sono d'accordo,**
	but I think two aspirins	**ma penso che due pastiglie di aspirina**
	will be enough.	**saranno sufficienti.**
	When Peter came out	**Quando Peter è uscito**
	of the chemist's	**dalla farmacia**
	he wasn't sure which way to go	**non era sicuro da che parte andare**
	back to the hotel.	**per ritornare all'albergo.**
	Along the pavement, a young man	**Sul marciapiede, un giovanotto**
	was coming towards him.	**veniva verso di lui.**
	Peter stopped him.	**Peter lo ha fermato.**
Peter:	Excuse me,	**Scusi,**
	can you tell me the way	**può indicarmi la strada**
	to via Milano?	**per via Milano?**
Youth:	I'm sorry, but I'm not from Rome.	**Mi dispiace, ma non sono di Roma.**
	I don't know that street.	**Non conosco quella via.**
	Why don't you ask	**Perchè non domanda**
	at the newspaper kiosk?	**all'edicola dei giornali?**
Peter:	Thank you, I will.	**Sì, grazie.**
	Peter went to the kiosk	**Peter è andato all'edicola**
	and asked the newsagent.	**e ha domandato alla giornalaia.**
Peter:	Excuse me, can you tell me	**Scusi, può indicarmi la strada**
	the way to the Hotel Tre Palme,	**per l'Hotel Tre Palme,**
	in via Milano?	**in via Milano?**
Newsagent:	Sure, go to the end	**Certo, vada in fondo**
	of the street,	**alla strada,**
	as far as the traffic lights.	**fino al semaforo.**
	Then take the second street	**Poi prenda la seconda via**
	on the left:	**a sinistra;**
	that's via Milano.	**quella è via Milano.**
Peter:	Thanks, is it far?	**Grazie, è lontana?**
Newsagent:	No, it's quite near:	**No, è abbastanza vicina:**
	about 500 (five hundred) metres.	**a circa 500 metri.**
	At last Peter got back	**Finalmente Peter è arrivato**
	to the hotel.	**all'hotel.**
	He went straight to his room,	**È andato subito in camera,**
	had a shower,	**ha fatto la doccia,**
	and dressed for dinner.	**e si è vestito per la cena.**
	His headache had gone.	**Il mal di testa era passato.**
	He felt on form once more.	**Si sentiva di nuovo in forma.**

ATTO 5 (i)

Bella ha portato Peter al Caffè degli Artisti.

Dove un tempo si incontravano, artisti, scrittori e poeti.

Davanti al caffè, sul marciapiede, attorno al tavolini, c'erano grandi vasi di terracotta.

Il profumo dei fiori si mescolava con l'aroma dei gelati e gli odori del traffico.

C'era un'enorme palma verdissima.

Peter pensava che era molto divertente rimanere qui seduto, a guardare la gente.

I camerieri erano molto occupati, e correvano di qua e di là.

Davanti al caffè, un anziano pittore con la barba bianca dipingeva la gente seduta ai tavolini.

Che cosa prende, Peter, tè o caffè

Una bella voce di tenore cantava una famosa aria dal Rigoletto.

Al latte o al limone?

Mi dica, Bella, che cosa c'era nel pacchetto?

Non si preoccupi. Peter, non siamo obbligati a mangiarle tutte!

Niente. Solo documenti.

ATTO 5 (iii)

Andiamo al cinema,

o a teatro?

O preferisce andare a ballare?

Non vorrei rimanere in casa a guardare la televisione!

Hanno guardato l'elenco degli spettacoli sul giornale.

Fanno ottima cucina casalinga.

Bella ha messo la mano sul braccio di Peter.

ATTO 5 (iv)

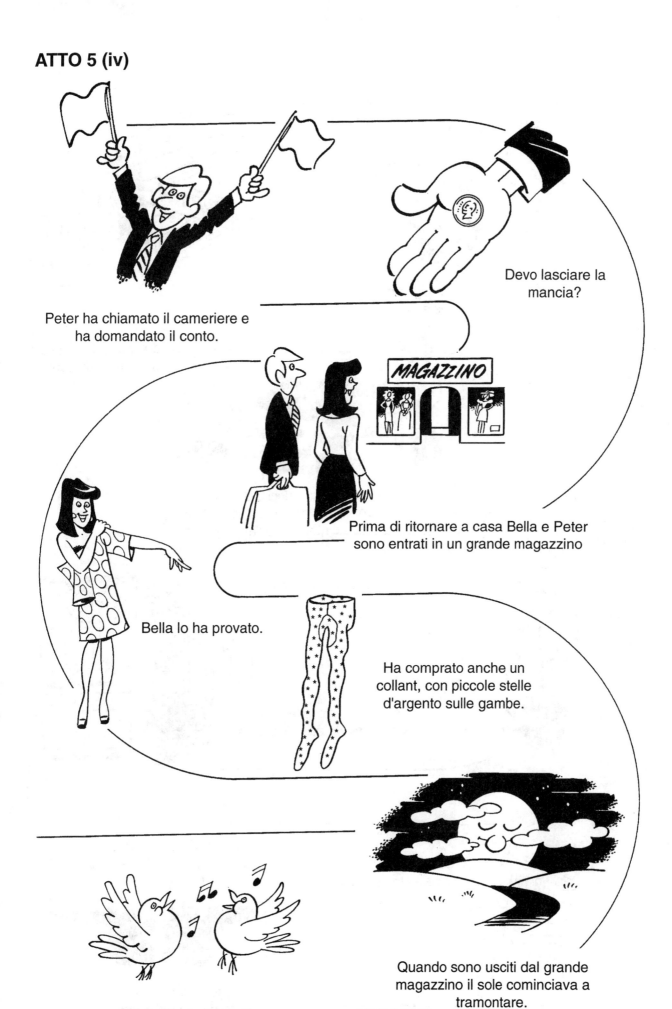

Peter ha chiamato il cameriere e ha domandato il conto.

Devo lasciare la mancia?

Prima di ritornare a casa Bella e Peter sono entrati in un grande magazzino

Bella lo ha provato.

Ha comprato anche un collant, con piccole stelle d'argento sulle gambe.

Quando sono usciti dal grande magazzino il sole cominciava a tramontare.

Sugli alberi gli uccelli sembravano molto eccitati.

ATTO 5 (v)

Vorrei qualche pastiglia per il mal di testa.

Sì, sono d'accordo, ma penso che due pastiglie di aspirina saranno sufficienti.

Quando Peter è uscito dalla farmacia non era sicuro da che parte andare per ritornare all'albergo.

Scusi, può indicarmi la strada per via Milano?

Peter è andato all'edicola e ha domandato alla giornalaia.

È andato subito in camera, ha fatto la doccia.

Certo, vada in fondo alla strada, fino al semaforo.

Si sentiva di nuovo in forma.

Intonation and Pronunciation

Concentrate on the rhythm and stress patterns of the past tenses in Italian. Speak aloud all the sentences in the text of Scenes 1 and 2 containing past tenses (underlined), reading them fluently, without hesitation, noting where the stress falls: e.g. **c'erano; si incontravano; si mescolava; correvano.**

Note also that the '**h**' in **ha** and **hanno** is silent:

1. **ha portato**
2. **ha assaggiato**
3. **ha guardato**
4. **hanno deciso**
5. **hanno guardato**

Hanno guardato l'elenco degli spettacoli sul giornale.

Functional Dialogues

1. At the Caffé degli Artisti. **Al Caffè degli Artisti.**

Peter:	It's very amusing here.	**È molto divertente qui.**
	I like watching the people.	**Mi piace guardare la gente.**
Bella:	Yes, it's very amusing.	**Sì, è molto divertente.**
	What will you have, Peter,	**Che cosa prende, Peter,**
	tea or coffee?	**tè o caffè?**
Peter:	I'll have a tea.	**Io prendo un tè.**
Cam:	With milk or lemon?	**Al latte o al limone?**
Peter:	With milk please.	**Al latte, per favore.**
Bella:	I'll have lemon tea.	**Per me un tè al limone.**
Cam:	Yes, signorina.	**Sì, signorina.**
Bella:	And bring us some cakes too,	**E ci porti anche qualche pasta,**
	please.	**per favore.**
Cam:	There you are, chocolate cakes,	**Ecco, ci sono paste al cioccolato,**
	cream cakes and cakes with liqueur.	**alla panna e al liquore.**
Bella:	Go on, try one Peter.	**Prego, ne assaggi una, Peter.**
	They're the house speciality.	**Sono la specialità della casa.**
Peter:	Mmm, delicious!	**Mmm, che squisita!**

2. Peter and Bella make plans. **Peter e Bella fanno i piani.**

Peter:	What shall we do this evening?	**Che cosa facciamo questa sera?**
Bella:	I don't know.	**Non lo so.**
Peter:	Shall we go to the cinema, or	**Andiamo al cinema o**
	to the theatre? Or would you rather	**a teatro? O preferisce**
	go dancing?	**andare a ballare?**
Bella:	I like everything: cinema,	**Mi piace tutto: il cinema,**
	theatre, dancing. You choose.	**il teatro, il ballo. Scelga lei.**
Peter:	Do you want to stay at home	**Vuole rimanere in casa**
	and watch television?	**a guardare la televisione?**
Bella:	No, I'd rather go out.	**No, preferisco uscire.**
Peter:	Let's go out to dinner, then.	**Allora, andiamo fuori a cena.**
Bella:	Yes, let's! I know a trattoria	**Sì, andiamo! Conosco una trattoria**
	in Trastevere – small, but nice,	**a Trastevere, piccola, ma simpatica,**
	and very intimate...	**e molto intima...**

*Un piatto pieno di paste
al cioccolato, alla panna, e al liquore.*

3.   At the chemist's.   **In farmacia.**

Chemist   **Farmacista = Farm:**

Farm:	Good evening, can I help you?	**Buonasera, desidera?**
Peter:	I've got a headache.	**Ho mal di testa.**
	I'd like some pills.	**Vorrei qualche pastiglia.**
	I don't feel too bad.	**Non sto molto male.**
	But I'd sooner take	**Ma preferisco prendere**
	something straight away.	**qualcosa subito.**
Farm:	Yes, I agree. I think	**Sì, d'accordo. Penso che**
	two aspirins	**due pastiglie di aspirina**
	will be enough.	**saranno sufficienti.**
Peter:	OK., thanks.	**Va bene, grazie.**

4.   Asking the way.   **La strada per...**

Young man   **Giovane = Gio:**

Peter:	Excuse me, can you tell me the way to via Milano?	**Scusi, può indicarmi la strada per via Milano?**
Gio:	I'm sorry, I don't know that street.	**Mi dispiace, non conosco quella via.**
Peter:	OK, thanks...	**Va bene, grazie...**
	Excuse me, can you tell me the way to the Hotel Tre Palme, via Milano?	**Scusi, può indicarmi la strada per l'Hotel Tre Palme, in via Milano?**
Gio:	Sure, go to the end of the street as far as the traffic lights	**Certo, vada in fondo alla strada... fino al semaforo...**
Peter:	As far as the traffic lights?	**...fino al semaforo...?**
Gio:	Yes, then take the second street on the left ...	**Sì, poi prenda la seconda via a sinistra ...**
Peter:	...the second on the left ...	**...la seconda a sinistra ...**
Gio:	That's via Milano ...	**Quella è via Milano.**
Peter:	Thanks, is it far?	**Grazie, è lontana?**
Gio:	No, it's very near.	**No, è vicinissima.**

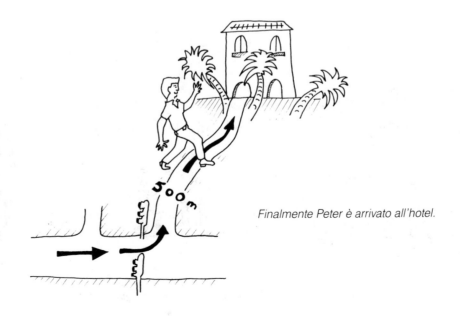

Finalmente Peter è arrivato all'hotel.

Personalised Dialogues

1. Decisions, decisions. You're having a relaxing time at an outdoor cafè, watching the world go by. Your companion insists you try the local specialities.
(**Compagna**/Companion)

Lei:	(It's very amusing here. You like watching the people.)
Compagna:	**Sì, è molto divertente. Che cosa prende, tè, caffè, whisky?**
Lei:	(You'll have a tea.)
Cameriera:	**Al latte o al limone?**
Lei:	(With lemon, please.)
Compagna:	**Per me un whisky e ci porti anche qualche pasta, per favore.**
Cameriera:	**Sì, signorina.**

Later:

Cameriera:	**Ecco, paste al cioccolato, alla panna, e al liquore.**
Lei:	(It's not possible!)
Compagna:	**Non siamo obbligati a mangiarle tutte! Prego, ne assaggi una. Sono la specialità della casa.**
Lei:	(All right, you'll have a liqueur cake.)
Compagna:	**Le piace?**
Lei:	(Mmm, it's delicious!)
Compagna:	**Sono tutte squisite!**

2. The best laid plans... You and a friend are planning the perfect evening out.

Lei:	(What shall we do this evening?)
Amica:	**Non lo so.**
Lei:	(Shall we go to the cinema, or the theatre? Ask her if she'd rather go dancing.)
Amica:	**Non lo so. Mi piace tutto.**
Lei:	(Ask her if she wants to stay home and watch television.)
Amica:	**No, preferisco uscire.**
Lei:	(Suggest going out to dinner, then.)
Amica:	**Sì, andiamo! Conosco una trattoria molto simpatica e molto intima. Si chiama "A Trastevere".**
Lei:	(Excellent.)
Amica:	**Ah, ma oggi è domenica. È chiusa.**

Mi piace tutto: il cinema, il teatro, il ballo.

3. Italian verbs, or one too many liqueur cakes, have given you a headache. The chemist is cautious.

(Farmacista/Chemist)

Farmacista: **Buonasera, desidera?**
Lei: (You've got a headache.) (You'd like some pills.)
Farmacista: **Sta molto male?**
Lei: (You're not feeling too bad. But you'd rather have something straight away.)
Farmacista: **Sono d'accordo. Penso che due pastiglie saranno sufficienti.**
Lei: (OK thanks.)

4. You've lost the way to the hotel. You try some friendly passers-by.

(Passante/Passer-by)

Lei: (Say Excuse me. Can she tell you the way to via Condotti?)
Passante: **Mi dispiace, non sono di Roma. Non conosco quella via.**
Lei: (OK, thanks.)

Lei: (Say Excuse me, and ask her the way to the Hotel Ritz, via Condotti.)
Passante: **Certo, vada in fondo alla strada...fino al semaforo...**
Lei: (As far as the traffic lights.)
Passante: **Sì, poi prenda la prima via a sinistra.**
Lei: (...the first on the left...)
Passante: **Quella è via Condotti.**
Lei: (Thanks, is it far?)
Passante: **No, è vicinissima.**

Vorrei qualche pastiglia
per il mal di testa.

Grammar

1. VERBS – IMPERFECT TENSE (Contd.)

As noted before in the Grammar section of Act 4, No. 2, the Italian imperfect is used to express past states or repeated or continuous actions.

It is formed as follows:

-ARE verbs : **cantare** **cant<u>avo</u>** I...

  cant<u>ava</u> he/she... you ...

  cant<u>avamo</u> we...

  cant<u>avano</u> they...

Story examples:

> **...una bella voce di tenore <u>cantava</u> una famosa aria dal Rigoletto.**
> (was singing)

> **...dove un tempo <u>si incontravano</u> artisti**...
> (used to meet)

-ERE verbs: **dipingere** **diping<u>evo</u>** I...

  diping<u>eva</u> he/she, you...

  diping<u>evamo</u> we...

  diping<u>evano</u> they...

Story examples:

> **...un anziano pittore ... <u>dipingeva</u> la gente** ...
> (was painting)

> **...una trattoria che Bella <u>conosceva</u>.**
> (knew, used to know)

-IRE verbs	**venire**	**ven<u>ivo</u>**	I...
		ven<u>iva</u>	he/she, you...
		ven<u>ivamo</u>	we...
		ven<u>ivano</u>	they...

Story examples:

> **...un giovanotto <u>veniva</u> verso di lui**
> (was coming)

> **...si <u>sentiva</u> di nuovo in forma**
> (he felt)

The only irregular form in the imperfect is **essere**:

	ero	I...
	era	he/she, you...
	eravamo	we...
	erano	they...

Story examples:

> **...il cielo <u>era</u> rosso vivo**

> **...i camerieri <u>erano</u> molto occupati**

2. C'ERA... C'ERANO

The imperfect of **c'è** is **c'era**:

> **c'era molta gente**　　　　　　　　　there was...

> **non c'era niente d'interessante**

The imperfect of **ci sono is <u>c'erano:</u>**

> **c'erano grandi vasi**　　　　　　　　there were...

3. POSITION

davanti a	in front of	**davanti al caffè**
attorno a	around	**attorno ai tavolini**
di fianco a	beside	**di fianco al caffè**
fuori	outside	**andare fuori**
su	on top of	**sugli alberi**
verso di	towards	**veniva verso di lui**
fino a	as far as	**fino al semaforo**

Note also the phrases:	Is it far?	**È lontano?**
	Is it near?	**È vicino?**

When referring to a specific location which is feminine (e.g. **la via, la stazione**), they change accordingly:
È lontana? No, è vicina.

4. **STARE**

Peter's feeling ill.	**Peter sta male**.
I'm not (feeling) too ill.	**Non sto molto male**.
It was very pleasant.	**Si stava molto bene**.

5. **CHE**

Che (that, which, what) is one of those little words that (which) go a long way:

Peter pensava che era molto divertente ...

La cravatta che mi ha comprato lei ...

... un vestito che voleva comprare

Che ottima idea!

6. PERCHÈ

Perchè (?) means both 'why?' and 'because...':

Perchè non ci diamo del tu? ('**tu'** – you – is used between friends)

... **perchè i verbi italiani sono un osso duro!**

7. DAYS OF THE WEEK

In Italian **domenica** (Sunday) is considered the last day of the week.
The other days are as follows:

lunedì

martedì

mercoledì

giovedì

venerdì

sabato

Except for **domenica** and **sabato** the stress always falls on the last syllable.

Perchè non ci diamo del 'tu'?

Games

1. SPOT THE PAST

The past tenses are underlined (or otherwise indicated) in Scenes 1 and 2 of Act 5, but not in Scenes 3 and 4. Use your marker pen to highlight the past tenses in Scenes 3 and 4.

2. SCRIPT EDITOR

The scriptwriter has mistakenly left the script in the present tense. Convert the following lines into the past (perfect, or imperfect as in the text of Act 5).

2. 1	**Peter paga il conto.**
2. 2	**Peter chiama il cameriere.**
3. 3	**... una trattoria che Bella conosce...**
3. 4	**Bella mette la mano sul braccio di Peter.**
3. 5	**Guardano l'elenco degli spettacoli.**
3. 6	**Che cosa c'è nel pachetto?**
3. 7	**Peter sorride di nuovo.**
3. 8	**Il cameriere torna poco dopo.**
3. 9	**Una bella voce di baritono canta una famosa aria dal Rigoletto.**
3.10	**Peter assaggia una pasta al liquore.**

3. AH! YES, I REMEMBER IT WELL

The times are changing, but you like to remember things the way they were. Use **c'era** or **c'erano**...

3. 1	**C'è un'enorme palma verdissima.**
3. 2	**Ci sono grandi vasi di terracotta.**
3. 3	**Non c'è niente d'interessante.**
3. 4	**C'è molta gente.**
3. 5	**Che cosa c'è nel pacchetto?**
3. 6	**Ci sono solo documenti.**

4. SIGN LANGUAGE

Use words instead of the following signs:

1

2

3

4

5

6

7

8

5. **CHE**

Four examples of **che** are given in No. 5.of the Grammar Section of this Act. There are eight others in the text. See if you can find them. Note the different meanings.

6. MYSTERY

6. 1	**Il Caffé degli Artisti è famoso. Perchè?**
6. 2	**C'era molta gente seduta ai tavolini. Perchè?**
6. 3	**I camerieri erano molto occupati. Perchè?**
6. 4	**Bella è scoppiata a ridere. Perchè?**
6. 5	**Bella e Peter hanno deciso di andare fuori a cena. Perchè?**
6. 6	**Peter non ha lasciato la mancia. Perchè?**
6. 7	**Il cielo era rosso vivo. Perchè?**
6. 8	**Peter si è fermato in una farmacia. Perchè?**

What if...? **Se invece...**

Your secret rendezvous may be in a cafè in Lisbon, Lima or Leningrad. Wherever it is, it's a cafè with a past. Who used to go there? What did they do? What were they like?

White-bearded revolutionaries perhaps, plotting the overthrow of governments, dreaming of power and the perfect society. Seductive courtesans surreptitiously plying their high-class trade. Poor students paying for their studies by playing the guitar or the harmonica for rich clients, singing a plaintive song of romance or protest...

It's a place to make plans for the future, and to try the local specialities — food and drink found nowhere else.

It's the scene of an intimate friendship being formed...

Later you may decide to go shopping, for clothes or for medicines, for example, something to make sure you're feeling on top form for the evening ahead.

Act 6 **Atto 6**

Scene 1 **Scena 1**

Bella and Peter go out to dinner. **Bella e Peter vanno fuori a cena.**

At 8 o'clock exactly Peter went to pick up Bella. **Alle 8 in punto Peter è andato a prendere Bella.**

Peter: Shall we take a taxi to go to Trastevere? **Prendiamo un taxi per andare a Trastevere?**

Bella: Yes. The restaurant is called *'Da Alfredo'.* **Sì, il ristorante si chiama 'Da Alfredo'.**
I booked a table for 8.30. **Ho prenotato un tavolo per le otto e trenta.**

There were already a lot of people in the restaurant. **Al ristorante c'era già molta gente.**
From the kitchen came the smell of barbecued meat. **Dalla cucina veniva il profumo della carne alla brace.**
There were lots of paintings on the walls. **C'erano molti quadri alle pareti.**

On every table there was a lighted candle. **Su ogni tavolo c'era una candela accesa.**
There was also a small vase of red carnations. **C'era anche un vasetto di garofani rossi.**
The tablecloths and napkins were pink, **Le tovaglie e i tovaglioli erano rosa;**
and the glasses were large, made of crystal. **e i bicchieri erano grandi, di cristallo.**

In one corner a singer played the guitar. **In un angolo, un cantante suonava la chitarra.**
A waiter sat them outside, **Un cameriere li ha fatti sedere fuori,**
in the garden, where Bella had booked the table. **in giardino, dove Bella aveva prenotato il tavolo.**

Peter: What a beautiful place, such a romantic atmosphere! **Che bel posto, e che atmosfera romantica!**

Bella: Do you like eating outside? **Ti piace mangiare fuori?**
Peter: Yes, Very much. **Moltissimo.**
In England, unfortunately, it's very rare to eat outside. **In Inghilterra, purtroppo, si mangia fuori molto raramente.**

Un cantante suonava la chitarra.

	English	Italian

Scene 2 — **Scena 2**

Alfredo, the owner, a tall man with a black moustache and a friendly smile, came up to their table. — **Alfredo, il padrone, un signore alto coi baffi neri e un sorriso simpatico, si è avvicinato al loro tavolo.**

Alfredo: Good evening, signorina Bruni, It's a pleasure to see you again. — **Buonasera, signorina Bruni. È un piacere rivederla.**

Good evening, sir. — **Buonasera, signore.**

Bella: Good evening, signor Alfredo. What nice things have you got this evening? — **Buonasera, signor Alfredo. Che cosa c'è di buono questa sera?**

Alfredo: For the first course we have an excellent risotto with mushrooms, or home-made noodles, *penne all'arrabbiata* ... — **Come primo piatto abbiamo un ottimo risotto ai funghi, oppure fettuccine fatte in case, penne all'arrabbiata ...**

Bella: Well, to start with I'll have a mushroom risotto. And you, Peter? — **Beh, per cominciare io prendo un risotto ai funghi. E tu, Peter?**

Peter: What are the *penne all'arrabbiata* like? — **Come sono le penne all'arrabbiata?**

Alfredo: They're done with a tomato sauce, garlic, and chilli peppers. — **Sono con salsa al pomodoro, aglio e peperoncino.**

Peter: They're very hot, aren't they? — **Sono molto piccanti, non è vero?**

Alfredo: Fairly. — **Abbastanza.**

They're very appetising. — **Sono molto appetitose.**

Peter: I love hot sauces. So for me, *penne all'arrabbiata* to start with. — **Amo le salse piccanti. Allora, per me penne all'arrabbiata per cominciare.**

Bella: And as a main dish what do you advise? — **E come secondo piatto, che cosa ci consiglia?**

Alfredo: There's barbecued meat, *osso buco,* roast mushrooms with garlic and rosemary ... — **C'è carne alla brace, osso buco ... ci sono funghi arrosto, con aglio e rosmarino.**

Peter: What's *osso buco?* — **Che cos'è l'osso buco?**

Alfredo: It's veal on the bone, cooked in wine, onion and parsley. — **È vitello con osso, cotto con vino, cipolla e prezzemolo.**

Bella:	The English produce the best beef,	**Gli inglesi producono il miglior manzo,**
	the French the best lamb,	**i francesi il miglior agnello,**
	and the Italians produce the best veal.	**e gli italiani producono il miglior vitello.**
	In this restaurant you can eat	**In questo ristorante si mangia**
	the best *osso buco* in Italy!	**il miglior osso buco d'Italia!**
Alfredo:	The lady is right.	**La signorina ha ragione.**
	Will you try the *osso buco*, sir?	**Vuole provare l'osso buco, signore?**
Bella:	I don't think he will.	**Non credo.**
	Osso buco for me,	**Osso buco per me,**
	but my guest doesn't eat meat,	**ma il mio ospite non mangia carne:**
	he's vegetarian.	**è vegetariano.**
Peter:	But I love mushrooms.	**Però amo molto i funghi.**
Alfredo:	So, for the gentleman we can do	**Allora per il signore possiamo fare**
	roast mushrooms with potatoes,	**funghi arrosto con patatine**
	and a nice dish	**e un bel piatto**
	of barbecued vegetables.	**di verdura alla brace.**
Peter:	Excellent. I've never eaten	**Ottimo. Non ho mai mangiato**
	barbecued vegetables.	**verdura alla brace.**
Bella:	They're very good:	**È buonissima:**
	it's another one	**è un'altra specialità**
	of Alfredo's specialities.	**del signor Alfredo.**
Alfredo:	Shall we bring	**Portiamo**
	a little asparagus	**un po' di asparagi**
	as a starter?	**come antipasto?**
Peter:	Are they hot or cold?	**Sono caldi o freddi?**
Alfredo:	As you like,	**Come li preferisce:**
	warm in melted butter,	**caldi, al burro fuso,**
	or cold in vinaigrette.	**oppure freddi, all'agro.**
Bella:	I prefer them in vinaigrette.	**Io li preferisco all'agro.**
Peter:	In melted butter for me please.	**E io al burro fuso, per favore.**
Alfredo:	And to drink? Shall we bring	**E da bere? Portiamo**
	a bottle of Frascati?	**una bottiglia di Frascati?**
Bella:	No, bring us	**No, ci porti**
	your house wine, the white.	**il suo vino bianco della casa.**
	You'll see, Peter,	**Vedrà, Peter,**
	it's the best wine in Rome.	**è il miglior vino di Roma.**
	It comes from their vineyards.	**Viene dalle loro vigne.**
	The waiter brought a carafe	**Il cameriere ha portato una caraffa**
	of white wine, and a bottle of	**di vino bianco, e una bottiglia di**
	mineral water.	**acqua minerale.**
Bella:	Taste the wine Peter,	**Assaggia il vino, Peter.**
	see how light it is.	**Senti com'è delicato.**
	Peter lifted his glass.	**Peter ha alzato il bicchiere.**
Peter:	To your health, Bella!	**Alla tua salute, Bella.**
Bella:	Cheers!	**Cin-cin!**

		Scene 3	**Scena 3**
Peter:		Tell me about yourself, Bella.	**Parlami di te Bella.**
		What town do you come from?	**Da che città vieni?**
		Where were you born?	**Dove sei nata?**
Bella:		Well, I was born in Brazil,	**Beh, io sono nata in Brasile,**
		of Italian parents.	**da genitori italiani.**
		Then, when I was five,	**Poi, quando avevo cinque anni,**
		my parents returned to Italy.	**i miei genitori sono ritornati in Italia.**
		Now I live with my uncle,	**Ora abito con mio zio,**
		here in Rome.	**qui a Roma.**

But my father and mother — **Ma mio padre e mia madre**
live in Gardone Riviera, — **abitano a Gardone Riviera,**
on Lake Garda. — **sul lago di Garda.**
It's an ideal place for them, — **È un posto ideale per loro:**
there are mountains, the lake — **ci sono le montagne, il lago,**
and it's very quiet. — **ed è molto tranquillo.**
I go there often, to rest. — **Io ci vado spesso, per riposarmi.**

Twenty years ago my father founded — **Vent'anni fa mio padre ha fondato**
an import-export firm — **una ditta di importazioni ed esportazioni**
with South America. — **con l'America del Sud.**
Now he's retired, — **Ora lui è andato in pensione,**
and I work for the firm. — **e io lavoro per la ditta.**
I'm a major shareholder. — **Sono un'importante azionista.**
My uncle is the General Manager — **Mio zio è il Direttore Generale**
– the boss. — **– il capo.**

There was another major shareholder, — **C'era un altro importante azionista,**
an Englishman. — **un inglese.**
But unfortunately — **Ma purtroppo**
he died a month ago — **è morto un mese fa,**
in Venezuela, — **in Venezuela,**
in a plane crash. — **in un incidente aereo.**

Peter: — I'm sorry … — **Mi displace …**
Bella: — I didn't know him very well. — **Io non lo conoscevo molto bene.**
but, of course, it was — **Ma naturalmente è stato**
a very sad event — **un avvenimento molto triste**
for my family … — **per la mia famiglia …**

Ma mio padre e mia madre abitano
sul lago di Garda.

LAGO DI GARDA

	Scene 4	**Scena 4**
Peter:	What work do you do for the firm?	**Che lavoro fai per la ditta?**
Bella:	I'm the Sales Manager.	**Sono la Direttrice Vendite.**
	It's an interesting job,	**È un lavoro interessante,**
	which allows me to travel	**che mi permette di viaggiare**
	and meet lots of people.	**e di incontrare molta gente.**
	"Bella must be very good	**"Bella deve essere molto brava**
	at her job," thought Peter.	**nel suo lavoro." Peter ha pensato.**
	She seems very sure of herself.	**"Sembra molto sicura di sè.**
	She inspires a lot of trust,	**Inspira molta fiducia,**
	even if she is still so young	**anche se è ancora così giovane**
	for such an important job.	**per un lavoro tanto importante.**
Bella:	And you? What are your plans	**E tu? Che piani hai**
	for the future?	**per il tuo futuro?**
	I don't suppose you want	**Immagino non vorrai**
	to go around delivering packages	**andare in giro a consegnare pacchetti**
	for a living?	**come professione?**
Peter:	Certainly not.	**No di certo.**
	I've just finished studying	**Ho appena finito di studiare**
	Economics	**Scienze Economiche**
	at the University of London.	**all'Università di Londra.**
	Now I'm waiting for my exam results,	**Ora sto aspettando il risultato degli esami,**
	and I'm looking for a job.	**e sto cercando un lavoro.**
Bella:	That's interesting.	**È interessante.**
	I also studied Economics,	**Anch'io ho studiato Scienze Economiche,**
	at the University of Rome.	**all'Università di Roma.**
Peter:	Have you any brothers or sisters?	**Hai fratelli o sorelle?**
Bella:	No. I'm an only child. And you?	**No, sono figlia unica. E tu?**
Peter:	I've a brother and a sister.	**Ho un fratello e una sorella.**
	My brother's a doctor.	**Mio fratello è medico.**
	He's married and has two children	**È sposato e ha due bambini:**
	– a boy and a girl.	**un maschio e una femmina.**
	My sister's a nurse,	**Mia sorella è infermiera,**
	she works in a hospital.	**lavora in ospedale.**
	I'm the youngest.	**Io sono il più giovane.**
	We're a very close family.	**Siamo una famiglia molto unita.**
Bella:	It's nice	**È bello**
	to feel close to your family.	**sentirsi uniti alla famiglia.**

Siamo una famiglia molto unita.

Alle 8 in punto Peter è andato a prendere Bella.

Prendiamo un taxi per andare a Trastevere?

Ho prenotato un tavolo per le otto e trenta.

C'era anche un vasetto di garofani rossi.

Su ogni tavolo c'era una candela accesa.

In un angolo, un cantante suonava la chitarra.

Alfredo, il padrone, un signore alto coi baffi neri e un sorriso simpatico, si è avvicinato al loro tavolo.

Menu   Vinos

C'è carne alla brace.

Un ottimo risotto al funghi.

ATTO 6 (ii)

ATTO 6 (iii)

Quando avevo cinque anni,
i miei genitori sono ritornati in Italia.

Ma mio padre e mia madre
abitano a Gardone Riviera,
sur lago di Garda.

Io ci vado spesso, per riposarmi.

Ma purtroppo è morto un mese fa,
in Venezuela in un incidente aereo.

Mio zio è il Direttore
Generale - il capo.

Ma naturalmente è
stato un avvenimento
molto triste per la mia
famiglia.

Intonation and Pronunciation

From now on there will be no detailed notes on pronunciation.

The most important thing is to listen carefully to, and reproduce as closely as you can, the sounds and intonation patterns of the dialogues on the cassettes.

Try reading the narrative pieces aloud to yourself, fluently without hesitation, without worrying about making mistakes.

Concentrate on the pure vowel sounds, and the musical flow of the language.

Enter into the spirit of enthusiasm: che bel posto! che atmosfera romantica! che bella lingua! che bravo studente!

Ho appena finito di studiare all'Università di Londra.

Functional Dialogues

1.   Bella and Peter go out to dinner.   **Bella e Peter vanno fuori a cena.**

Bella:	Hello Peter! What's the time?	**Ciao, Peter! Che ore sono?**
Peter:	It's eight o'clock exactly.	**Sono le otto in punto.**
	Shall we take a taxi to go	**Prendiamo un taxi per andare**
	to Trastevere?	**a Trastevere?**
Bella:	Yes, it's quite a long way.	**Sì, è abbastanza lontano.**
	The restaurant is called	**Il ristorante si chiama**
	'da Alfredo'.	**'da Alfredo'.**
Peter:	Have you booked a taxi?	**Hai prenotato un tavolo?**
Bella:	Yes, I've booked a table	**Sì, ho prenotato un tavolo**
	for eight thirty.	**per le otto e mezza.**
Peter:	What a beautiful place!	**Che bel posto!**
Bella:	And what a romantic atmosphere!	**E che atmosfera romantica!**
	Do you like eating outside?	**Ti piace mangiare fuori?**
Peter:	Very much. In England,	**Moltissimo. In Inghilterra,**
	unfortunately,	**purtroppo,**
	it's very rare to eat outside.	**si mangia fuori molto raramente.**
Bella:	What a pity!	**Che peccato!**

2.   At Alfredo's restaurant.   **Da Alfredo.**

Alfredo:	Good evening, signorina Bruni.	**Buonasera, signorina Bruni.**
	Good evening, sir.	**Buonasera, signore.**
Bella:	Good evening signor Alfredo.	**Buonasera, signor Alfredo.**
	What nice things have you got	**Che cosa c'è di buono**
	this evening?	**questa sera?**
Alfredo:	For the first course we have	**Come primo piatto abbiamo**
	an excellent risotto	**un ottimo risotto**
	with mushrooms or noodles,	**ai funghi, oppure fettucine,**
	penne all'arrabbiata...	**penne all'arrabbiata...**
Bella:	I'll have risotto with mushrooms.	**Io prendo risotto ai funghi.**
	And you, Peter?	**E tu Peter?**
Peter:	For me *penne all'arrabbiata.*	**Per me penne all'arrabbiata.**
Bella:	And as a main dish,	**E come secondo,**
	what do you advise?	**che cosa ci consiglia?**
Alfredo:	There's barbecued meat,	**C'è carne alla brace, osso buco,**
	there's roast mushrooms,	**ci sono funghi arrosto,**
	with garlic and rosemary.	**con aglio e rosmarino.**
Bella:	*Osso buco* for me.	**Osso buco per me.**

C'è carne alla brace.

Peter:	I don't eat meat.	**Io non mangio carne.**
Alfredo:	Well, we can do roast mushrooms with potatoes, and a nice dish of barbecued vegetables.	**Allora, possiamo fare funghi arrosto con patatine, e un bel piatto di verdura alla brace.**
Peter:	Excellent.	**Ottimo.**
Alfredo:	And to drink?	**E da bere?**
Bella:	Bring us your house white, please.	**Ci porti il suo vino bianco della casa, per piacere.**
	Taste the wine Peter.	**Assaggia il vino, Peter.**
Peter:	To your health, Bella!	**Alla tua salute, Bella!**
Bella:	Cheers!	**Cin-cin!**

3.	A conversation at Alfredo's.	**Una conversazione da Alfredo.**
Peter:	Tell me about yourself, Bella. Where were you born?	**Parlami di te, Bella. Dove sei nata?**
Bella:	I was born in Brazil.	**Io sono nata in Brasile.**
Peter:	What town do you come from?	**Da che città vieni?**
Bella:	I come from Rio. But when I was five years old, my parents returned to Italy.	**Vengo da Rio. Però, quando avevo cinque anni, i miei genitori sono ritornati in Italia.**
Peter:	Where do you live?	**Dove abiti?**
Bella:	Now I live here in Rome, with my uncle.	**Ora abito qui a Roma, con mio zio.**
Peter:	And your parents, where do they live?	**E i tuoi genitori, dove abitano?**
Bella:	They live in Gardone Riviera, on Lake Garda.	**Abitano a Gardone Riviera, sul lago di Garda.**
Peter:	What job does your father do?	**E tuo padre, che cosa fa di professione?**
Bella:	My father founded an import-export firm with South America.	**Mio padre ha fondato una ditta di importazioni ed esportazioni con l'America del Sud.**
Peter:	And what work do you do for the firm?	**E tu, che lavoro fai per la ditta?**
Bella:	I'm the Sales Director.	**Sono la Direttrice Vendite.**
Peter:	How interesting!	**Che interessante!**

Poi, quando avevo cinque anni, i miei genitori sono ritornati in Italia.

4. Plans for the future. **I piani per il futuro.**

Bella:	And you, what plans have you got for the future?	**E tu, che piani hai per il tuo futuro?**
Peter:	I don't know. I've just finished my studies.	**Non lo so. Ho appena finito di studiare.**
Bella:	What did you study?	**Che cos'hai studiato?**
Peter:	I studied economics.	**Ho studiato scienze economiche.**
Bella:	Where?	**Dove?**
Peter:	At the University of London.	**All'Università di Londra.**
Bella:	That's interesting. I studied economics too.	**È interessante. Anch'io ho studiato scienze economiche.**
Peter:	Where?	**Dove?**
Bella:	At the University of Rome.	**All'Università di Roma.**

5. The family. **La famiglia.**

Peter:	Have you any brothers or sisters?	**Hai fratelli o sorelle?**
Bella:	No, I'm an only child. And you?	**No, sono figlia unica. E tu?**
Peter:	I've got a brother and a sister.	**Ho un fratello e una sorella.**
Bella:	What does your brother do?	**Tuo fratello, che cosa fa?**
Peter:	He's a doctor.	**È medico.**
Bella:	And your sister?	**E tua sorella?**
Peter:	She's a nurse. She works in a hospital.	**È infermiera, lavora in ospedale.**

Mio fratello è medico.

Mia sorella è infermiera.

Personalised Dialogues

1. You're taking a friend out to dinner. Being English you're very punctual.

Amica:	**Ciao! Che ore sono?**
Lei:	(Say hello. It's 9 o'clock on the dot.)
Amica:	**Prendiamo un taxi per andare al ristorante?**
Lei:	(Say yes, it's quite a long way to go.)
Amica:	**Come si chiama il ristorante?**
Lei:	(Say it's called **"La Dolce Vita".**)
Amica:	**Hai prenotato un tavolo?**
Lei:	(Say you've booked a table for 9.30.)
	(Let's go!)

Later:

Amica:	**Che bel posto!**
Lei:	(And what a romantic atmosphere! Ask if she likes eating outside.)
Amica:	**Moltissimo!**

2. At **"La Dolce Vita"** restaurant. You impress your friend by knowing the manageress, and the house specialities.

La Manager:	**Buonasera, signore. Buonasera, signorina.**
Lei:	(Say good evening. Ask what nice things she's got this evening.)
La Manager:	**Come primo piatto abbiamo un ottimo risotto ai funghi... oppure fettucine... penne all'arriabbiata...**
Lei:	(You'll have the risotto. Ask your friend what she'd like.)
Amica:	**Per me penne all'arrabbiata.**
Lei:	(And what would she advise for the main course?)
La Manager:	**C'è carne alla brace, osso buco, ci sono funghi arrosto.**
Amica:	**Osso buco per me.**
Lei:	(You're a vegetarian. You don't eat meat. For you roast mushrooms and potatoes.)
La Manager:	**E da bere?**
Lei:	(Ask her to bring you her house white wine please.)
La Manager:	**Sì, signore.**

Prendiamo un taxi per andare a Trastevere?

3. Getting to know you. You're now on familiar terms with your friend (the house wine was very good) and your curiosity gets the better of you. (It's assumed the friend is a woman, but you may change this if you wish.)

Lei:	(Ask her to talk about herself. Where was she born?)
Amica:	**Io sono nata in Messico.**
Lei:	(What city does she come from?)
Amica:	**Vengo da Acapulco.**
Lei:	(Where does she live now?)
Amica:	**Abito a Roma.**
Lei:	(And where do her parents live?)
Amica:	**Abitano a Venezia.**
Lei:	(And what job does her father do?)
Amica:	**Mio padre è giornalista.**
Lei:	(And what job does she do?)
Amica:	**Sono giornalista anch'io.**
Lei:	(How interesting!)

4. Your thoughts turn to the future. She wants to know about your past.

Lei:	(What plans has she got for the future?)
Amica:	**Non lo so. E tu, che cos'hai studiato?**
Lei:	(You studied Italian.)
Amica:	**Dove hai studiato?**
Lei:	(You studied at the University of Cambridge.)
Amica:	**Che cosa fai di professione?**
Lei:	(You're a...)
Amica:	**È interessante. Dove abiti?**
Lei:	(You live in London.)
Amica:	**Vorrei tanto visitare Londra!**

5. All in the family. You try to find out more about her, but she turns the tables.

Lei:	(Has she got any brothers or sisters?)
Amica:	**No, sono figlia unica. E tu?**
Lei:	(You've got one brother and one sister.)
Amica:	**Tuo fratello, che cosa fa?**
Lei:	(He's a journalist.)
Amica:	**E tua sorella?**
Lei:	(She's a journalist too – she works in television.)

Grammar

1. REFLEXIVE VERBS

Some Italian verbs must always have a direct object even when this is not necessary in English. In such cases they are 'reflexive':

Il ristorante <u>si chiama</u> 'da Alfredo'

È bello <u>sentirsi</u> uniti alla famiglia

The reflexive is frequently not translated in English, though sometimes can be rendered by 'one' ... or 'you' ... (impersonal):

In Inghilterra <u>si mangia</u> fuori molto raramente

In questo ristorante <u>si mangia</u> il miglior osso buco d'Italia

In the perfect tense reflexive verbs are always used with **essere:**

Alfredo si è avvicinato al loro tavolo

2. SONO NATO ... È MORTO

The verbs **nascere, morire** also use **essere:**

Sono nato/a	I was born
È morto/a	he/she died

3. VERBS – FAMILIAR FORMS

Until now in the course most verb forms have used the formal address for 'you'. Now that Bella and Peter are getting to know each other, the informal **tu** form is being used:

ti piace...	**Ti piace mangiare fuori?**
vieni...	**Da che città vieni?**
sei...	**Dove sei nata?**
fai...	**Che lavoro fai per la ditta?**
hai...	**Che piani hai per il tuo futuro?**
	Hai fratelli o sorelle?

Sono nata in Brasile.

4. SUPERLATIVES

To say 'the ...est' in Italian, use **il più**:

il più giovane   the youngest

or **la più**:

la più vecchia   the oldest

To say 'the best' use **il miglior:**

il miglior vitello
il miglior vino

or **la migliore:**

la migliore casa di Roma

5. **CI**

Note the use of **ci** meaning 'there':

Ci vado spesso   I go there often.
Ci si mangia bene   You eat well there.

6. EXPRESSIONS OF TIME

sono le otto	It's 8 o'clock
è l'una	1.00
sono le nove e venti	9.20
alle otto	at 8 o'clock
alle otto e un quarto	at 8.15
per le otto e mezza	for 8.30
quando avevo cinque anni	When I was... (literally 'had') five years old.
vent'anni fa	20 years ago
un mese fa	a month ago
sono le nove meno un quarto	8.45/It's a quarter to nine.

7. **STO...**

The verb **stare** is used together with the **gerund** to indicate an ongoing or continuous process, roughly similar to the English usage 'I'm...ing', 'he's...ing' etc.

aspettare	**sto aspettando il risultato degli esami**
cercare	**sto cercando un lavoro**
mangiare	**sto mangiando troppo**
bere	**sta bevendo troppo**

Games

1. DEAD OR ALIVE

Classify the following famous Italians as dead (**è morto/a**) or alive (**è vivo/a**):

1. 1   **Giusseppe Garibaldi**
1. 2   **Giulietta Masina**
1. 3   **Federico Fellini**
1. 4   **Leonardo da Vinci**
1. 5   **Dante**
1. 6   **Beatrice**
1. 7   **Marcello Mastroianni**
1. 8   **Lucrezia Borgia**
1. 9   **Claudia Cardinale**
1.10   **Mona Lisa**

2. AD MAN

Write an enthusiastic advertisement for Alfredo's restaurant. It has:

2. 1   The best veal.
2. 2   The best pasta.
2. 3   The best antipasti.
2. 4   The most handsome waiter.
2. 5   The most beautiful waitress.
2. 6   The best wine.
2. 7   The best bread.
2. 8   The biggest glasses.
2. 9   The most beautiful garden.
2.10   The best music.

3. SOUNDS FAMILIAR

Fill in the gaps with familiar forms of the verb:

3. 1   **Dove _ _ _ nata?**

3. 2   **Che piani _ _ _ per il tuo futuro?**

3. 3   **_ _ piace mangiare fuori?**

3. 4   **Da che città _ _ _ _ _ _?**

3. 5   **Che lavoro _ _ _ per la ditta?**

3. 6   **_ _ _ _ _ _ _ _ _ _ vino bianco o vino rosso?**

3. 7   **_ _ _ fratelli o sorelle?**

3. 8   **_ _ _ così giovane.**

3. 9   **_ _ _ finito di studiare?**

3.10   **_ _ _ sposata?**

4. **CHE ORE SONO?**

4. 1

4. 2

4. 3

4. 4

4. 5

Using an alarm clock with a memorable ring rehearse appointments on the hour and half hour, asking the question **che ore sono**? and giving the answer **sono le ...** aloud each time the alarm bell goes off. Start with 2 o'clock. 'It's one o'clock' is: **è l'una.**

5. RESISTANCE

Resist all attempts to interrupt you. Use **sto... ando, ...endo** as appropriate.

    5. 1   No, ... I'm eating *penne all'arrabbiata.*
    5. 2   No, ... I'm drinking the best wine in Rome.
    5. 3   No, ... I'm waiting for Godot.
    5. 4   No, ... I'm looking for Bella.
    5. 5   No, ... I'm writing a book.
    5. 6   No, ... I'm preparing a salad.
    5. 7   No, ... I'm studying Italian.
    5. 8   No, ... I'm watching television.

Make up some excuses of your own. Practise them with your wife, husband or partner.

What if...? **Se invece...**

Concoct your own culinary alternative to Alfredo's restaurant.

Invent your own romantic atmosphere – the music might be classical, rock or jazz. The perfumes may be artificial or tropical, the food exotic or plain, the drinks fantastic cocktails or healthy fruit juices.

The company may be friendly or hostile, ugly or beautiful, young or old, fascinating or boring. And your companion (a business colleague, a detective, an old flame?) may reveal the most extraordinary secrets about their past... or about their plans for the future. **Buon appetito!**

Scene 1 **Scena 1**
Getting to know each other. **Imparare a conoscersi.**

During the evening **Durante la serata**
Peter and Bella **Peter e Bella**
talked a lot about themselves, **hanno parlato molto di sè stessi,**
about their favourite hobbies, **dei loro hobby,**
and sports. **e dei loro sport preferiti.**

Bella:

I'm interested to hear **M'interessa sentire**
you do a lot of sport. **che fai molto sport.**
I love tennis. **Io amo molto il tennis.**
It doesn't matter **Non m'importa**
if I win or lose. **se vinco o perdo.**
I always feel better **Mi sento sempre meglio**
after a game, **dopo aver giocato,**
especially after a day's work **specialmente dopo una giornata di lavoro**
in the office. **in ufficio.**
I think we all need **Penso che abbiamo tutti bisogno**
to do some sport **di fare un po' di sport**
in order to relax, **per poterci rilassare,**
don't you think so? **non credi?**

Peter looked at Bella in silence **Peter guardava Bella silenzioso.**
He listened to her voice **Ascoltava la sua voce,**
and to the music. **e ascoltava la musica.**
The candle on the table **La candela sul tavolo**
lit up her face. **illuminava il suo viso.**
Her eyes shone as she spoke. **Le brillavano gli occhi mentre parlava.**

Bella:

At the moment I'm studying **Ora sto anche studiando**
English as well. **l'inglese.**
I find English grammar easy, **Trovo che la grammatica inglese è facile,**
but the pronunciation **ma la pronuncia**
is very difficult. **è molto difficile.**

After dinner **Dopo cena**
the waiter brought two Sambuca **il cameriere ha portato due Sambuca**
on the house. **offerti dalla casa.**

Peter had realised **Peter aveva capito**
that Bella **che Bella**
was not only a nice, **era una donna non solo simpatica**
attractive woman, **e attraente,**
but was also very intelligent. **ma anche molto intelligente.**
He wanted to be her friend. **Voleva esserle amico.**
But why was her uncle **Ma perchè suo zio**
so mysterious? **era così misterioso?**

Bella:	What are you thinking about?	**A cosa stai pensando?**
Peter:	I'm thinking that I'm very happy to be here in Rome.	**Sto pensando che sono molto felice di essere qui, a Roma.**
	Maybe, if your uncle doesn't come back tomorrow, we can go for a trip in the hills, or to the sea.	**Forse, se tuo zio non ritorna domani, possiamo andare a fare una gita in collina, o al mare.**
	If you're free tomorrow, of course.	**Se sei libera, domani, naturalmente.**
Bella:	What a good idea!	**Che buona idea!**
	Yes, tomorrow I'm free.	**Sì, domani sono libera.**
Peter:	We can hire a car.	**Possiamo noleggiare una macchina.**
	There's a car hire near the hotel.	**C'è un autonoleggio vicino all'hotel.**
Bella:	That won't be necessary, we can go in my car.	**Non è necessario, andiamo con la mia macchina.**
	I'll come and pick you up at the hotel tomorrow morning.	**Ti vengo a prendere all'albergo domani mattina.**

Scene 2	**Scena 2**
They paid the bill and left the restaurant.	**Hanno pagato il conto e sono usciti dal ristorante.**
In the streets and cafés of Trastevere there were lots of people.	**Nelle strade e nei caffè di Trastevere c'era ancora molta gente.**
Peter looked at the old houses with their faded facades, lit up by the street lamps.	**Peter guardava le vecchie case con le facciate scolorite, e illuminate dai lampioni delle strade.**

Peter:	What a marvellous city!	**Che città meravigliosa!**
	I'd like to walk around all night, look at everything, listening to the people, taking in the smells and sounds of the city ... waiting for dawn.	**Vorrei camminare tutta la notte, guardare tutto, ascoltare la gente, sentire gli odori della città, i suoni ... aspettare l'alba.**
Bella:	Yes, but tomorrow we have to get up early!	**Sì, però domani dobbiamo alzarci presto!**

They walked in silence as far as *Piazza di Santa Maria* in Trastevere.	**Hanno camminato in silenzio fino a Piazza di Santa Maria in Trastevere.**

Bella:	Come on, I'll treat you to an *affogato*.	**Vieni, ti offro un affogato.**
Peter:	What's that?	**Che cos'è?**
Bella:	It's another Roman speciality.	**È un'altra specialità romana.**

Una gita in collina, o al mare.

124

	They sat at a café	**Si sono seduti a un caffè**
	in the square.	**in piazza.**
	Bella ordered	**Bella ha ordinato**
	two *affogati* in brandy.	**due affogati al cognac.**
	A little later	**Poco dopo**
	the waiter came back	**il cameriere è tornato**
	with two enormous ice-creams,	**con due gelati enormi,**
	soaked in brandy.	**impregnati di cognac.**

| **Bella:** | Well, do you like it? | **Allora, ti piace?** |
| **Peter:** | I'm speechless. It's delicious. | **Sono senza parole. È squisito.** |

	In the centre of the square	**Nel centro della piazza**
	children were playing	**i bambini giocavano**
	around a monument.	**attorno a un monumento.**
	It was nearly one o'clock	**Era quasi l'una**
	when they returned home by taxi.	**quando sono ritornati a casa in taxi.**
	Bella got out first.	**Bella è scesa per prima.**
	Then the taxi took	**Poi il taxi ha portato**
	Peter to the hotel.	**Peter all'albergo.**

	Scene 3	**Scena 3**
	The next morning,	**La mattina dopo,**
	just before nine,	**poco prima delle nove,**
	Bella went to pick up	**Bella è andata a prendere**
	Peter at the hotel.	**Peter all'albergo.**
	She had put on a yellow dress,	**Aveva messo un vestito giallo,**
	off the shoulder.	**con le spalle nude.**
	Over her shoulders	**Sulle spalle**
	she wore a white shawl.	**portava uno scialle bianco.**
	Peter was already in the reception.	**Peter era già nella hall.**

Bella: Are you ready? — **Sei pronto?**

Peter: Ready. — **Prontissimo.**
Would you like a coffee — **Vuoi prendere un caffè**
before leaving? — **prima di partire?**

Bella: No, I just had breakfast, — **No, ho appena fatto colazione,**
thanks. — **grazie.**

Peter had put on his new trousers — **Peter aveva messo i pantaloni nuovi**
and the blue sports shirt. — **e la camicia azzurra sportiva.**

Bella: Do you want to drive? — **Vuoi guidare tu?**
Have you got a licence? — **Hai la patente?**

Peter: Of course. — **Certo.**
Do you trust me? — **Ti fidi?**
I've never driven on the right. — **Non ho mai guidato alla destra.**

Bella looked at him seriously. — **Bella lo ha guardato seria.**

Bella: I trust you. — **Mi fido.**
That way I can look at the map — **E poi così io posso guardare la mappa**
and give you directions. — **e indicarti la strada.**

Peter: Are you insured for me too? — **Sei assicurata anche per me?**

Bella: Don't worry, — **Stai tranquillo,**
I've got comprehensive insurance. — **ho l'assicurazione globale.**
Show me your licence. — **Mostrami la tua patente.**

Peter took out his wallet — **Peter ha tirato fuori il portafoglio**
and showed his licence — **e ha mostrato la patente**
to Bella. — **a Bella.**

Peter: There you are, all in order. — **Ecco, tutto in regola.**
Shall we go? — **Possiamo partire?**

Bella: Yes, I've already filled up — **Sì, ho già fatto il pieno**
with petrol and oil. — **della benzina e messo l'olio.**

Io posso guardare la mappa
e indicarti la strada.

126

	Scene 4	**Scena 4**

| | There was a lot of traffic on the roads. | **Per le strade c'era molto traffico.** |
| | It seemed to Peter as if everyone in Rome must own either a car, or a motorbike. | **Peter ha pensato che forse tutti a Roma devono avere o la macchina, o la motocicletta.** |

They took the ring road
to avoid the traffic
in the centre.
In a short while
they were already
on the motorway
leading out of Rome.

**Hanno preso il raccordo anulare
per evitare il traffico
del centro.
In poco tempo
erano già
sull'autostrada
che portava fuori Roma.**

The sun was high on the hills.
Through the open windows
came the smell of the fields.

**Il sole era alto sulle colline.
Dai finestrini aperti
entrava il profumo dei campi.**

Bella:

Be careful, Peter,
you're going too fast.
There are a lot of police
around here.
The speed limit on the motorways
is 130 kilometres an hour.

**Fai attenzione, Peter,
stai andando troppo forte.
C'è molta polizia
da queste parti.
Il limite di velocità sulle autostrade
è di 130 chilometri all'ora.**

Peter slowed down straight away.
Bella was right.
A few kilometres ahead
were two police cars
checking the traffic.
They had stopped a car
with a Rome registration.

**Peter ha rallentato subito.
Bella aveva ragione:
pochi chilometri più avanti
c'erano due macchine della polizia
che controllavano il traffico.
Avevano fermato una macchina
targata Roma.**

They passed countryside,
vineyards and castles.
From time to time
they could even see the sea.

**Hanno passato campagna,
vigneti e castelli.
Di tanto in tanto
si vedeva anche il mare.**

Per le strade c'era molto traffico.

Bella:	Bravo, you're a good driver.	**Bravo, guidi bene.**
	But slow down now,	**Ora però rallenta;**
	in a short time we'll be	**fra poco usciamo**
	leaving the motorway.	**dall'autostrada.**
	Can you see that little village	**Vedi quel paesino**
	up there on the hill?	**lassù, sulla collina?**
Peter:	Yes, it looks very beautiful.	**Sì, sembra molto bello.**
Bella:	If you take the next exit	**Se prendi la prossima uscita,**
	I'll take you up there.	**ti porto lassù.**

	They left the motorway	**Sono usciti dall'autostrada.**
	Bella paid the toll.	**Bella ha pagato il pedaggio.**
	They took a little narrow road	**Hanno preso una stradina stretta,**
	leading up to	**che saliva**
	the top of the hill.	**sulla collina.**

Bella:	At the next crossroad	**Al prossimo incrocio**
	you'll find a traffic light.	**troverai un semaforo.**
	Go straight on.	**Vai pure diritto.**
	Then on your left	**Poi, sulla sinistra,**
	There'll be a café	**ci sarà un caffè**
	with tables outside.	**coi tavolini fuori.**
	On the right,	**Sulla destra,**
	you'll see a small hospital.	**vedrai un piccolo ospedale.**
	Then a square.	**Poi una piazza.**
	If you park in the square,	**Se parcheggi nella piazza,**
	we'll stop to buy	**ci fermiamo**
	everything we need	**a comprare il necessario**
	for a nice picnic.	**per fare un bel picnic.**

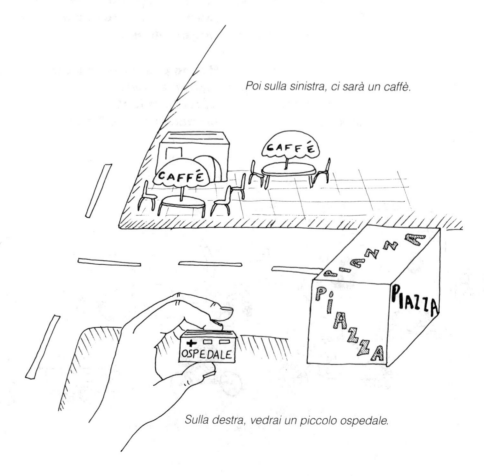

Poi sulla sinistra, ci sarà un caffè.

Sulla destra, vedrai un piccolo ospedale.

ATTO 7 (i)

Io amo molto il tennis.

Durante la serata Peter e Bella hanno parlato molto di sè stessi, dei loro hobby, e dei loro sport preferiti.

Penso che abbiamo tutti bisogno di fare un po' di sport per poterci rilassare.

Ora sto anche studiando l'inglese.

ma anche molto intelligente.

Peter aveva capito che Bella era donna non solo simpatica e attraente

Ma perchè suo zio era così misterioso?

ATTO 7 (ii)

ATTO 7 (iii)

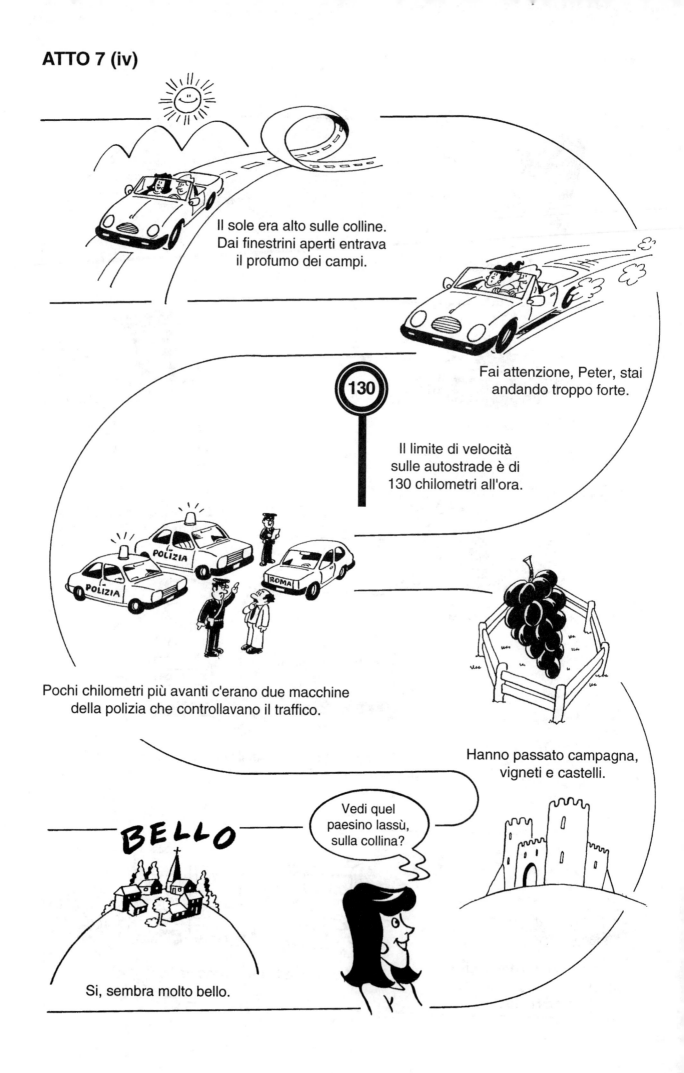

Il sole era alto sulle colline. Dai finestrini aperti entrava il profumo dei campi.

Fai attenzione, Peter, stai andando troppo forte.

Il limite di velocità sulle autostrade è di 130 chilometri all'ora.

Pochi chilometri più avanti c'erano due macchine della polizia che controllavano il traffico.

Hanno passato campagna, vigneti e castelli.

BELLO

Vedi quel paesino lassù, sulla collina?

Si, sembra molto bello.

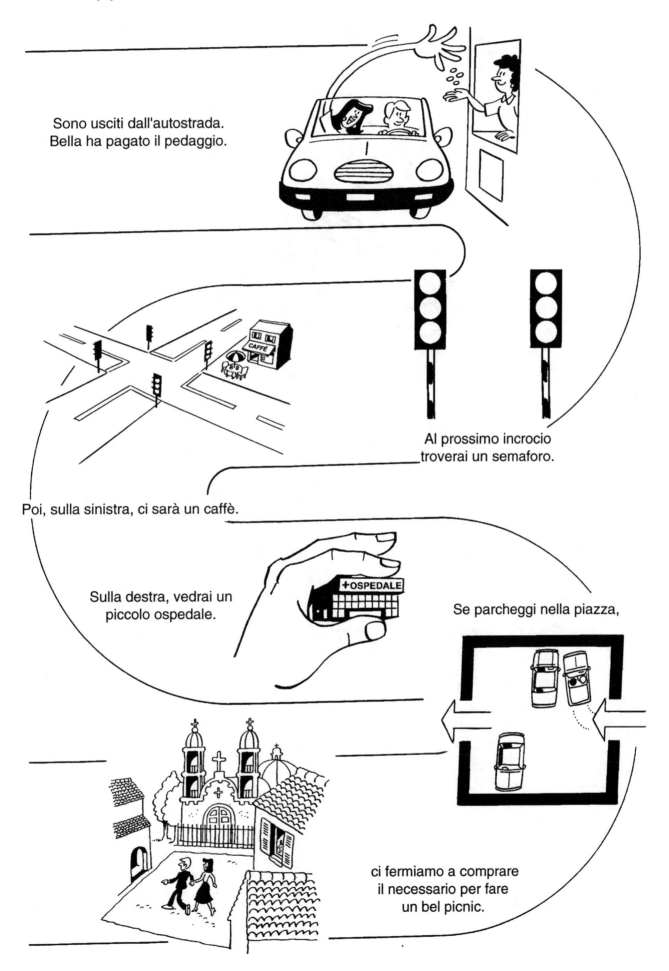

Sono usciti dall'autostrada.
Bella ha pagato il pedaggio.

Al prossimo incrocio troverai un semaforo.

Poi, sulla sinistra, ci sarà un caffè.

Sulla destra, vedrai un piccolo ospedale.

Se parcheggi nella piazza,

ci fermiamo a comprare il necessario per fare un bel picnic.

Intonation and Pronunciation

Use the pause button on your cassette player to interrupt and repeat the dialogue sections of Act 7. Imitate pace, intonation and vowel sounds as closely as possible. Record your own version separately. Play it back and compare it with the original: you'll be pleasantly surprised at the progress you've made in the pronunciation of Italian.

Stai andando troppo forte.

Functional Dialogues

1.   Getting to know each other.   **Imparare a conoscersi.**

          Peter and Bella at the restaurant.   **Peter e Bella al ristorante.**

Bella:	Do you do a lot of sport?	**Fai molto sport?**
Peter:	Yes, I like cricket, gymnastics, tennis.	**Sì, mi piacciono il cricket, la ginnastica, il tennis.**
Bella:	I love tennis too. I always feel better after a game...	**Anch'io amo molto il tennis. Mi sento sempre meglio dopo aver giocato...**
Peter:	We all need to do some sport.	**Abbiamo tutti bisogno di fare un pò' di sport.**
Bella:	At the moment I'm studying English too: the grammar is easy, but the pronunciation is very difficult.	**Ora sto anche studiando l'inglese: la grammatica è facile, ma la pronuncia è molto difficile.**
Peter:	I'm studying Italian – the grammar is not easy but the pronunciation is not very difficult.	**Io sto studiando l'italiano – la grammatica non è facile ma la pronuncia non è molto difficile.**
Bella:	What are you thinking about?	**A cosa stai pensando?**
Peter:	I'm thinking that I'm very happy to be here in Rome.	**Sto pensando che sono molto felice di essere qui a Roma.**
Bella:	Me too!	**Anch'io!**
Peter:	Shall we go for a trip tomorrow, to the hills, or to the sea?	**Andiamo a fare una gita domani, in collina o al mare?**
Bella:	What a good idea!	**Che buona idea!**
Peter:	We can hire a car.	**Possiamo noleggiare una macchina.**
Bella:	That's not necessary. We'll go with my car.	**Non è necessario. Andiamo con la mia macchina.**

2.   Rome by night.   **Roma di notte.**

Peter:	What a marvellous city! Rome is very beautiful by night.	**Che città meravigliosa! Di notte Roma è molto bella.**
Peter:	I'd like to walk all night!	**Vorrei camminare tutta la notte!**
Bella:	Me too, but tomorrow we have to get up early...	**Anch'io, però domani dobbiamo alzarci presto...**
Bella:	Come on, I'll treat you to an *affogato*.	**Vieni, ti offro un affogato.**
Peter:	What's that?	**Che cos'è?**
Bella:	It's another Roman speciality.	**È un'altra specialità romana.**
Bella:	Well, do you like it?	**Allora, ti piace?**
Peter:	I'm speechless. It's delicious.	**Sono senza parole. È squisito.**

Io amo molto il tennis.

3. A country ride. **Una gita in campagna.**

Bella: Are you ready? **Sei pronto?**
Peter: Ready. **Prontissimo.**
Bella: Well, let's go. **Allora andiamo.**
Do you want to drive? **Vuoi guidare tu?**
Peter: Yes, of course. **Sì, certo.**
Bella: Have you got a licence? **Hai la patente?**
Peter: Of course. Do you trust me? **Certo. Ti fidi?**
I've never driven on the right. **Non ho mai guidato a destra.**
Bella: I trust you. **Mi fido.**
Peter: Are you insured for me too? **Sei assicurata anche per me?**
Bella: Don't worry. I've got **Stai tranquillo, ho**
comprehensive insurance. **l'assicurazione globale.**
Peter: Can we go then? **Allora possiamo partire?**
Bella: Yes, I've already filled up **Sì, ho già fatto il pieno**
with petrol and oil. **della benzina e messo l'olio.**

4. On the road. **Per la strada.**

Bella: Let's take the ring road. **Prendiamo il raccordo anulare.**
That way we can avoid **Così possiamo evitare**
the traffic in the centre. **il traffico del centro.**
Peter: OK. **Va bene.**
Bella: Be careful, Peter, **Fai attenzione, Peter,**
You're going too fast. **stai andando troppo forte.**
Peter: Are there a lot of police **C'è molta polizia**
around here? **da queste parti?**
Bella: Yes, and the speed limit **Sì, ed il limite**
on the motorways **di velocità sulle autostrade**
is 130 kilometres an hour. **è di 130 chilometri all'ora.**
Bella: Bravo, you're a good driver... **Bravo, guidi bene...**
But slow down now. **Ora però rallenta.**
Peter: Why? **Perchè?**
Bella: Because in a short time **Pechè fra poco**
we'll be leaving the motorway. **usciamo dall'autostrada.**
Peter: Shall I take the next exit? **Prendo la prossima uscita?**
Bella: Yes. **Sì.**

5. In the village. **Nel paesino.**

Bella: At the next crossroads you'll find **Al prossimo incrocio troverai**
a set of traffic lights. **un semaforo.**
Peter: Here are the traffic lights. **Ecco il semaforo.**
Bella: Go straight on. Then on the left **Vai pure diritto. Poi sulla sinistra**
there'll be a café. **ci sarà un caffè.**
Peter: Here's the café. **Ecco il caffè.**
Bella: On the right you'll see **Sulla destra vedrai**
a small hospital. **un piccolo ospedale.**
Then a square. **Poi una piazza.**
Peter: Here's the square. **Ecco la piazza.**
Bella: Let's park in the square. **Parcheggiamo nella piazza.**
We'll stop and buy **Ci fermiamo a comprare**
everything we need for a picnic. **il necessario per fare un bel picnic.**

Personalised Dialogues

1. Getting to know you. You're in a romantic restaurant.
   Swop small talk.
   (**Lui-Lei**/He-She)

Lui/Lei:	**Fai molto sport?**
Lei:	(Yes, you like cricket and tennis.)
Lui/Lei:	**Anch'io amo molto il tennis.**
Lei:	(We all need to do a little sport.)

Lui/Lei:	**Ora sto studiando l'inglese.**
Lei:	(You're studying Italian.)
Lui/Lei:	**La grammatica inglese è facile, ma la pronuncia è molto difficile.**
Lei:	(Italian grammar isn't easy, but the pronunciation isn't very difficult.)

Lei:	(What is he thinking about?)
Lui/Lei:	**Sto pensando che sono molto felice.**
Lei:	(How about an outing tomorrow, to the hills or to the sea?)
Lui/Lei:	**Che buona idea! Possiamo noleggiare una macchina.**
Lei:	(That's not necessary. You can go in yours.)

2. Rome by night. A local speciality.

Lei:	(You're impressed by the city. What do you say?)
Lui/Lei:	**Di notte Roma è molto bella.**
Lei:	(You'd like to walk all night!)
Lui/Lei:	**Anch'io!**
Lei:	(Let's go and see the *Fontana di Trevi.*)

Lui/Lei:	**Vieni, ti offro un affogato.**
Lei:	(What's that? you ask.)
Lui/Lei:	**È una specialità romana.**

Lui/Lei:	**Allora, ti piace?**
Lei:	(You like it a lot. You're speechless. It's delicious.)

3. You're going for a ride in the country. Your cautious companion's a stickler for the rules — and a bit of a backseat driver.

Lei:	(Are you ready?)
Lui/Lei:	**Prontissimo.**
Lei:	(Well, let's go.)
Lui/Lei:	**Vuoi guidare tu?**
Lei:	(Yes of course.)
Lui/Lei:	**Hai la patente?**
Lei:	(Of course. You have a licence. Doesn't he trust you?)
Lui/Lei:	**Sì ma... hai mai guidato a destra?**
Lei:	(No, you've never driven on the right.)
Lui/Lei:	**Sei assicurata anche per me?**
Lei:	(Tell him not to worry, you've got comprehensive insurance.)
Lui/Lei:	**Allora, possiamo partire?**
Lei:	(Yes, you've already filled up with petrol and oil.)

4. On the road — it doesn't get any better.

Lui/Lei:	**Prendiamo il raccordo anulare.**
Lei:	(OK)
Lui/Lei:	**Così possiamo evitare il traffico del centro.**
Lei:	(Yes, yes.)
Lui/Lei:	**Fai attenzione!**
Lei:	(Why, are you going too fast?)
Lui/Lei:	**Sì.**
Lei:	(What's the speed limit on the motorways?)
Lui/Lei:	**Il limite di velocità sulle autostrade è di 130 chilometri all'ora.**

5. You arrive at your destination. But there are more instructions to come. You repeat them — to make sure you've understood, and to humour your companion.

Lui/Lei:	**Prendi la prossima uscita.**
Lei:	(I take the next exit.)
Lui/Lei:	**Al prossimo incrocio troverai un semaforo.**
Lei:	(At the next crossroad I'll find a traffic light.)
Lui/Lei:	**Vai pure diritto.**
Lei:	(I go straight on.)
Lui/Lei:	**Poi sulla sinistra ci sarà un caffè.**
Lei:	(There'll be a cafè on the left.)
Lui/Lei:	**Sulla destra vedrai un ospedale.**
Lei:	(On the right I'll see a hospital.)
Lui/Lei:	**Poi una piazza.**
Lei:	(Then a square... ah, there's the square. Where shall we park?)
Lui/Lei:	**Parcheggiamo nella piazza.**

Non ho mai guidato alla destra.

Grammar

1. VERBS – PAST WITH **AVERE/ESSERE**

There are many examples of past tenses in Act 7, using both **avere** and **essere**, especially in the third person plural ('they...').

REMEMBER verbs which take an object ('transitive verbs') use **avere:**

> **Hanno parlato molto.**
>
> **Hanno pagato il conto.**
>
> **Hanno preso il raccordo anulare.**

Verbs which do not take an object ('intransitive verbs'), usually verbs of movement, use **essere:**

> **Sono usciti dal ristorante.**
>
> **Si sono seduti a un caffè.**
>
> **Sono ritornati a casa in taxi**.

REMEMBER, too, that the past participle, used with **essere**, agrees like an adjective:

> **Il cameriere è tornato.**
>
> **Bella è andata.**
>
> **Sono usciti.**

2. VERBS – PLUPERFECT WITH **AVERE**

'To describe events further back in the past ('had gone', 'had understood', etc.), the pluperfect form of the verb is used.

The formation is simple:

use the imperfect of **avere (avevo, aveva** etc.), plus the past participle:

Peter aveva capito...	had understood
Peter aveva messo...	had put
avevano fermato una macchina...	(they) had stopped

Era quasi l'una quando sono ritornati a casa in taxi.

139

3. VERBS – FUTURE

In Italian you can talk about the future by mostly using the present tense:

Domani vado a Roma.   Tomorrow I'm going to Rome

When referring to a specific point in the future, however, the future tense is usually used:

troverai un semaforo   you'll find ...

ci sarà un caffè   there'll be ...

vedrai un ospedale   you'll see ...

4. VERBS – **POTERE, DOVERE, VOLERE** + INFINITIVE

In Italian if you want to say 'you can', 'must', 'would like to do' something, use forms of **potere** (can) ... **dovere** (must) ... **volere** (want) plus the infinitive:

potere	**posso** I can	**posso andare**
Story example:	**possiamo andare al mare...**	
dovere	**devo** I must	**devo uscire**
Story example:	**dobbiamo alzarci presto**	
volere	**voglio** I want	**voglio prendere**
Story example:	**vuoi prendere un caffè?**	
	vorrei	**vorrei camminare**
Story examples:	**vorrei camminare tutta la notte**	
	vorrei aspettare l'alba	

5. AVERE BISOGNO DI ...

To say you need something use forms of **avere bisogno di:**

ho bisogno di musica
ha bisogno di amore
abbiamo bisogna di aria

If you need to do something, use the infinitive:

Story example: **Abbiamo tutti bisogno di fare un po' di sport.**

6. PRIMA DI ... DOPO

6.1 Followed by nouns: **prima di pranzo**
dopo cena

6.2 Followed by verbs: **prima di partire**
dopo aver giocato

6.3 Expressions of time: **poco prima delle nove**
la mattina dopo

7. PER...

7.1 **Per** + noun/pronoun = 'for':

Sei assicurata anche per me?

Per me un affogato al cognac.

7.2 **Per** + INF : = 'in order to':

...per poterci rilassare

...per evitare il traffico

Games

1. WITNESS

Bonnie and Clyde have just made a quick getaway. You are the key witness to their every action.

   1. 1   They talked a lot.
   1. 2   They ate two **affogati**.
   1. 3   They drank coffee.
   1. 4   They paid the bill.
   1. 5   They left the restaurant.
   1. 6   They took a taxi.
   1. 7   They took the ring road.
   1. 8   They were already on the motorway in no time at all.
   1. 9   They stopped a car with a Rome registration.
   1.10   They took a narrow road up into the hills.

2. MALE/FEMALE

   2. 1   He went out.
   2. 2   She came back.
   2. 3   She went out.
   2. 4   He came back.
   2. 5   He went to a cafè in the square.
   2. 6   She went to a cafè in the square.
   2. 7   They sat down.
   2. 8   They got up.
   2. 9   They walked all night.
   2.10   They returned home by taxi.

3. GUIDED TOUR

Your taking a small group of tourists round Rome. First you suggest things to see and do. Use **possiamo**.

   3. 1   ... see the Vatican.   **(il Vaticano)**
   3. 2   ... visit the Colosseum.   **(il Colosseo)**
   3. 3   ... look at the Sistine Chapel.   **(la Capella Sistina)**
   3. 4   ... listen to the music in **Trastevere**.
   3. 5   ... hire a car and go for a trip to the sea.

There are certain things which must be done. Use **dobbiamo**.

   3. 6   ... get up early.
   3. 7   ... eat breakfast.
   3. 8   ... drink coffee.
   3. 9   ... have an aperitive.
   3.10   ... eat an **affogato**.

4. BEFORE AND AFTER

Fill in the gaps:

   4. 1   **Vuoi** _ _ _ _ _ _ _ _ _ **un caffè** _ _ _ _ _ _ _ **partire?**

   4. 2   **La mattina** _ _ _ _ **;** _ _ _ _ _ **delle nove** _ _ _ _ _ _**.**

   4. 3   _ _ _ _ **cena il cameriere** _ _ _ _ _ _ _ _ _ _**.**

   4. 4   **Poco** _ _ _ _ _ **il cameriere** _ _ _ _ _ _ _ _ _ _ **con due gelati enormi.**

   4. 5   **Ora però rallenta** _ _ _ _ _ _ _ _ **usciamo dell'autostrada.**

   4. 6   _ _ _ _ **sulla sinistra** _ _ _ _ _ _ _ **un caffè.**

What if...? **Se invece...**

The end of a perfect evening, small talk mingled with seductiveness – or sedition, conspiracy or plot. Over the brandy, grappa or rum punch you plan your next move – an invitation, an excursion, an all-night vigil, a walk about town, a ride to the seaside, or into the country, the mountains.

The next day you dress for the occasion, you hire, buy, borrow the right car in the right colour. Perhaps you're caught by the police for speeding. But nothing can stop you embarking, with your mysterious colleague (companion, rival, Dr. Watson, Mata Hari, Isadora Duncan, Sherpa Ten Sing) on a magical mystery tour ino the unknown...

An excellent way to learn and revise vocabulary is to make up your own 'Word Webs'. There is one below. You simply take a topic, in this case shopping, and choose some sub-heads on that subject. We chose shopping for clothes, at the chemist, for food and at the cafe, since these subjects have been covered already.

Then you just write in the words that occur to you when you think of that topic - free assocation. You'll find you soon build up logical groups of associated words which is a great way to build vocabulary.

We strongly suggest you add words to this Word Web. Better yet, go back and make up some of your own Word Webs for the previous four Acts. And continue to make up at least one Word Web per Act. It's a very memorable way to create a visual memory for your language.

Act 8 **Atto 8**

Scena 1
The picnic and the castle. **Il picnic e il castello.**

The village was small,
with narrow streets.
The old houses
were a pastel colour
faded by time.

**Il paese era piccolo,
con le vie strette.
Le vecchie case
color pastello
erano scolorite dal tempo.**

Here and there women in black
sat in doorways.
In the beautiful old square,
the church was full of people.
A choir was singing 'Ave Maria'.
The air smelt of incense.

**Qua e là donne in nero
erano sedute sulle porte.
Nella bella piazza antica,
la chiesa era piena di gente.
Un coro cantava l'Ave Maria.
L'aria aveva odore d'incenso.**

Bella and Peter went into
a grocer's shop.
They bought rolls, wine,
cheese and olives.
There was also fresh pizza,
still warm.
They bought two large slices.
They also bought
peaches and apples.

**Bella e Peter sono entrati
in un negozio di alimentari.
Hanno comprato panini, vino,
formaggio e olive.
C'era anche la pizza fresca,
ancora calda.
Ne hanno preso due grandi fette.
Hanno comprato anche
pesche e mele.**

Then they went back to the car.
Just outside the village,
on the hill,
was a small castle
in red stone
surrounded by vineyards
and olive groves.

**Poi sono ritornati in macchina.
Appena fuori dal paese,
sulla collina,
c'era un piccolo castello
di pietra rossa,
circondato da vigneti
e oliveti.**

All around, the countryside
was bright green.
In the fields
grazed cows and horses.
There were also
a few peasant houses.
In the distance you could hear
the ringing of bells.

**Tutto intorno, la campagna
era verdissima.
Nei campi
c'erano vacche e cavalli al pascolo.
C'erano anche
alcune case di contadini.
Da lontano si sentiva
il suono delle campane.**

Da lontano si sentiva il suono delle campane.

Bella:	Let's stop here,	**Fermiamoci qua,**
	and park the car.	**parcheggiamo la macchina.**
	There's an avenue	**C'è un viale**
	leading up to the castle.	**che porta su al castello.**
	Peter took the picnic basket,	**Peter ha preso la borsa del picnic,**
	and they went up on foot.	**e sono saliti a piedi.**
	On the right	**Sulla destra**
	there was a tiny wood,	**c'era un piccolo bosco,**
	and on the left a waterfall	**e sulla sinistra una cascata**
	poured down from the hillside.	**scendeva dalla collina.**
	Bella and Peter stopped	**Bella e Peter si sono fermati**
	to listen to the birdsong,	**per ascoltare il cinguettio degli uccelli**
	and the running of the water.	**e il rumore dell'acqua.**
	The sky was blue and clear.	**Il cielo era azzurro, limpido.**
	Beneath the trees	**Sotto gli alberi**
	the air was cool.	**l'aria era fresca.**
	Peter breathed deeply.	**Peter ha respirato profondamente.**
Peter:	Such peace.	**Che pace.**
	I'd like to stay here forever.	**Vorrei rimanere qui per sempre.**

	Scene 2	**Scene 2**
Bella:	Are you hungry?	**Hai fame?**
Peter:	Yes, I'm hungry and thirsty.	**Sì, ho fame e sete.**
	Where shall we stop	**Dove ci fermiamo**
	for the picnic?	**a fare il picnic?**
Bella:	Let's stop here, in the wood.	**Fermiamoci qui, nel bosco.**
	Or there, by the waterfall.	**Oppure là, vicino alla cascata.**
Peter:	I prefer by the waterfall.	**Preferisco andare alla cascata.**
	Did you know that waterfalls	**Sai che le cascate**
	have healing powers?	**hanno un potere curativo?**
Bella:	I didn't know that.	**Non lo sapevo.**
	Let's go to the waterfall then.	**Allora andiamo alla cascata.**
	They sat on the grass.	**Si sono seduti sull'erba.**
	From close by	**Da vicino**
	the castle seemed bigger.	**il castello sembrava più grande.**
Peter:	I wonder who lives	**Chissà chi ci abita**
	in that castle?	**in quel castello?**
	Bella didn't reply.	**Bella non ha risposto.**
	She gave him a look	**Lo ha guardato**
	and a mysterious smile.	**e ha sorriso misterioso.**
	They had some food and drink.	**Hanno mangiato e bevuto.**
	Near the waterfall	**Vicino alla cascata**
	there was also a pine forest.	**c'era anche una pineta.**
	You could smell the pine trees.	**Si sentiva il profumo dei pini.**
	Down there, through the trees,	**Laggiù, fra gli alberi,**
	you could see the sea.	**si vedeva il mare.**
Bella:	Do you like the sea?	**Ti piace il mare?**
Peter:	Very much. And you?	**Moltissimo. E a te?**
Bella:	I would like to live	**Vorrei vivere**
	on an island,	**su un'isola,**
	a very, very small one,	**piccola piccola,**
	and be surrounded forever	**per essere sempre circondata**
	by the sea.	**dal mare.**

	Suddenly	**D'improvviso**
	Bella got up.	**Bella si è alzata in piedi.**
Bella:	Do you want to visit the castle?	**Vuoi visitare il castello?**
Peter:	Yes, but ...	**Sì ma ...**
	don't people live there?	**non è abitato?**
Bella:	Yes, but the owners	**Sì, però ora i proprietari**
	are away at the moment.	**sono via.**
	Come on, I'll introduce you	**Vieni, ti presento**
	to my cousin.	**mio cugino.**
	That's why I brought you here.	**È per questo che ti ho portato qui.**
	Once again Peter was taken aback	**Ancora una volta Peter è rimasto sorpreso**
	by Bella's behaviour.	**dal comportamento di Bella.**
	She organised everything.	**Organizzava tutto.**
	Everything had	**Tutto aveva**
	a precise motive for her.	**un motivo specifico per lei.**
Bella:	Well, then, are you coming?	**Allora, vieni?**
	Peter got up and followed her.	**Peter si è alzato e l'ha seguita.**
	In front of the large wooden door	**Davanti al grande portone di legno**
	was an antique doorbell.	**c'era un campanello antico.**
	Bella pulled the cord,	**Bella ha tirato la corda,**
	and they waited in silence.	**e hanno aspettato in silenzio.**
	They could hear	**Si sentiva**
	the buzzing of insects	**il ronzìo degli insetti**
	and the singing of birds.	**e il cinguettio degli uccelli.**
	A dog was sleeping quietly	**Un cane dormiva tranquillo**
	in the shadow of a tree.	**all'ombra di un albero.**
	From inside came	**Dall'interno veniva**
	the sound of footsteps.	**il rumore di passi.**
	A man of about thirty	**Un uomo di circa trent'anni**
	opened the door.	**ha aperto il portone.**

*Un cane dormiva tranquillo
all'ombra di un albero.*

	Scene 3	**Scene 3**
	The man greeted Bella.	**L'uomo ha salutato Bella.**
	Then he shook hands with Peter	**Poi ha dato la mano a Peter**
	and introduced himself.	**e si è presentato.**
Enrico:	I'm Enrico Lanza,	**Sono Enrico Lanza,**
	Bella's cousin.	**il cugino di Bella.**
	Do come in.	**Prego, entrate.**
	They entered an enormous,	**Sono entrati in un salone enorme,**
	rather dark lounge.	**piuttosto buio.**
	And then went into a large,	**E poi in una grande sala,**
	brightly lit room.	**piena di luce.**
	The floor was made of marble,	**Il pavimento era di marmo,**
	and the ceiling covered	**e il soffitto era coperto**
	in antique frescoes.	**di affreschi antichi.**
	There was very little furniture.	**C'erano pochissimi mobili.**
	The huge windows overlooked	**Le grandi finestre guardavano**
	a garden of flowers	**su un giardino pieno di fiori**
	and fruit trees.	**e di alberi da frutta.**
	While Bella went to make	**Mentre Bella è andata a preparare**
	some coffee,	**il caffè,**
	Peter and Enrico	**Peter ed Enrico**
	sat on the sofa.	**si sono seduti sul divano.**
	Enrico asked Peter	**Enrico ha fatto molte**
	lots of questions	**domande a Peter**
	about his family,	**sulla sua famiglia,**
	his interests.	**e sui suoi interessi.**
Enrico:	What are your ambitions	**Che ambizioni ha**
	for the future?	**per il futuro?**
Peter:	I don't know exactly ...	**Non so esattamente ...**
	I'd like to work in business.	**Vorrei lavorare nel campo commerciale.**
	Enrico also talked about himself	**Anche Enrico ha parlato di sè**
	and his family.	**e della sua famiglia.**
	He said he's been married	**Ha detto che è sposato**
	for five years	**da cinque anni,**
	and has two children:	**e che ha due bambini:**
	a boy and a girl.	**un maschio e una femmina.**
	Peter was surprised	**Peter è rimasto sorpreso**
	when Enrico said he worked	**quando Enrico ha detto che lavorava**
	in an import-export firm.	**in una ditta di importazioni ed esportazioni.**
Peter:	Strange, so does Bella.	**Strano, anche Bella.**
Enrico:	I know. We work together.	**Lo so. Lavoriamo insieme.**

Scene 4	**Scena 4**
The sun was already going down	**Il sole scendeva già**
behind the hills	**dietro le colline**
when Bella and Peter	**mentre Bella e Peter**
walked back to the car.	**camminavano verso la macchina.**
The air was warm.	**L'aria era calda,**
There was a pleasant wind.	**c'era un vento piacevole.**

Peter:

Why didn't you tell me	**Perchè non mi hai detto**
Enrico works with you?	**che Enrico lavora con te?**

Bella smiled.	**Bella ha sorriso.**

Bella:

I didn't think of it.	**Non ci avevo pensato.**

When they arrived	**Quando sono arrivati**
at Bella's home	**a casa di Bella**
There was a message	**c'era un messaggio**
from Signor Bruni:	**dal signor Bruni:**
''For business reasons	**"Per ragioni d'affari**
I'm held up another day.	**devo ritardare ancora un giorno.**

Ask Peter	**Domanda a Peter**
if he can stay in Rome.	**se può rimanere a Roma.**

Take him to visit the city.''	**Portalo a visitare la città."**
''Strange,'' thought Peter,	**"Strano," ha pensato Peter**
as he walked	**mentre camminava**
back to the hotel.	**verso l'albergo.**
But he was happy.	**Ma era felice.**
He could spend another day	**Poteva passare un'altra giornata**
with Bella.	**con Bella.**

ATTO 8 (i)

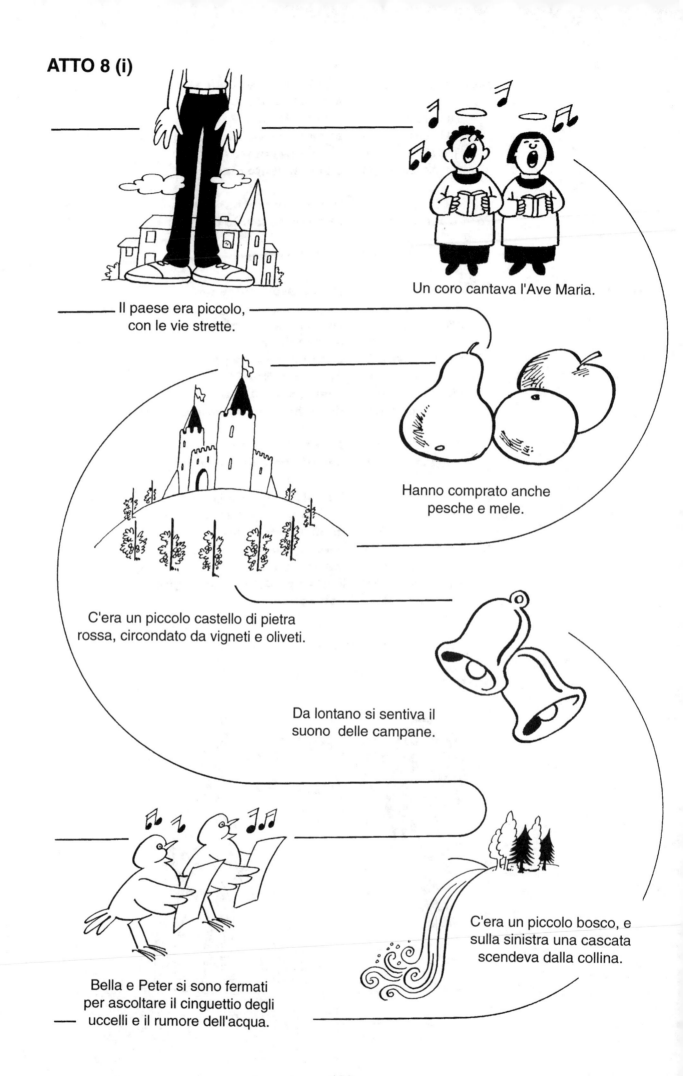

Il paese era piccolo, con le vie strette.

Un coro cantava l'Ave Maria.

Hanno comprato anche pesche e mele.

C'era un piccolo castello di pietra rossa, circondato da vigneti e oliveti.

Da lontano si sentiva il suono delle campane.

C'era un piccolo bosco, e sulla sinistra una cascata scendeva dalla collina.

Bella e Peter si sono fermati per ascoltare il cinguettio degli uccelli e il rumore dell'acqua.

ATTO 8 (ii)

Dove ci fermiamo a fare il picnic?

L'aria era fresca. Peter ha respirato profondamente.

Si sono seduci sull'erba.

Hanno mangiato e bevuto.

Vuoi visitare il castello?

Vieni, ti presento mio cugino.

Ancora una volta Peter è rimasto sorpreso dal comportamento di Bella.

Davanti al grande portone di legno c'era un campanello antico.

ATTO 8 (iii)

Si sentiva il ronzìo degli insetti e il cinguettìo degli uccelli.

Un uomo di circa trent'anni ha aperto il portone.

Un cane dormiva tranquillo all'ombra di un albero.

Poi ha dato la mano a Peter e si è pressantato.

Le grandi finestre guardavano su un giardino pieno di flori e di alebri da frutta.

Ha detto che è sposato da cinque anni,

Enrico ha fatto molte domande a Peter sulla sua famiglia, e sui suoi interessi.

Intonation and Pronunciation

Concentrate on the poetic sound of the description in Scene 1. Read them to yourself as if they were poetry, then read them aloud, make your own recording and compare it with the original. By now you should be starting to master the flow of the Italian language. Try repeating the following lines aloud several times:

1. **Le vecchie case color pastello erano scolorite dal tempo.**
2. **Un coro cantava l'Ave Maria.**
3. **L'aria aveva odore d'incenso.**
4. **Da lontano si sentiva il suono delle campane.**
5. **Si sentiva il ronzio degli insetti..., e il cinguettio degli uccelli.**
6. **Il cielo era azzurro, limpido.**

Il ronzio degli insetti.

Il cinguettio degli uccelli.

Functional Dialogues

1.

	Peter and Bella go into a grocer's.	**Peter e Bella entrano in un negozio di alimentari.**
	Shopkeeper	**Negoziante = Negoz:**

Bella:	I'd like four rolls, please.	**Vorrei quattro panini, per piacere.**
Negoz:	Yes, Miss. Here they are. Anything else?	**Sì, signorina. Eccoli. Vuole altro?**
Bella:	Yes, I'd like a bottle of white wine – cold, please.	**Sì, vorrei una bottiglia di vino bianco – freddo, per favore.**
Negoz:	A bottle of white wine, yes Miss. We have the wine from the Castle. Will that do?	**Una bottiglia di vino bianco, sì signorina. Abbiamo il vino del Castello. Va bene?**
Bella:	Excellent.	**Ottimo.**
Peter:	Have you any local cheese?	**Ha formaggio locale?**
Negoz:	Yes sir, we've got this cheese which is very good, very soft.	**Sì signore, abbiamo questo formaggio, che è molto buono, molto dolce.**
Peter:	We'll take 200 grams please.	**Ne prendiamo due etti, per favore.**
Bella:	There's a smell of fresh pizza, Peter! Let's take a pizza!	**Senti, Peter, c'è l'odore della pizza fresca! Prendiamo una pizza!**
Peter:	It's very big. Two slices are enough, don't you think?	**È molto grande. Bastano due fette, non credi?**
Bella:	What fruit have you got?	**Che frutta c'è?**
Negoz:	There are peaches, and apples.	**Ci sono pesche e mele.**
Bella:	All right, a kilo of peaches, and two apples, please.	**Va bene, un chilo di pesche, e due mele, per favore.**
Negoz:	Is that all?	**Basta così?**
Bella:	Yes, that's all, thank you.	**Sì, basta così, grazie.**

2.

	Peter and Bella have a picnic.	**Peter e Bella fanno il picnic.**

Peter:	Such peace. I'd like to stay here forever.	**Che pace! Vorrei rimanere qui per sempre.**
Bella:	Its a beautiful place. I come here often... are you hungry?	**È un posto molto bello... Ci vengo spesso... hai fame?**
Peter:	Yes, I'm hungry, and thirsty. Where shall we stop for the picnic?	**Sì, ho fame e sete. Dove ci fermiamo a fare il picnic?**
Bella:	Let's stop here, in the wood. Or there, near the waterfall.	**Fermiamoci qui, nel bosco. Oppure là, vicino alla cascata.**
Peter:	I'd rather go to the waterfall. Let's sit here on the grass.	**Preferisco andare alla cascata. Sediamoci qui sull'erba.**
Peter:	Mmm, the pizza's good!	**Mmm, è buona la pizza!**
Bella:	The cheese is good too – very good. Do you like the wine?	**Anche il formaggio è buono – buonissimo. Ti piace il vino?**
Peter:	Very much – it's delicious!	**Mi piace molto – è squisito!**
Bella:	Do you want to visit the castle?	**Vuoi visitare il castello?**
Peter:	Yes, but isn't it inhabited?	**Sì, ma non è abitato?**
Bella:	Come on, I'll introduce you to my cousin.	**Vieni, ti presento mio cugino.**

Sì, ho fame e sete.

3. Peter meets Bella's cousin. **Peter incontra il cugino di Bella.**

Enrico:	I'm Enrico Lanza, Bella's cousin.	**Sono Enrico Lanza, il cugino di Bella.**
Peter:	I'm Peter West.	**Io sono Peter West.**
	I come from England.	**Vengo dall'Inghilterra.**
Enrico:	Yes, I know...	**Sì, lo so...**
	please make yourself at home.	**prego, s'accomodi.**
	Lets sit on the sofa.	**Sediamoci sul divano.**
	Well, Peter, do you like	**Allora, Peter, le piace**
	our little house?	**la nostra casetta?**
Peter:	It's very imposing!	**È molto imponente!**
Enrico:	And where do you live?	**E lei, dove abita?**
Peter:	I live in a small flat	**Abito in un piccolo appartamento,**
	in London, in Chelsea.	**a Londra, nel quartiere di Chelsea.**
Enrico:	And what do you do for a living?	**E che cosa fa di professione?**
Peter:	I'm a student. I've just finished	**Sono studente. Ho appena finito di**
	studying economics,	**studiare scienze economiche,**
	at the University of Cambridge.	**all'Università di Cambridge.**
Enrico:	Excellent. And your family?	**Ottimo. E la sua famiglia?**
Peter:	My parents live	**I miei genitori abitano**
	near London.	**vicino a Londra.**
	My mother's of Italian origin.	**Mia madre è di origine italiana.**
	I have a brother and a sister.	**Ho un fratello e una sorella.**
Enrico:	Good, good. Do you like Italy?	**Bene, bene, le piace l'Italia?**
Peter:	It's a marvellous country.	**È un paese meraviglioso.**
	I feel at home in Italy.	**Mi sento a casa in Italia.**
	And what do you do for a living?	**E lei, che cosa fa di professione?**
Enrico:	Me? I work in an	**Io? Lavoro in una ditta di**
	import-export company.	**importazioni e exportazioni.**
Peter:	Strange, so does Bella.	**Strano, anche Bella.**
Enrico:	I know, we work together.	**Lo so, lavoriamo insieme.**

4. The telegram. **Il telegramma.**

Domestic **Domestica = Dom:**

Dom:	Signorina Bruni,	**Signorina Bruni,**
	there's a telegram for you.	**C'è un telegramma per lei.**
Bella:	Thank you.	**Grazie.**
	Ah, a message from my uncle.	**Ah, un messaggio da mio zio.**
Peter:	Has he arrived?	**È arrivato?**
Bella:	No, he hasn't arrived.	**No, non è arrivato.**
	He says that for business reasons	**Dice che, per ragioni d'affari,**
	he's held up another day.	**deve ritardare ancora un giorno.**
Peter:	And what must I do?	**E io, che cosa devo fare?**
Bella:	Can you stay another day in Rome?	**Puoi rimanere a Roma ancora un giorno?**
Peter:	Yes I can, but...	**Sì, posso, ma...**
Bella:	I'll take you to visit the city,	**Ti porto a visitare la città,**
	if you like.	**se vuoi.**

Personalised Dialogues

1. You're shopping for a picnic. Unfortunately your companion doesn't share your tastes.

Negoziante:	**Buongiorno, signora, desidera?**
Lei:	(Hello. You'd like three rolls, please.)
Compagne:	**Non basta. Prendiamone quattro.**
Lei:	(OK, four rolls. And you'd like a bottle of white wine.)
Compagne:	**No, io preferisco vino rosso.**
Lei:	(OK, you'd like a bottle of red wine.) (Have they got any local cheese?)
Compagne:	**Non mi piacciono i formaggi locali. Preferisco il formaggio francese.**
Lei:	(OK, You'll take 200 grams of French cheese – and a fresh pizza.)
Compagne:	**È molto grande. Bastano due fette.**
Lei:	(OK, you'll take two slices of pizza. What fruit have they got?)
Negoziante:	**Abbiamo pesche e mele.**
Lei:	(You'd like a kilo of peaches, please.)
Compagne:	**Ma non mi piacciono le pesche. Prendiamo le mele.**
Lei:	(Let's go to a restaurant instead.)

2. The restaurant was closed, so you decided on a picnic after all. As you might predict, deciding where to picnic isn't all that straightforward.

Lei:	(Where shall we park? There?)
Compagne:	**No, parcheggiamo qui. È più comodo.**
Lei:	(How peaceful!)
Compagne:	**Che rumore!**
Lei:	(How beautiful!)
Compagne:	**Che brutto!**
Lei:	(You're hungry.)
Compagne:	**Io non ho fame ancora.**
Lei:	(You're thirsty.)
Compagne:	**Io no, aspettiamo un po'.**
Lei:	(Shall we stop here, in the wood?)
Compagne:	**Preferisco andare alla cascata.**
Lei:	(Let's go to the waterfall, then.)
	(Mmm, the pizza's good.)
Compagne:	**È troppo fredda.**
Lei:	(The cheese is very good.)
Compagne:	**È un po' duro.**
Lei:	(Ask him if he likes the wine.)
Compagne:	**È troppo caldo.**
Lei:	Ask him if he likes picnics.)
Compagne:	**No, non mi piacciono. Preferisco andare al ristorante.**

Fermiamoci qui, nel bosco.

3. You've been hired by Bruni & Co to do some market research. As you discover, it's not as easy as it looks.

Lei:	(Where do you live?)
Passante:	**Abito a Padova.**
Lei:	(Do you live in a flat?)
Passante:	**No, abito in un castello.**
Lei:	(Is that so?)
Compagne:	**No, non è vero, ma è più interessante così, non è vero?**

Lei:	(What job do you do?)
Passante:	**Non lavoro. Sono miliardaria.**
Lei:	(Is that so?)
Passante:	**No, non è vero, però mi piace sognare.**
Lei:	(Have you got brothers or sisters?)
Passante:	**Sì, ho dieci fratelli e otto sorelle.**
Lei:	(Is that so?)
Passante:	**Sì, sono socialista. Siamo tutti fratelli e sorelle. Che ne dice?**
Lei:	**(Mamma mia!)**

4. You receive a telegram with instructions which upset all your plans. What's more, the telegram answers back.

Telegramma: Deve rimanere a Roma.	
Lei:	(But you can't stay in Rome.)
Telegramma: Deve rilassarsi un po'.	
Lei:	(But you can't relax!)
Telegramma: Deve visitare la città.	
Lei:	(But you can't visit the city.)
Telegramma: Deve guardare la televisione.	
Lei:	(But you can't watch television.)
Telegramma: Perchè no?	
Lei:	(Because you haven't got a television.)

Grammar

1. VERBS – PAST DESCRIPTION/PAST ACTION

Note the use of the imperfect to describe:

1.1 States:

Il paese era piccolo.

Le vecchie case erano scolorite dal tempo.

Il castello sembrava più grande.

1.2 Ongoing process:

L'aria aveva odore d'incenso.

Un coro cantava l'Ave Maria.

Una cascata scendeva dalla collina.

1.3 Repeated actions:

Bella organizzava tutto. (i.e. again and again ...)

Contrast the use of the perfect to indicate specific completed actions:

Sono entrati in un negozio di alimentari.

Hanno comprato panini.

Peter ha respirato profondamente.

Hanno mangiato e bevuto.

Bella si è alzata in piedi.

Un coro cantava l'Ave Maria.

2. SI ...

Note the use of the reflexive **si** + imperfect for the impersonal 'you ...':

Si sentiva il profumo dei pini.

Si vedeva il mare.

Si sentiva il ronzio degli insetti.

3. SUGGESTION

Note the use of the **-iamo** form of the verb to express 'let's'..:

Andiamo alla cascata.
Fermiamoci qua.
Parcheggiamo la macchina.

4. **LO SO ... LO SAPEVO**

The **lo** is not translated in English:

lo so...	**lo sapevo**	(I know ... I knew)
no lo so...	**non lo sapevo**	(I don't know.., I didn't know...)

5. **CHISSÀ?**

Chissà? Literally 'who knows'? Used in the sense of 'I wonder' ...

> **Chissà chi ci abita in quel castello?**
> **Chissà quanto costa la pizza?**

6. **HO FAME ... HO SETE**

Note the use of these idioms:

in the present:

ho fame	**hai fame?**
ho sete	**hai sete?**

in the past:

avevo fame
avevo sete

7. **DA ...**

To say how long you've been doing something, use **da** + present tense:

> **Enrico è sposato da cinque anni.**
> **Abito a Londra da dieci anni**

Games

1. TRUE OR FALSE?

È vero?   È falso?

1. **Bella ha una sorella.**
2. **Peter è sposato.**
3. **Peter è figlio unico.**
4. **Enrico è sposato da quattro anni.**
5. **Un coro cantava l'Ave Maria.**
6. **Il paese era piccolo.**
7. **Il castello era di pietra bianca.**
8. **Si sono fermati nel bosco.**
9. **Vicino alla cascata c'era una pineta.**
10. **Nella sala del castello c'erano molti mobili.**

2. TELEGRAM

Fill in this telegram, sending it to a friend in Italy, giving the following information:

2. 1 You must stay in London another couple
       of days for business reasons.
2. 2 You have a headache.
2. 3 You don't like London.
2. 4 There's too much noise.
2. 5 The hotel isn't comfortable.
2. 6 There's no sun.
2. 7 You'd like to come home, but you can't.
2. 8 Wish him/her Happy Birthday : *Buon compleanno!*

TELEGRAM

3. FUTURE STOCK

Fill in the gaps:

3. 1   **Vorrei** _ _ _ _ _ _ _ _ _ **nel campo commerciale.**

3. 2   **Vorrei** _ _ _ _ _ _ _ _ _ **qui per sempre.**

3. 3   **Vorrei** _ _ _ _ _ _ _ **su un' isola.**

3. 4   **Che** _ _ _ _ _ _   _ _ _ _ **per il futuro?**

3. 5   **Vorrei** _ _ _ _ _ _ _ **sempre circondata dal mare.**

4. COMPUTER BREAKDOWN

The computer has wrongly converted all perfect tenses in your script to the imperfect. Convert them back again.

4. 1   **Compravano panini.**
4. 2   **Entravano in un negozio di alimentari.**
4. 3   **Peter si alzava e la seguiva.**
4. 4   **Aspettavano in silenzio.**
4. 5   **Mangiavano e bevevono.**
4. 6   **Ritornavano in macchina.**

5. SECRET CODE

Decode the following jumbled messages:

5. 1   **DNAMOIA LALA CATSCAA.**

5. 2   **GGARCPHEIOMA AL HINAMACC.**

5. 3   **MOCIFERMAI AUQ.**

5. 4   **VOED TIRDARERA CORNAA NU ORNIOG.**

5. 5   **UÒP MANEREIR A MORA?**

What if...? **Se invece...**

Compose an alternative picnic, with your favourite food and drink, and choose your own ideal picnic location – by the sea, on top of a mountain, in bed if you're feeling lazy! Choose your company carefully, and go visiting strange places – a haunted castle, perhaps, the skyscrapers of Chicago, the silver-lined clouds of heaven. Who do you meet there? What do they do? What plans do they have – for themselves, for you?

A last-minute message (in a bottle in the sea, in a secret code, a Valentine) changes all your plans...

Act 9 **Atto 9**

Scene 1 **Scena 1**
Sightseeing. **Visita alla città**

It was breakfast time
next morning at the Hotel Tre Palme.
Peter called the waitress over.

**Era l'ora di colazione
la mattina dopo all'Hotel Tre Palme.
Peter ha chiamato la cameriera.**

Peter: Have you got today's paper,
please?
I'd like to see
what the weather's going to be like.

**Ha il giornale di oggi,
per favore?
Vorrei vedere
che tempo farà.**

The waitress brought him
the newspaper.
Peter studied the page
with the weather forecast.
It will be hot and sunny
in the whole of Italy.
In London, however,
it will be cloudy,
with wind and rain.
After breakfast
Peter phoned Bella.

**La cameriera gli ha portato
il giornale.
Peter ha studiato la pagina
con le previsioni del tempo.
Farà caldo e ci sarà il sole
in tutta Italia.
A Londra invece
sarà nuvoloso,
con vento e pioggia.
Dopo colazione
Peter ha telefonato a Bella.**

Peter: What are we doing today?
Bella: What, don't you remember?
We decided
to go and visit the city.
We'll start with the Colosseum,
then we'll go
to St. Peter's Square,
Then to the Sistine Chapel.
We can go by underground,
if you like.
It's quicker than the bus,
and cheaper than a taxi.

**Che cosa facciamo oggi?
Come, non ricordi?
Abbiamo deciso
di andare a visitare la città.
Cominciamo con il Colosseo,
poi andiamo
in piazza San Pietro,
e dopo, alla Cappella Sistina.
Possiamo andare in metropolitana,
se vuoi.
È più veloce dell'autobus,
e più economica del taxi.**

Peter ha telefonato a Bella.

They met	**Si sono incontrati**
at an underground station,	**ad una stazione della metropolitana,**
half way	**a metà strada**
beteween the Hotel Tre Palme	**fra l'Hotel Tre Palme**
and Bella's house.	**e la casa di Bella.**

Bella:

You buy the tickets,	**Compra tu i biglietti,**
you need to practise	**hai bisogno di far pratica**
your Italian.	**d'italiano.**

Peter:

Shall I buy just a single,	**Compro solo andata,**
or return?	**o andata e ritorno?**

Bella:

Buy two singles.	**Compra due andate.**

Peter went to the	**Peter è andato**
ticket office.	**allo sportello dei biglietti.**

Peter:

Two singles for the Colosseum,	**Due andate per il Colosseo,**
please.	**per favore.**

A few minutes later	**Dopo pochi minuti**
they were already	**erano già**
at the stop for the Colosseum.	**alla fermata del Colosseo.**

	Scene 2	**Scena 2**
	Outside	**Fuori**
	the sun was shining beautifully,	**c'era un sole splendido,**
	but it wasn't too hot.	**ma non faceva troppo caldo.**

Peter: I've always dreamed of visiting Rome.
Ho sempre sognato di visitare Roma.

Bella: You see, Rome is divided into three parts: ancient, medieval and modern ...
Vedi, Roma è divisa in tre parti; Roma antica, Roma medioevale, e Roma moderna ...

At the Colosseum there were lots of tourists, speaking all the languages of the world.
Al Colosseo c'erano molti turisti; parlavano tutte le lingue del mondo.

Peter: It's very imposing ... I feel quite small ... When was it built?
Com'è imponente ... mi sento piccolo piccolo ... Quando è stato costruito?

Bella: It was built between 72 AD and 80 AD. Look around you, imagine what it was like in ancient times: there, in the centre, sits the emperor. Surrounding him are the senators, and the imperial family.
È stato costruito fra il 72 e l'80 d.c. (dopo Cristo). Guardati attorno, immaginalo com'era ai tempi antichi: là, al centro, siede l'imperatore. Attorno a lui ci sono i senatori e la famiglia imperiale.

The Christians come out down there, the people are waiting. There is a moment of silence. Then, from the back over there, come the wild animals ... If you close your eyes you can hear the roaring of the lions and the screaming of the crowds, the applause and ...
Da laggiù escono i cristiani. La gente aspetta. C'è un attimo di silenzio. Poi, da là in fondo, arrivano le bestie feroci ... Se chiudi gli occhi puoi sentire il ruggito dei leoni, e le grida della folla che applaude e ...

Arrivano le bestie feroci.

Peter:	That's enough – it's terrible!	**Basta, è terribile!**
Bella:	Yes, but it's all history now,	**Sì, ma ora è tutta storia,**
	and in history	**e nella storia**
	there are sad things	**ci sono cose tristi**
	and beautiful things.	**e cose belle.**

After the Colosseum,	**Dopo il Colosseo,**
they went to the Roman Forum,	**sono andati al Foro Romano,**
to St. Peter's	**a San Pietro**
and, finally,	**e, infine,**
to the Sistine Chapel.	**alla Cappella Sistina.**
Bella knew a lot about history,	**Bella conosceva bene la storia,**
and also had	**aveva anche**
quite an imagination ...	**molta fantasia ...**

Peter listened to her in silence	**Peter l'ascoltava in silenzio**
as she talked about the monuments,	**mentre parlava dei monumenti,**
the statues, the fountains	**delle statue, delle fontane**
and, now, the frescoes	**e, ora, degli affreschi**
of the Sistine Chapel.	**della Cappella Sistina.**

Bella:	Here is my	**Ecco la mia**
	favourite work of art,	**opera preferita:**
	''The Creation of Man''.	**"La Creazione dell'Uomo".**
	The Creator is on the point	**Il Creatore è sul punto**
	of touching Man with his finger,	**di toccare l'Uomo con un dito,**
	to give him soul and life.	**per dargli anima e vita.**
	You must look	**Devi guardare**
	at this work of art	**quest'opera**
	in silence,	**in silenzio,**
	observe the colours.	**osservare i colori,**
	the power and delicateness	**la forza e la dolcezza**
	of the lines.	**delle linee.**
	In my opinion	**Secondo me,**
	it's really one of the greatest	**è veramente uno dei più grandi**
	masterpieces in the world.	**capolavori del mondo.**

	Scene 3	**Scena 3**
	They walked, tired,	**Camminavano, stanchi,**
	along the banks of the river Tiber.	**sul Lungotevere.**

Peter: Rome is so rich in history and art ...
Roma è una città così ricca di storia e di arte ...

Bella: Yes, there's so much more to see.
Sì, c'è ancora tanto da vedere.

Peter: I'd like to visit Caracalla, the Fontana di Trevi, Tivoli, the Pincio ...
Vorrei visitare Caracalla, la Fontana di Trevi, Tivoli, il Pincio ...

Bella: We can go to the Fontana di Trevi now, if you like.
Possiamo andare ora alla Fontana di Trevi, se vuoi.

Peter: And when can I meet this mysterious uncle of yours?
E quando sarà possibile incontrare questo tuo misterioso zio?

Bella: He's not mysterious at all. He'll be back this evening, don't worry.
Non è per niente misterioso. Sarà di ritorno questa sera, non preoccuparti.

Further on, on the bank of the river, was a group of people. A woman was shouting. Peter went up immediately to the group.
Più avanti, sulla riva del fiume, c'era un gruppo di gente. Una donna gridava. Peter è andato subito vicino al gruppo.

Peter: What happened?
Che cosa è successo?

Woman: A young boy fell into the water We pulled him out.
Un giovane è caduto in acqua. L'abbiamo tirato fuori.

Peter: Is he alive?
È vivo?

Woman: He looked dead, but luckily he's breathing now.
Sembrava morto, ma per fortuna ora respira.

Peter: Can we do anything, call a doctor or an ambulance?
Possiamo fare qualcosa; chiamare un medico, un'ambulanza?

Woman: There's no need. We've already called an ambulance. He's hurt a leg, but it's nothing serious.
Non è necessario. Abbiamo già chiamato un'ambulanza. Si è fatto male a una gamba, ma non è niente di grave.

Camminavano, stanchi, sul Lungotevere.

167

Before returning home	**Prima di ritornare a casa**
Bella and Peter	**Bella e Peter**
went to visit	**sono andati a visitare**
the Fontana di Trevi.	**La Fontana di Trevi.**
Peter threw a coin	**Peter ha buttato un soldo**
into the water.	**in acqua.**
Then closed his eyes	**Poi ha chiuso gli occhi**
and thought that, maybe,	**e ha pensato che, forse,**
all this was really a dream.	**tutto questo era davvero un sogno.**
There were lots of things	**C'erano molte cose**
he still didn't understand.	**che ancora non capiva.**
There was the mystery,	**C'era il mistero,**
and there was Bella ...	**e c'era Bella ...**
But who knows, maybe one day	**Però ... chissà, forse un giorno,**
he really would come back to Rome ...	**sarebbe ritornato davvero a Roma ...**

Bella:	Peter, did you express a wish?	**Peter, hai espresso un desiderio?**
Peter:	Yes, to come back to Rome.	**Sì, di ritornare a Roma.**
Bella:	But now let's go home.	**Però ora, andiamo a casa.**
	I'm very tired!	**Sono stanchissima!**

At Bella's house	**A casa di Bella**
a tall, large man	**un uomo grande e grosso**
was waiting in the living room.	**aspettava nel soggiorno.**
Bella embraced him.	**Bella lo ha abbracciato.**

Bella:	Uncle Mario! At last!	**Zio Mario! Finalmente!**

Zio Mario! Finalmente!

ATTO 9 (i)

Peter ha chiamato la cameriera.

Ha il giornale di oggi, per favore? Vorrei vedere che tempo farà

Peter ha studiato la pagina con le previsioni del tempo.

Farà caldo e ci sarà il sole in tutta Italia.

A Londra invece sarà nuvoloso, con vento e pioggia.

Dopo colazione Peter ha telefonato a Bella.

Possiamo andare in metropolitana.

È più veloce dell'autobus,

e più economica del taxi.

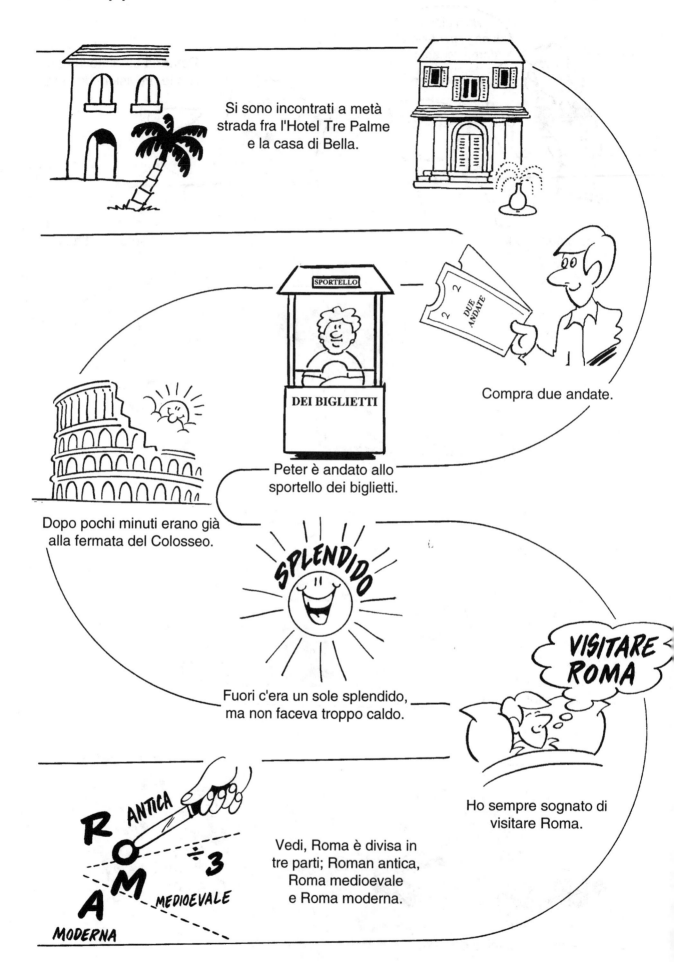

Si sono incontrati a metà strada fra l'Hotel Tre Palme e la casa di Bella.

Compra due andate.

Peter è andato allo sportello dei biglietti.

Dopo pochi minuti erano già alla fermata del Colosseo.

Fuori c'era un sole splendido, ma non faceva troppo caldo.

Ho sempre sognato di visitare Roma.

Vedi, Roma è divisa in tre parti; Roman antica, Roma medioevale e Roma moderna.

ATTO 9 (iii)

Al Colosseo c'erano molti turisti; parlavano tutte le lingue del mondo.

Com'è imponente... mi sento piccolo piccolo.

Là, al centro, siede l'imperatore.

Da laggiù escono i cristiani.

Poi, da là in fondo, arrivano le bestie feroci ...

SAN PIETRO

Basta, è terribile!

E nella storia ci sono cose tristi.

Dopo il Colosseo, sono andati al Foro Romano, a San Pietro e, infine, alla Cappella Sistina.

171

ATTO 9 (iv)

E quando sarà possibile incontrare questo tuo misterioso zio?

Camminavano, stanchi, sul Lungotevere.

Più avanti, sulla riva del fiume, c'era un gruppo di gente

Un giovane è caduto in acqua. L'abbiamo tirato fuori.

Poi ha chiuso gli occhi e ha pensato che, forse, tutto questo era davvero un sogno.

VISITARE ROMA

Abbiamo già chiamato un ambulanza?

Sono stanchissima!

Un uomo grande e grosso aspettava nel soggiorno.

Intonation and Pronunciation

Concentrate on Bella's speeches in Scene 2 describing the Colosseum and the Sistine Chapel. Listen to the way the descriptions are paced, phrase by phrase. Speak them aloud, paying attention to this phrasing, as if you were conveying the meaning to someone who's never been to Rome.

Functional Dialogues

1.	Breakfast time.	**L'ora di colazione.**

Cam:	Good morning, Mr West.	**Buongiorno, Signor West.**
	Coffee with milk?	**Caffè latte?**
Peter:	Good morning. Yes, please.	**Buongiorno. Sì, grazie.**
	Have you got today's paper, please?	**Ha il giornale di oggi, per favore?**
Cam:	Yes, of course. Here it is.	**Sì, certo. Eccolo.**
Peter:	I'd like to see	**Vorrei vedere**
	what the weather's going to be like.	**che tempo farà.**
Cam:	I've already heard, on the radio:	**Ho già sentito, alla radio:**
	it'll be hot and sunny	**farà caldo e ci sarà il sole**
	in the whole of Italy. Again...	**in tutta Italia. Ancora...**
Peter:	How lovely!	**Che bello!**
Cam:	And what's the weather	**E a Londra,**
	going to be like in London?	**che tempo farà?**

Farà caldo e ci sarà

Peter:	Let's have a look. Here we are...	**Guardiamo un pò. Ecco...**
	In London, on the other hand	**A Londra, invece**
	it's going to be cloudy	**sarà nuvoloso**
	with wind and rain.	**con vento e pioggia.**
Cam:	How wonderful! I'd like so much to	**Che meraviglia! Vorrei tanto**
	visit London!	**visitare Londra!**

2.	Peter phones Bella.	**Peter telefona a Bella.**

Bella:	Hello!	**Pronto!**
Peter:	Hello. It's Peter.	**Pronto, sono Peter.**
Bella:	Hello Peter, how are you?	**Ciao, Peter, come stai?**
Peter:	Fine thanks. What are we going	**Bene grazie. Che cosa**
	to do today?	**facciamo oggi?**
Bella:	What, you don't remember?	**Come, non ricordi?**
	We decided to go	**Abbiamo deciso di andare**
	and visit the city.	**a visitare la città.**

il sole in tutta Italia.

Peter:	Ah yes, that's right.	**Ah sì, è vero.**
	Where shall we start?	**Dove cominciamo?**
Bella:	We'll start with the Colosseum.	**Cominciamo con il Colosseo.**
	Then we'll go to St.Peter's square,	**Poi andiamo in piazza S.Pietro,**
	and afterwards,	**e dopo,**
	to the Sistine Chapel.	**alla Cappella Sistina.**
Peter:	How will we get there?	**Come ci andiamo?**
Bella:	We can go by underground,	**Possiamo andare in metropolitana,**
	if you like.	**se vuoi.**
	It's quicker than the bus,	**È più veloce dell' autobus,**
	and cheaper than a taxi.	**e più economica del taxi.**
Peter:	OK, where shall we meet?	**Va bene, dove c'incontriamo?**

Bella:	We'll meet	**Ci vediamo**
	at the underground station	**alla stazione della metropolitana**
	near your hotel. It's halfway.	**vicino al tuo albergo. È a metà strada.**
Peter:	When shall we meet?	**Quando c'incontriamo?**
Bella:	In half an hour. 'Bye.	**Fra mezz'ora. Ciao!**
Peter:	'Bye, see you later.	**Ciao, a fra poco.**

3.   At the underground station.   **Alla stazione della metropolitana.**

Peter: Hi, Bella. Have you already bought the tickets?   **Ciao, Bella. Hai già comprato i biglietti?**

Bella: No, you buy them. You need to practise your Italian!   **No, comprali tu. Hai bisogno di far pratica d'italiano!**

Peter: Shall I buy just a single, or a return?   **Compro solo andata, o andata e ritorno?**

Bella: Buy two singles.   **Compra due andate.**

Peter: Two singles for the Colosseum, please.   **Due andate per il Colosseo, per favore.**

4.   Peter and Bella visit Rome.   **Peter e Bella visitano Roma.**

Peter: I've always dreamt of visiting Rome.   **Ho sempre sognato di visitare Roma.**

Bella: It's a city so rich in history and art.   **È una città così ricca di storia e di arte.**

Peter: Yes, there's so much to see. I'd like to visit the *Fontana di Trevi*, *Tivoli*, the *Pincio*.   **Sì, c'è tanto da vedere. Vorrei visitare la Fontana di Trevi, Tivoli, il Pincio.**

Bella: We can go now to the *Fontana di Trevi* if you like. You see, here you have to throw a coin into the water, and make a wish. Did you make a wish?   **Possiamo andare ora alla Fontana di Trevi se vuoi. Vedi, qui devi buttare un soldo in acqua, ed esprimere un desiderio. Hai espresso un desiderio?**

Peter: Yes, to come back to Rome.   **Sì, di ritornare a Roma.**

Personalised Dialogues

1. You're having breakfast in the hotel. Pass the time of day with the waitress, who's rather starry-eyed about London.

Cameriera:	**Buongiorno, signore, come sta?**
Lei:	(Good morning, fine thanks.)
Cameriera:	**Cappuccino?**
Lei:	(No thanks, today you'll have tea with lemon.)
Cameriera:	**Un tè al limone, si signore.**
Lei:	(Ask her if she's got today's paper, please.)
Cameriera:	**Sì, certo, eccolo.**
Lei:	(You'd like to see what the weather's going to be like.)
Cameriera:	**Ho già sentito alla radio: farà caldo e ci sarà il sole in tutta Italia. Ancora...**
Lei:	(How lovely!)
Cameriera:	**E a Londra che tempo farà?**
Lei:	In London, on the contrary, it's going to be cloudy, windy and rainy.)
Cameriera:	**Che meraviglia! Vorrei tanto visitare Londra!**

2. It's your second day in Rome. Last night's companion gave you his phone number. You phone to check the plans for today.

(**Compagno** – masculine/Companion)

Compagno:	**Pronto!**
Lei:	(Hello, it's...)
Compagno:	**Ciao, come stai?**
Lei:	(Fine thanks, how's he.)
Compagno:	**Benissimo.**
Lei:	(Ask him what you're both going to do today.)
Compagno:	**Come, non ricordi? Abbiamo deciso di andare a visitare la città.**
Lei:	(Ah, yes, you'd forgotten. You drank a lot of wine yesterday evening.)
Compagno:	**Sì, è vero.**
Lei:	(Where shall we start?)
Compagno:	**Cominciamo con il Colosseo.**
Lei:	(How will we get there?)
Compagno:	**Possiamo andare in metropolitana, se vuoi.**
Lei:	(Fine, where shall we meet?)
Compagno:	**Ci vediamo alla stazione della metropolitana vicino al tuo albergo.**
Lei:	(When shall we meet?)
Compagno:	**Fra mezz'ora. D'accordo?**
Lei:	(OK, 'bye, see you soon.)

3. Your new friend, whose name is Silvana, seems to think your Italian needs practice, and is waiting for you to buy the tickets for the underground.

Lei:	(Hi, Silvana, have you already bought the tickets?)
Silvana:	**No, comprali tu. Hai bisogno di far pratica d'italiano!**
Lei:	(Oh no, you've left your wallet (**il portafoglio**) in the hotel.)
Silvana:	**Non importa, ecco i soldi.**
Lei:	(Thanks. Shall you buy just a single or return?)
Silvana:	**Compra due andate.**
Lei:	(Two singles for the Colosseum, please.)
Impiegata:	**Due andate per il Colosseo, sì signore/a.**
Lei:	(Thanks very much. Good day. Let's go!)

4. The Colosseum and the Sistine Chapel are behind you, but there's still so much you'd like to see. Luckily, Silvana is a romantic too!

Lei:	(You've always dreamed of visiting Rome.)
Silvana:	**È una città così ricca di storia e di arte.**
Lei:	(Yes, there's so much to see. You'd like to visit *Caracalla*, *Tivoli*, the *Pincio*, the *Fontana di Trevi*...)
Silvana:	**Possiamo andare ora alla Fontana di Trevi, se vuoi.**
Lei:	(What a good idea!)
Silvana:	**Vedi, qui devi buttare un soldo in acqua... devi esprimere un desiderio.**
Lei:	(You have only one wish.)
Silvana:	**Sì?**
Lei:	(To come back to Rome.)

Grammar

1. VERBS – IMPERATIVES

The imperative is used to make requests or give orders or instructions when addressing people informally in the **tu** form:

The 2nd person singular of verbs ending in **are** ends in **-a**:

comprare	**compra**	**compra tu i biglietti**
guardare	**guarda**	**guardati attorno**

Pronouns and adverbs are attached to the end of the imperative:

compra<u>li</u> tu	<u>you</u> buy <u>them</u>
guarda<u>ti</u> attorno	look around (yourself)
immagina<u>lo</u> com'era	imagine <u>it</u>

2. NEGATIVE IMPERATIVE

The negative imperative in the singular is formed with **non** + the infinitive:

compra	**non comprare**
bevi	**non bere**

Story example: **non preoccuparti** (from **preoccuparsi**)

In the plural it's formed with **non** + imperative:

entrate	**non entrate**

3. VERBS: FUTURE

Note the following future idioms:

è	**sarà**	**sarà di ritorno**	(he'll be back)
fa	**farà**	**farà caldo**	(it'll be hot)

(Imperfect: **faceva:**   **non faceva troppo caldo)**

The future of **c'è** is **ci sarà: ci sarà il sole**

4. VERBS – PAST PARTICIPLES

Note the following examples of the past participle:

decidere	**deciso**	**Abbiamo deciso di andare.**
succedere	**successo**	**Che cosa è successo?**
chiudere	**chiuso**	**Ha chiuso gli occhi.**
esprimere	**espresso**	**Hai espresso un desiderio?**
essere	**stato**	**È stato costruito.**

Note also the placing of adverbs between forms of **avere** (or **essere**) and the past participle:

ho sognato	**Ho sempre sognato di visitare Roma.**
abbiamo chiamato	**Abbiamo già chiamato un'ambulanza.**
è caduto	**È già caduto in acqua.**

Finally, note the placing of direct and indirect pronouns:

Bella lo ha abbracciato.
Peter l'ascoltava in silenzio.
L'abbiamo tirato fuori.
La cameriera gli ha portato il giornale. (i.e. 'to him')

5. COMPARATIVES

Use **più di:**

La metropolitana è più veloce dell'autobus.
più economica del taxi

Less than = **meno di:**

L'autobus costa meno del taxi.

Note also the superlative form **il più:**

il più grande capolavoro	the greatest...
uno dei più grandi capolavori	one of the greatest...

Also **la più:**

la più brutta donna	the ugliest...
una delle più brutte donne	one of the ugliest...

6. OPINIONS

secondo me	in my opinion

Secondo me "la Creazione dell'Uomo" è un capolovoro.

preferito/a	the one I like best

La mia preferita è la Cappella Sistina.

Games

1. OPINIONS

Agree **(sì)** or disagree **(no)** with the following opinions:

1. 1   **Secondo me Dostoevsky era un autore italiano.**
1. 2   **Secondo me Sophia Loren è morta.**
1. 3   **Secondo me "La Dolce Vita" è un film francese.**
1. 4   **Secondo me Brigitte Bardot è un'attrice italiana.**
1. 5   **Secondo me Melina Mercouri è un'attrice italiana.**
1. 6   **Secondo me il tempo in Italia è più buono del tempo in Inghilterra.**
1. 7   **Secondo me Milano è la capitale d'Italia.**
1. 8   **Secondo me Roma è la capitale d'Italia.**
1. 9   **Secondo me Ravel era un compositore francese.**
1.10   **Secondo me Manito de Platas è un chitarrista italiano.**

2. CHE SARÀ, SARÀ

Fill in the gaps with **sarà, farà, saranno** as appropriate:

2. 1   **In agosto in Italia _ _ _ _ caldo.**

2. 2   **In aprile a Londra ci _ _ _ _ la pioggia.**

2. 3   **A New York a novembre _ _ _ _ freddo.**

2. 4   **A Mosca in dicembre ci _ _ _ _ la neve.**

2. 5   **Al mare domani ci _ _ _ _ vento.**

2. 6   **Domani in montagna ci _ _ _ _ _ _ _ le nuvole.**

3. ORDERS ARE ORDERS

But you're in charge, so countermand the following instructions (using **non**):

3. 1   **Compra due biglietti.**
3. 2   **Bevi il vino.**
3. 3   **Entra!**
3. 4   **Va via!**
3. 5   **Guardami!**
3. 6   **Mangia gli spaghetti.**
3. 7   **Entrate.**
3. 8   **Mangiate tutto.**

4. MORE OR LESS

Fill in the gaps using **più di** or **meno di**:

4. 1   **Milano è _ _ _ grande _ _ Roma.**

4. 2   **Sophia Loren è _ _ _ bella _ _ Jeanne Moreau.**

4. 3   **L'autobus costa _ _ _ _   _ _ _ taxi.**

4. 4   **La metropolitana è _ _ _ veloce _ _ _ _ _ autobus.**

4. 5   **La televisione è _ _ _ interessante _ _ _ _ _ radio.**

4. 6   **La Cina è _ _ _ grande _ _ _ _ _ America.**

5. CITY TOUR

Unscramble the following Rome sights and monuments:

5. 1   **AL PEPACLAL TINSISA**

5. 2   **LI LOSSEOSO**

5. 3   **ZIAPZA SNA TOREPI**

5. 4   **LI ROOF MORNAO**

5. 5   **AL ANATNOF ID REVTI**

What if...? **Se invece...**

What if you and your companion (accomplice, guide, lover) were not in Rome at all, but in Rio, San Francisco, Bangkok, Paris, Moscow? What alternative sights can be seen, by day and by night, what monuments can be visited, what people might you pass the time of day (or night) with?

How will you travel there? How will you get about once you're there? What incident or accident will interrupt the routine? What mysterious figure will appear at the end of the day – and will you be relieved, surprised, disappointed or afraid?

A REMINDER

Are you still doing the 'extra exercises' we described on page xxvii :

1. Making up post cards to revise with.

2. Acting out the Dialogues expressively.

3. Putting up post-it notes around the house or office or even in the car!

4. Representing at least 10 words visually.

5. Selecting the 10 most useful words per Act. (That gets you reviewing them all!)

6. Underlining, highlighting and <u>writing down</u> key words and sentences.

7. Describing the scenes out loud in your new language.

8. Making a Word Web for each Act.

Atto 10

Scene 1 | **Scena 1**
Uncle Mario | **Lo zio Mario.**

Uncle Mario really was | **Lo zio Mario era veramente**
a big man. | **grande e grosso.**
Indeed he was rather fat. | **Infatti era piuttosto grasso.**
Probably the result | **Probabilmente il risultato**
of many years of good living! | **di molti anni di dolce vita!**
He was over 6 feet tall, well-dressed, | **Era alto due metri, ben vestito,**
and wore dark glasses. | **e portava gli occhiali scuri.**
He seemed very happy to see them. | **Sembrava molto felice di vederli.**

U Mario: Well, Peter, do you like Rome? | **Allora, Peter, le place Roma?**
I'm sorry I'm late, | **Mi dispiace di essere in ritardo,**
but I was held up | **ma sono stato trattenuto**
by business out of town. | **fuori città dagli affari.**
Peter: It doesn't matter, | **Non importa,**
I've been having a good time. | **mi sono divertito molto.**
In fact, I like being a tourist! | **Infatti mi piace fare il turista!**
U Mario: I'm sure! | **Lo credo!**
Unfortunately, however, | **Purtroppo però**
I have another job for you. | **ho un altro lavoro per lei.**

Uncle Mario went | **Lo zio Mario si è avvicinato**
to the safe. | **alla cassaforte.**
Opened it. | **L'ha aperta.**
Took out two packages: | **Ha tirato fuori due pacchetti:**
the one Peter brought | **quello che Peter ha portato**
from London, | **da Londra,**
and another, larger package. | **e un altro pacchetto più grande.**

U Mario: I want you to take | **Voglio che lei porti**
these packages to Zurich, | **questi pacchetti a Zurigo,**
and deliver them personally | **e li consegni di persona**
to a client of mine. | **a un mio cliente.**
Naturally | **Naturalmente**
I'll pay all the expenses. | **pago io tutte le spese.**

Peter: Sorry if I seem cheeky, | **Scusi se sembro impertinente,**
but why don't you post them | **ma perchè invece non li manda**
instead? | **per posta?**
It costs less, | **Costa meno caro,**
and I must admit | **e poi devo confessarle**
I'm worried about the contents | **che il contenuto dei pacchetti**
of the packages. | **mi preoccupa.**

L'indirizzo è sui pacchetti.

	Uncle Mario didn't get angry as Peter feared. Instead he smiled.	**Lo zio Mario non si è arrabbiato come Peter temeva. Invece ha sorriso.**
U Mario:	Don't worry, Peter, trust me. I understand why you're worried, but there's no need. Everything will be OK, you'll see. All you have to do is deliver the packages in person to a certain Mr. Braun. The address is on the packages.	**Non si preoccupi, Peter, si fidi di me. Capisco che lei sia preoccupato, ma non è il caso. Vedrà che tutto andrà bene. Lei deve solo consegnare i pacchetti di persona a un certo signor Braun. L'indirizzo è sui pacchetti.**
	Peter was still hesitant, but he agreed. Mario Bruni put the packages in a very expensive brown briefcase, and gave it to Peter. They all had dinner together.	**Peter era ancora esitante, ma ha consentito. Mario Bruni ha messo i pacchetti in una costosissima valigetta marrone, e l'ha data a Peter. Hanno cenato tutti assieme.**
U Mario:	Your flight is already booked for tomorrow at 10, but you'll have to go and pick up the ticket at the Alitalia Terminus, before going to the airport.	**Il suo volo è già prenotato per domani alle 10, ma dovrà andare a ritirare il biglietto al Terminus dell'Alitalia, prima di andare all'aeroporto.**

Il suo volo è già prenotato per domani alle 10.

184

	Scene 2	**Scena 2**
	The next morning Peter paid the hotel bill with the money given to him by Signor Bruni. Then he took a taxi to the Alitalia Terminus.	**La mattina dopo Peter ha pagato il conto dell'albergo con i soldi che gli ha dato il signor Bruni. Poi ha preso un taxi ed è andato al Terminus dell'Alitalia.**
Peter:	Excuse me please, I'd like to collect my return ticket to Zurich. My name is Peter West.	**Scusi, per favore, vorrei ritirare il mio biglietto di andata e ritorno per Zurigo. Il mio nome è Peter West.**
Clerk:	Of course, Mr. West, your ticket is ready. How would you like to pay: by credit card or cash?	**Certamente, signor West, il suo biglietto è pronto. Come vuole pagare: con carta di credito, o in contanti?**
Peter:	I'll pay cash. Can you tell me if the flight is on time?	**Pago in contanti. Mi può dire se il volo è in orario?**
Clerk:	Yes, it's on time. The bus for Fiumicino leaves from here at 8.45. You can check in here at the Terminus. Have you any luggage?	**Sì, è in orario. L'autobus per Fiumicino parte da qui alle 8.45. Può fare il check-in qui al Terminus. Ha bagagli?**
Peter:	No, only hand baggage.	**No, solo un bagaglio a mano.**
Clerk:	Smoking?	**Fuma?**
Peter:	No, Non Smoking. Can I confirm my return flight? leaving from Zurich at 17.00?	**No, non fumo. Posso confermare il volo di ritorno che parte da Zurigo alle 17?**
Clerk:	Yes, it arrives in Rome at 18.15.	**Sì, arriva a Roma alle 18.15.**
	There was still a quarter of an hour to go before the departure of the bus for the airport.	**C'era ancora un quarto d'ora prima della partenza dell'autobus per l'aeroporto.**
	Peter bought a postcard and a stamp, and wrote to his parents. He said he would be back in London next Saturday or Sunday. Then he went to catch the bus.	**Peter ha comprato una cartolina e un francobollo, e ha scritto ai suoi genitori. Ha detto che sarà di ritorno a Londra sabato o domenica prossimi. Poi è andato a prendere l'autobus.**

L'autobus per Fiumicino parte da qui alle 8.45.

ATTO 10 (i)

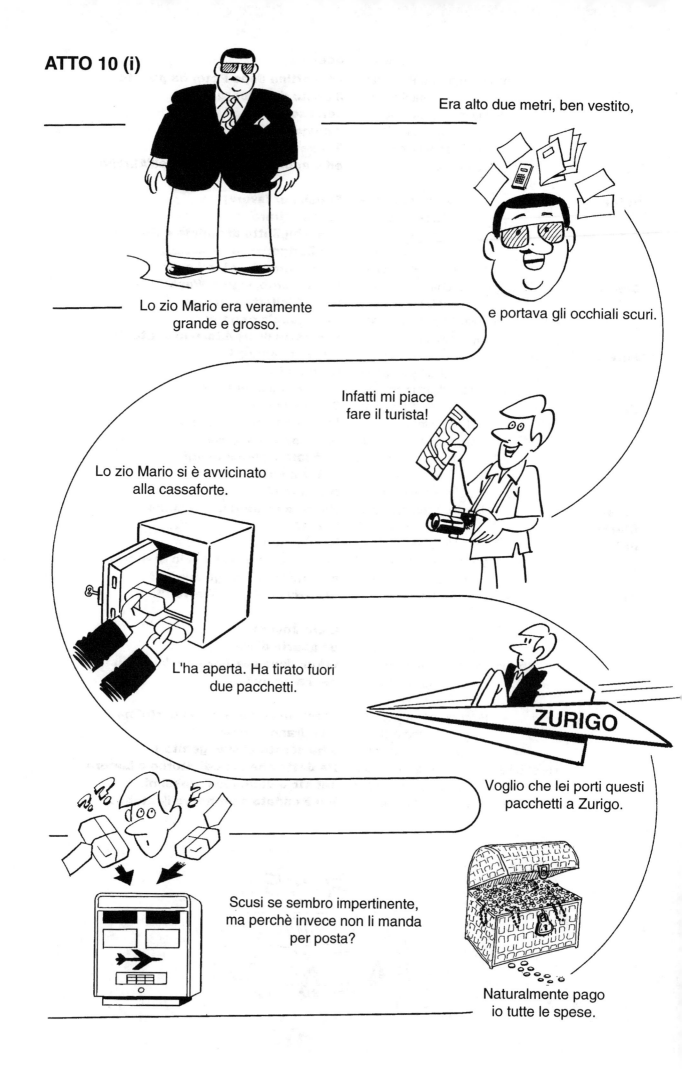

Era alto due metri, ben vestito,

Lo zio Mario era veramente
grande e grosso.

e portava gli occhiali scuri.

Infatti mi piace
fare il turista!

Lo zio Mario si è avvicinato
alla cassaforte.

L'ha aperta. Ha tirato fuori
due pacchetti.

ZURIGO

Voglio che lei porti questi
pacchetti a Zurigo.

Scusi se sembro impertinente,
ma perchè invece non li manda
per posta?

Naturalmente pago
io tutte le spese.

ATTO 10 (ii)

Lo zio Mario non si è arrabbiato.

Invece ha sorriso.

L'indirizzo è sui pacchetti.

Mario Bruni ha messo i pacchetti in una costosissima valigetta marrone.

Hanno cenato tutti assieme.

Il suo volo è già prenotato per domani alle 10,

ma dovrà andare a ritirare il biglietto.

Il suo biglietto è pronto.

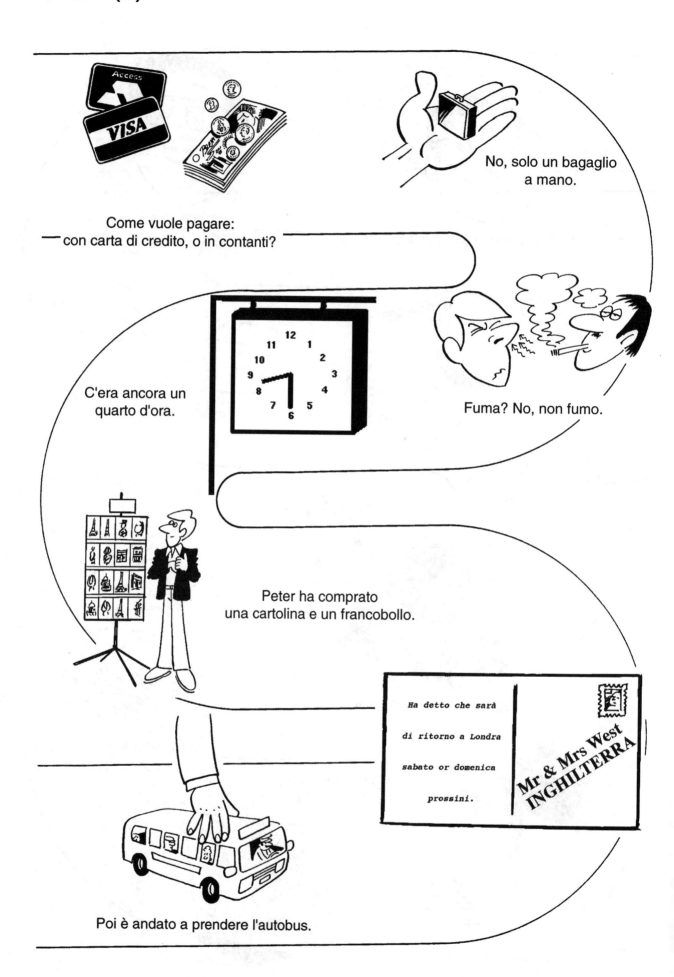

Come vuole pagare:
con carta di credito, o in contanti?

No, solo un bagaglio a mano.

C'era ancora un quarto d'ora.

Fuma? No, non fumo.

Peter ha comprato una cartolina e un francobollo.

Ha detto che sarà di ritorno a Londra sabato or domenica prossini.

Mr & Mrs West INGHILTERRA

Poi è andato a prendere l'autobus.

Intonation and Pronunciation

Concentrate on the speeches of Uncle Mario. Imitate the careful slow pattern of delivery, savouring the sound shape of each word and phrase, speaking with the same confidence and authority.

Functional Dialogues

1.

	Peter Meets Uncle Mario.	**Peter incontra lo zio Mario.**
		Uncle Mario = Mario:

Mario:	I'm very glad to see you!	**Sono molto felice di vedervi!**
	Well Peter, do you like Rome?	**Allora Peter, le piace Roma?**
	I'm sorry I'm late.	**Mi dispiace di essere in ritardo.**
Peter:	It doesn't matter.	**Non importa,**
	I've enjoyed myself very much.	**mi sono divertito molto.**
	In fact, I like being a tourist!	**Infatti, mi piace fare il turista!**
Mario:	I'm sure! Unfortunately, however,	**Lo credo! Purtroppo, però,**
	I have another job for you.	**ho un altro lavoro per lei.**
	I want you to take these packages	**Voglio che lei porti questi pacchetti**
	to Zurich.	**a Zurigo.**
Peter:	Sorry if I seem cheeky,	**Scusi se sembro impertinente,**
	but why don't you post them	**ma perchè invece non li manda**
	instead? It costs less.	**per posta? Costa meno.**
Mario:	Don't worry Peter, trust me.	**Non si preoccupi Peter, si fidi di me.**
	Everything will be OK, you'll see.	**Vedrà che tutto andrà bene.**
Peter:	Yes, but...	**Sì, ma...**
Mario:	All you have to do is deliver	**Lei deve solo consegnare**
	the packages in person	**i pacchetti di persona**
	to a certain Mr.Braun.	**a un certo signor Braun.**
	The address is on the packages.	**L'indirizzo è sui pacchetti.**

TURISTA

2.

	Peter pays the hotel bill.	**Peter paga il conto dell'albergo.**

S.A.:	Good morning, Mr.West.	**Buongiorno, Signor West.**
	So you have to leave?	**Allora lei deve partire?**
Peter:	Yes, unfortunately	**Sì, purtroppo**
	I have to leave straightaway.	**devo partire subito.**
	My flight is booked for 10 a.m.	**Il mio volo è prenotato per le dieci.**
	But I have to pick up the tickets	**Ma devo ritirare i biglietti**
	at *Alitalia* Terminus	**al Terminus dell' Alitalia**
	before going to the airport.	**prima di andare all' aeroporto.**
S.A.:	Don't worry.	**Non si preoccupi.**
	I've already prepared your bill...	**Ho già preparato il suo conto...**
	Here it is. Do you want to pay	**Eccolo. Vuole pagare**
	by credit card?	**con una carta di credito?**
Peter:	No, no, I don't like	**No, no, non mi piacciono**
	credit cards. I'd rather pay	**le carte di credito. Preferisco pagare**
	straight away.	**subito.**
	Here you are, 100,000 lire, OK?	**Ecco, 100,000 lire, va bene?**
S.A.:	All right, Mr West. Thank you.	**Va bene, Signor West. Grazie.**
	Goodbye then, and *bon voyage.*	**Allora arriverdeci, e buon viaggio.**

Mi piace fare il turist

Peter:	Thank you. Ah, where can I catch	**Grazie. Ah, dove posso prendere**
	a taxi?	**un taxi?**
S.A.:	I've already called one.	**Ne ho già chiamato uno.**
	It's waiting outside.	**Sta aspettando fuori.**
Peter:	Many thanks. Goodbye.	**Grazie mille. Arrivederci.**

3.   At the Terminal.   **Al Terminus.**

Clerk   **Impiegata = Imp:**

Peter:	Excuse me, please, I'd like to collect my return ticket to Zurich.	**Scusi, per favore, vorrei ritirare il mio biglietto di andata e ritorno per Zurigo.**
	My name is Peter West.	**Il mio nome è Peter West.**
Imp:	Of course, Mr West.	**Certamente, Signor West.**
	Your ticket is ready.	**il suo biglietto è pronto.**
	How do you want to pay?	**Come vuole pagare?**
	With credit card, or cash?	**Con carta di credito, o in contanti?**
Peter:	I'll pay cash.	**Pago in contanti.**
	Can you tell me if the flight is on time?	**Mi può dire se il volo è in orario?**
Imp:	Yes, it's on time.	**Sì, è in orario.**
Peter:	What time does the bus leave for Fiumicino?	**E a che ora parte l'autobus per Fiumicino?**
Imp:	It leaves here at 8.45.	**Parte da qui alle 8.45.**
	You can check in here at the Terminal.	**Può fare il check-in qui al Terminus.**
	Have you any luggage?	**Ha bagagli?**
Peter:	No, only hand luggage.	**No, solo un bagaglio a mano.**
Imp:	Smoking?	**Fuma?**
Peter:	No, Non Smoking.	**No, non fumo.**
	Can I confirm the return flight that leaves Zurich at 17.00?	**Posso confermare il volo di ritorno che parte da Zurigo alle 17.00?**
Imp:	Yes, it arrives in Rome at 18.15.	**Sì, arriva a Roma alle 18.15.**
	Here's your ticket. *Bon voyage.*	**Ecco il suo biglietto. Buon viaggio.**
Peter:	Thank you, goodbye.	**Grazie, arrivederci.**

4.   Peter buys a postcard.   **Peter compra una cartolina.**

Peter:	I'd like this postcard, please.	**Vorrei questa cartolina, per piacere.**
	How much is it?	**Quanto viene?**
Vend:	200 lire. Anything else?	**Duecento lire. Vuole altro?**
Peter:	Yes, have you any stamps?	**Sì, ha francobolli?**
Vend:	Yes, for what country?	**Sì, per che paese?**
Peter:	For England. Just one stamp.	**Per l'Inghilterra. Un francobollo solo.**
Vend:	There you are.	**Ecco.**
Peter:	How much is that altogether?	**Quant'è in tutto?**
Vend:	600 lire.	**Sono 600 lire.**
Peter:	Here you are. Thank you.	**Eccole, grazie.**

Come vuole pagare:

con carta di credito, o in contanti?

Personalised Dialogues

1. You're a rich businesswoman who's kept a young employee waiting. You're mildly apologetic, but he seems to have been having a good time with your secretary.

    (**Impiegato** – male/Employee)

Lei:	(You're sorry you're late.)
Impiegato:	**Non importa.**
Lei:	(You were held up by business out of town.)
Impiegato:	**Non importa. Mi sono divertito molto.**
Lei:	(You're sure. Ask him if he likes Rome.)
Impiegato:	**Mi piace molto.**
Lei:	(Ask him if he likes your secretary.)
Impiegato:	**Sì, è molto simpatica... e molto bella.**
Lei:	(Unfortunately you've got another job for him.)
Impiegato:	**Bene. Non mi piace fare il turista!**
Lei:	(You want him to take your secretary out to lunch.)
Impiegato:	**Ma...**
Lei:	(Tell him not to worry. Trust you, he'll see that everything will be fine.)

2. You have to check out of your hotel in a hurry. The receptionist is super-efficient.

    (**Ricezionista**/Receptionist). The English term 'Receptionist' is also frequently used in Italy.

Lei:	(You're sorry, but unfortunately you have to leave immediately.)
Ricezionista:	**Va bene, signore.**
Lei:	(Have they already prepared your bill?)
Ricezionista:	**Sì signore, un'attimo... eccolo. Vuole pagare con una carta di credito?**
Lei:	(No, you don't like credit cards. You'd rather pay straight away.)
Ricezionista:	**Benissimo.**
Lei:	(Your flight is booked for 10 o'clock. Where can you catch a taxi?)
Ricezionista:	**Ne ho già chiamato uno. Sta aspettando fuori.**
Lei:	(Many thanks. Goodbye.)

Peter ha pagato il conto dell'albergo.

3. You're at the terminal. The woman at the ticket desk is also super-efficient.

Lei:	(Say, excuse me please, you'd like to collect your return ticket to London.)
Impiegata:	**Certamente, signore. Il suo nome?**
Lei:	(Your name is...)
Impiegata:	**Ah sì, signore, il suo biglietto è pronto. Come vuole pagare: con carta di credito o in contanti?**
Lei:	(Cash. You don't like credit cards.) (Can she tell you if the flight is on time?)
Impiegata:	**Sì, è in orario.**
Lei:	(What time does the bus leave for Fiumicino?)
Impiegata:	**Parte da qui alle 8.30. Fra pochi minuti. Ha bagagli?**
Lei:	(No, only hand luggage.)
Impiegata:	**Fuma?**
Lei:	(No, you don't smoke. You hate smoke.)
Impiegata:	**Va bene signore.**
Lei:	(Can you confirm the return flight which leaves London at 18.00.)
Impiegata:	**Sì, arriva a Roma alle 20.30. Ecco il suo biglietto. Buon viaggio.**
Lei:	(Thank you. Goodbye.)

4. You have a few moments to spare before your flight, so you buy a postcard for the boss's secretary.

(**Commessa**/Assistant)

Lei:	(You'd like this postcard please. How much is it?)
Commessa:	**Cinquecento lire. Vuole altro?**
Lei:	(Yes, have they got any stamps?)
Commessa:	**Sì, per che paese?**
Lei:	(For England. Just one stamp.)
Commessa:	**Ecco. Altro, signore?**
Lei:	(Yes, have they got an English newspaper?)
Commessa:	**Mi dispiace, giornali inglesi non ne abbiamo.**
Lei:	(It doesn't matter. That's all. How much?)
Commessa:	**Sono mille lire.**
Lei:	(Here you are, thanks.)

*Peter ha comprato una cartolina
e un francobollo.*

Grammar

1. VERBS – PAST PARTICIPLES

Note these examples of the agreement of the past participle with the preceding direct object:

ha aperto la cassaforte   **l'ha apert<u>a</u>**
ha dato la valigetta a Peter   **l'ha dat<u>a</u> a Peter**

Note these irregular examples of the past participle:

prendere	**preso**	**ha preso un taxi**
scrivere	**scritto**	**ha scritto ai suoi genitori**
dire	**detto**	**ha detto che sarà di ritorno**
aprire	**aperto**	**l'ha apert<u>a</u>**

2. REFLEXIVES

The reflexive pronoun changes according to the subject, and in the past always goes with forms of **essere:**

avvicinarsi	**si è avvicinato**
divertirsi	**mi sono divertito**
arrabbiarsi	**non si è arrabbiato**

A woman would say: **mi sono divertit<u>a</u>**
Of a woman you would say   **non si è arrabbiat<u>a</u>**

3. SAYING SORRY

Scusi	**Scusi, per favore.**
	Scusi se sembro impertinente.
Mi dispiace	**Mi dispiace di essere in ritardo.**
Non importa	It doesn't matter.
	(in reply to an excuse or an apology)

4. MORE IMPERATIVES

non si preoccupi   the formal imperative.

Compare with:

non preoccuparti   informal
si fidi di me   (from **fidarsi** – to trust)

TERMINUS DELL' ALITALIA

5. POSSESSIVES

In Italian the article (**il, la, i, le**) is used to denote possession, in addition to the words for 'my', 'your', etc.:

singular:	**il mio volo**	my
plural:	**i miei biglietti;**	
	i suoi biglietti	your (his/her)
singular:	**il suo volo**	your (his/her)
singular:	**il suo biglietto**	your (his/her)
singular:	**la mia valigetta**	my
plural:	**le mie valigette**	
singular:	**la sua valigetta**	your (his/her)
plural:	**le sue valigette, etc.**	

6. PRONOUNS

Note these further examples of the pronoun attached to the infinitive:

	devo confessarle	(i.e. 'to you')
	sembrava molto felice di vederli	('them')
BUT:	**mi può dire se il volo è in orario?**	

You could say: **può dirmi se...?**

7. IDIOMS

Non ne è il caso	There's no need.
Lo credo	I'm sure (literally: 'I believe it')

Games

1. INDENTIKIT

The tall, the fat and the ugly... You're helping the police with their enquiries. Describe the one that got away.

1. 1   He's big.
1. 2   He's fat.
1. 3   He's over six feet tall.
1. 4   He's well dressed.
1. 5   He was wearing dark glasses.
1. 6   He's ugly.
1. 7   He's angry.
1. 8   He's nice.
1. 9   He's rather small.
1.10   He's handsome.

2. IDENTIKIT Contd...

Confused by your contradictory statement, the police turn to your wife, who is sure it was a woman...

2. 1   She was big
2. 2   She was fat.
2. 3   She was over six feet tall.
2. 4   She was well-dressed.
2. 5   She was wearing dark glasses.
2. 6   She was ugly.
2. 7   She was angry.
2. 8   She was nice.
2. 9   She was rather small.
2.10   She was beautiful.

3. MINE, ALL MINE

You and your wife can't agree about what belongs to whom. Fill in the gaps:

3. 1 **Questa è __ __ __ __ __ valigietta.**

3. 2 **No, è __ __ __ __ __ valigietta!**

3. 3 **Questo è __ __ __ __ __ biglietto.**

3. 4 **No, è __ __ __ __ __ biglietto!**

3. 5 **Questi sono __ __ __ __ __ pacchetti.**

3. 6 **No, sono __ __ __ __ __ pacchetti!**

3. 7 **Queste sono __ __ __ __ __ cartoline.**

3. 8 **No, sono __ __ __ __ __ cartoline!**

3. 9 **Questo è __ __ __ __ __ taxi.**

3.10 **No, è __ __ __ __ __ taxi!**

4. MIX-UP

The word processor's gone wrong again. This time all its past participles are in a twist.
Re-write the sentences the way they should be:

4. 1 **Ha scritto un taxi.**
4. 2 **Ha detto una cartolina.**
4. 3 **Ha comprato ai suoi genitori.**
4. 4 **Ha preso che sarà di ritorno domani.**
4. 5 **Ha aperto l'autobus.**
4. 6 **Ha prenotato la cassaforte.**
4. 7 **Ha confermato la valigia.**
4. 8 **Ha dato l'albergo per Peter.**

What if...? **Se invece...**

Invent a different mystery guest. It could be male or female, tall or small, beautiful or ugly. There could be several of them, all with dark glasses, or masked, or disguised. They may, or may not, have a package to give you, and the assignment (if there is one) may take you to Africa, South America, the Far East – though your return flight won't be the same day!

As your alternative story nears its own climax let the imagination run wild. Anything goes. And don't forget to write a postcard to the one(s) you've left behind – all clues may be helpful.

Act 11	**Atto 11**

Scene 1	**Scena 1**
The flight to Zurich.	**Il volo per Zurigo.**

The journey to Fiumicino airport took 45 minutes.	**Il viaggio per l'aeroporto di Fiumicino è durato 45 minuti.**
When Peter went through passport control,	**Quando Peter è passato al controllo passaporti,**
the officer looked carefully at his photograph.	**l'impiegato ha guardato attentamente la sua fotografia.**
Then he looked at the briefcase in Peter's hand.	**Poi ha guardato la valigetta che Peter aveva in mano.**
Finally he gave him back his passport.	**Infine gli ha restituito il passaporto.**

During the flight Peter felt ill at ease.	**Durante il volo Peter si sentiva a disagio.**
His hands were bathed in sweat.	**Aveva le mani bagnate di sudore.**
He listened to the announcements by the hostess without hearing a word.	**Ascoltava gli annunci della hostess senza sentire una parola.**
He looked nervously out of the window.	**Guardava nervoso fuori dal finestrino.**

Down below he could see the sea.	**Sotto si vedeva il mare.**
The golden beaches looked like velvet.	**Le spiagge dorate sembravano di velluto.**

Suddenly he heard a man's voice calling his name.	**D'improvviso ha sentito una voce maschile che chiamava il suo nome.**
Peter turned around in surprise.	**Peter si è girato sorpreso.**
It was Enrico, Bella's cousin.	**Era Enrico, il cugino di Bella.**

Enrico:	What a surprise! Are you going to Zurich as well?	**Che sorpresa! Vai a Zurigo anche tu?**

Peter didn't reply. He felt too confused.	**Peter non ha risposto, si sentiva troppo confuso.**

Enrico:	There's a free seat next to me, why don't you sit here?	**C'è un posto libero vicino a me, perchè non ti siedi qui?**

Without saying a word Peter got up and went to sit next to Enrico.	**Senza dire niente Peter si è alzato e si è andato a sedere vicino ad Enrico.**
Enrico called the hostess.	**Enrico ha chiamato la hostess.**

Enrico:	Excuse me, miss, would you bring us a bottle of champagne?	**Scusi, signorina, ci porta una bottiglia di champagne?**
Peter:	Not for me, thanks it's too early. But I'd like a cup of coffee.	**Non per me, grazie, è troppo presto. Però vorrei una tazza di caffè.**
	The coffee was good and very strong.	**Il caffè era buono e molto forte.**
Peter:	How come you're going to Zurich?	**Come mai, perchè vai a Zurigo?**
Enrico:	I've got an appointment with a very important client. He buys our products from South America. Then tomorrow I have to go to Frankfurt. I often do this journey. Usually two or three times a month. And you, why are you going to Zurich?	**Ho un appuntamento con un cliente molto importante. Compra i nostri prodotti dell'America del Sud. Poi domani devo andare a Francoforte. Faccio spesso questo viaggio. Di solito due o tre volte al mese. E tu, perchè vai a Zurigo?**
	Peter was sure Enrico already knew the reason for this journey of his, but didn't make any comment.	**Peter era certo che Enrico già sapeva la ragione di questo suo viaggio, ma non ha fatto commenti.**
Enrico:	Where are you staying in Zurich? I always stay at the Hotel Du Lac.	**Dove stai a Zurigo? Io sto sempre all'Hotel Du Lac.**
Peter:	I'm not staying the night in Zurich. In fact I'll be glad when I've delivered these packages and I'm back in Rome.	**Non rimango a Zurigo questa notte. Infatti sarò contento quando avrò consegnato questi pacchetti e sarò di ritorno a Roma.**
	Enrico was about to say something, but stopped himself when the hostess arrived with the breakfast. They ate in silence.	**Enrico stava per dire qualcosa, ma si è fermato quando è arrivata la hostess con la colazione. Hanno mangiato in silenzio.**
	From time to time the captain gave out some information about the flight. But Peter wasn't listening. He didn't even take in the taste of the food.	**Di tanto in tanto il capitano dava informazioni di volo. Ma Peter non ascoltava. Non sentiva nemmeno il sapore del cibo.**
	He was worried about the contents of the packages. Now he was sure there was something wrong. Maybe they're crooks, he thought, But I can't believe Bella is dishonest.	**Lo preoccupava il contenuto dei pacchetti. Ora era sicuro che c'era qualcosa che non andava. Forse sono dei criminali pensava, Ma non posso credere che Bella sia disonesta.**

| | The plane landed five minutes early. Peter said goodbye to Enrico Bruni. | **L'aereo è atterrato con cinque minuti di anticipo. Peter ha salutato Enrico Bruni.** |

Peter: I'm sorry, but I must dash, I have to be at an address in the centre before mid-day, and I don't want to arrive late.

Scusa, ma devo correre. Devo essere ad un indirizzo in centro prima di mezzogiorno e non voglio arrivare in ritardo.

Scene 2
Peter walked quickly towards customs. After all he had nothing to declare.

**Scena 2
Peter camminava in fretta verso la dogana. Dopo tutto, non aveva niente da dichiarare.**

C.O. Just a minute, sir, what have you got in your briefcase?

Un momento, signore, che cos'ha nella valigetta?

It was just what Peter was afraid of. His heart was beating wildly. He felt his forehead bathed in sweat, his mouth dry.

Era proprio ciò che Peter temeva. Il cuore gli batteva forte. Si sentiva la fronte bagnata di sudore, e la bocca secca.

Peter: Just two packages with papers inside.

Solo due pacchetti con dentro documenti.

C.O. Show me your passport.

Mi mostri il passaporto..

The man was looking at him fixedly, then looked at his photograph on the passport.

L'uomo lo guardava fisso, poi guardava la sua fotografia sul passaporto.

C.O. Show me the packages, please.

Mi mostri i pacchetti, per favore.

Peter opened the briefcase. His hands were trembling. I've had it, he thought.

Peter ha aperto la valigetta. Gli tremavano le mani. Ora sono finito, pensava.

C.O. Open them, please.

Li apra, per piacere.

Si sentiva la fronte bagnata di sudore.

201

First Peter opened the larger package, then the smaller one. He knew he had turned pale, and was shaking like a leaf.	**Peter ha aperto prima il pacchetto più grande, poi quello più piccolo. Sapeva di essere diventato pallido, e di tremare come una foglia.**
But no, Signor Bruni was right. The packages contained just papers. Now Peter felt more confused than ever. The customs officer was no longer interested in him.	**Ma no, il signor Bruni aveva ragione: i pacchetti contenevano solo documenti. Ora Peter si sentiva più che mai confuso. Il doganiere non era più interessato a lui.**

C.O.   Thank you, you may go.   **Grazie, può andare.**

Peter looked at his watch. It was 11.30. His appointment with Mr. Braun was for 12 o'clock exactly.	**Peter ha guardato l'orologio. Erano le 11.30. Il suo appuntamento col signor Braun era per le 12 in punto.**

Gli tremavano le mani.

ATTO 11 (i)

L'impiegato ha guardato attentamente.

Il viaggio per l'aeroporto di Fiumicino è durato 45 minuti.

Peter si è girato sorpreso.

Peter si sentiva a disagio. Aveva le mani bagnate di sudore.

Era Enrico, il cugino di Bella

Scusi, signorina ci porta una bottiglia di champagne?

Enrico ha chiamato la hostess.

C'è un posto libero vicino a me, perchè non ti siedi qui?

Ho un appuntamento con un cliente molto importante.

Compra i nostri prodotti dell'America del Sud.

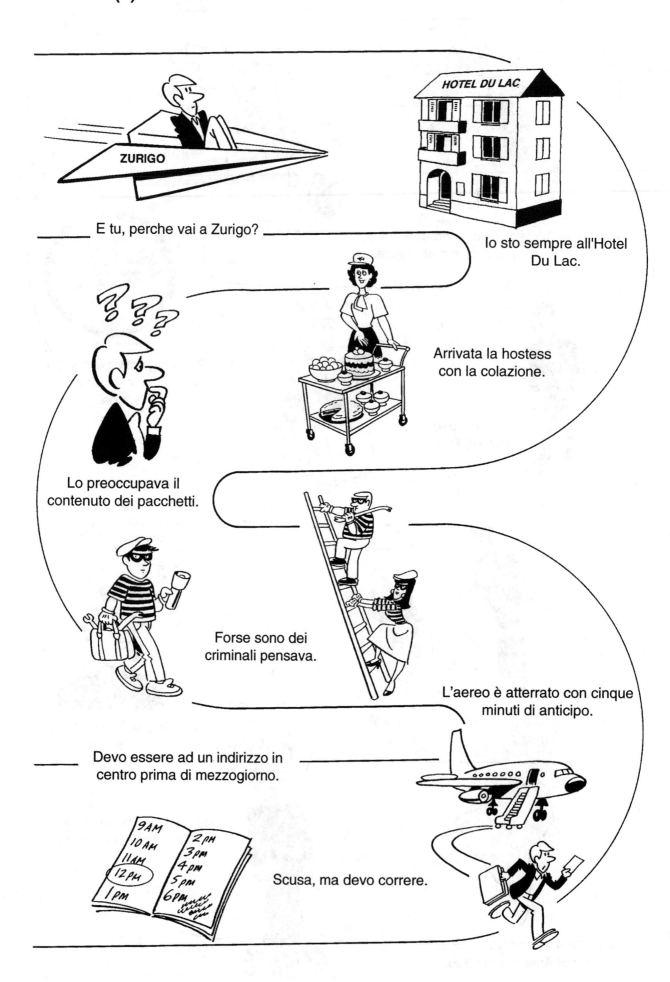

E tu, perche vai a Zurigo?

Io sto sempre all'Hotel Du Lac.

Arrivata la hostess con la colazione.

Lo preoccupava il contenuto dei pacchetti.

Forse sono dei criminali pensava.

L'aereo è atterrato con cinque minuti di anticipo.

Devo essere ad un indirizzo in centro prima di mezzogiorno.

Scusa, ma devo correre.

ATTO 11 (iii)

Peter camminava in fretta verso la dogana.

Dopo tutto, non aveva niente da dichiarare.

Un momento, signore, che cos'ha nella valigetta

Mi mostri i pacchetti, per favore.

Si sentiva la fronte bagnata di sudore, e la bocca secca.

L'uomo lo guardava fisso.

Gli tremavano le mani.

Li apra, per piacere.

ATTO 11 (iv)

Ora sono finito, pensava.

Peter ha aperto prima il pacchetto più grande,

poi quello più piccolo,

I pacchetti contenevano solo documenti.

Ma no, il signor Bruni aveva ragione.

Ora Peter si sentiva più che mai confuso.

Peter ha guardato l'orologio.

Erano le 11.30.

Il suo appuntamento col signor Braun era per le 12 in punto.

Functional Dialogues

1. Peter meets Enrico on the flight to Zurich.

Peter incontra Enrico sul volo per Zurigo.

Enrico:	What a surprise! Are you going to Zurich as well?	**Che sorpresa! Vai a Zurigo anche tu?**
Peter:	Enrico! I'm speechless!	**Enrico! Sono senza parole!**
Enrico:	There's a free seat next to me. Why don't you sit here?	**C'è un posto libero vicino a me. Perchè non ti siedi qui?**
Peter:	All right.	**Va bene.**
Enrico:	Excuse me, Miss. Would you bring us a bottle of champagne?	**Scusi, signorina, ci porta una bottiglia di champagne?**
Peter:	Not for me thanks. It's too early. But I'd like a cup of coffee. Mmm, the coffee's good. How come you're going to Zurich?	**Non per me, grazie. È troppo presto. Però vorrei una tazza di caffè. Mmm, il caffè è buono. Come mai vai a Zurigo?**
Enrico:	I've got an appointment with a very important client. I often do this journey. And why are you going to Zurich?	**Ho un appuntamento con un cliente molto importante. Faccio spesso questo viaggio. E tu, perchè vai a Zurigo?**
Peter:	I have to deliver two packages...	**Devo consegnare due pacchetti...**
Enrico:	Where are you staying in Zurich? I always stay at the Hotel du Lac.	**Dove stai a Zurigo? Io sto sempre all'Hotel du Lac.**
Peter:	I'm not staying in Zurich tonight. I'm going straight back to Rome.	**Non rimango a Zurigo questa notte. Torno subito a Roma.**

2. Peter makes his excuses.

Peter si scusa.

Enrico:	We're early. Five minutes early.	**Siamo arrivati in anticipo: con cinque minuti di anticipo.**
Peter:	Really, what time is it?	**Ah, si, che ore sono?**
Enrico:	It's 11.00.	**Sono le undici.**
Peter:	Excuse me, but I must run.	**Scusa, ma devo correre.**
Enrico:	What a pity! Why?	**Che peccato! Perchè?**
Peter:	Because I have to be at an address in the centre...	**Perchè devo essere ad un indirizzo in centro...**
Enrico:	I'm going into the centre too...	**Anch'io vado in centro...**
Peter:	Yes, but I must arrive before mid-day.	**Sì, ma devo arrivare prima di mezzogiorno.**
Enrico:	We can go to the centre together.	**Possiamo andare in centro insieme.**
Peter:	Thanks, but I'm sorry, I don't want to arrive late. Goodbye.	**Grazie, ma mi dispiace, non voglio arrivare in ritardo. Arrivederci.**

3. At the customs. **Alla dogana.**

Customs Officer **Doganiere = D:**

D:	Just a moment, sir.	**Un momento, signore.**
Peter:	I've got nothing to declare.	**Non ho niente da dichiarare.**
D:	What have you got in your briefcase?	**Che cos'ha nella valigetta?**
Peter:	Just two packages with papers inside.	**Solo due pacchetti con dentro documenti.**
D:	Show me your passport.	**Mi mostri il passaporto.**
Peter:	Yes, here it is.	**Sì, eccolo.**
D:	Where are you staying in Zurich?	**Dove sta a Zurigo?**
Peter:	I'm not staying in Zurich, I have to...	**Non rimango a Zurigo, devo...**
D:	Show me the packages please.	**Mi mostri i pacchetti, per favore.**
Peter:	Yes, here they are.	**Sì, eccoli.**
D:	Open them please.	**Li apra per piacere.**
Peter:	Yes, of course.	**Sì, certo.**
D:	Nothing. Thank you. You can go.	**Niente. Grazie. Può andare.**

4. In the taxi. **Nel taxi.**

Taxi driver **Tassista = T:**

T:	Good morning, Sir.	**Buongiorno, signore.**
Peter:	Good morning. The centre, please. Number 12 Bernestrasse.	**Buongiorno. Per il centro, per favore. Bernestrasse numero 12.**
T:	Yes sir.	**Sì, signore.**
Peter:	I've got an appointment at 1200. Will we arrive in time?	**Ho un appuntamento per le 12.00. Arriviamo in tempo?**
T:	Yes, of course, Sir, don't worry. We'll arrive early.	**Sì certo, signore, non si preoccupi. Arriveremo anche in anticipo.**
Peter:	Terrific. Thanks.	**Benissimo. Grazie.**

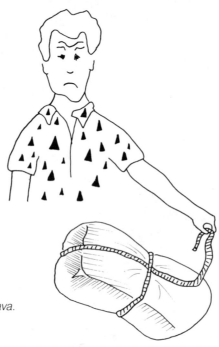

Ora sono finito, pensava.

Personalised Dialogues

1. On your flight to London you meet **Giancarlo**, a rather boring ex–colleague. He's pleased to see you, but you're rather more reticent.

Giancarlo:	**Che sorpresa! Vai a Londra anche tu?**
Lei:	(Giancarlo! You're speechless.)
Giancarlo:	**C'è un posto libero vicino a me. Perchè non ti siedi qui?**
Lei:	(All right.)
Giancarlo:	**Scusi, signora, ci porta una bottiglia di champagne?**
Lei:	(Not for you thanks, it's too early. But you'd like a cup of coffee.)
Giancarlo:	**Allora, una tazza di caffè e una bottiglia di champagne.**
Lei:	(How come he's going to London?)
Giancarlo:	**Ho un appuntamento con un cliente molto importante. E tu?**
Lei:	(You've also got an appointment with an important client. You often make this journey.)
Giancarlo:	**Dove stai a Londra? Io sto sempre al Dorchester.**
Lei:	(You don't know yet.)
Giancarlo:	**Possiamo cenare insieme. Ti invito io.**
Lei:	(You're sorry, but you have to visit your grandmother **la nonna.**)

2. Your plane arrives early and **Giancarlo** insists on your sharing a taxi. You make your excuses.

Giancarlo:	**Siamo arrivati con cinque minuti di anticipo.**
Lei:	(Really, what time is it?)
Giancarlo:	**Sono le undici e mezza.**
Lei:	(Excuse me but I must run.)
Giancarlo:	**Che peccato. Perchè?**
Lei:	(Because you have to be at an address in the centre.)
Giancarlo:	**Anch'io vado in centro.**
Lei:	(Yes, but you must arrive by mid-day.)
Giancarlo:	**Possiamo andare in centro insieme.**
Lei:	(Thanks, but you're sorry. You don't want to arrive late. Goodbye.)
Giancarlo:	**Ma...**

Scusa, ma devo correre.

3. You don't know what it is, but for some reason you always get picked on at customs.

(**Doganiere**/Customs Officer)

Doganiere:	**Un momento, signora.**
Lei:	(But you've nothing to declare.)
Doganiere:	**Che cos'ha nella valigetta?**
Lei:	(Only papers.)
Doganiere:	**Mi mostri il passaporto.**
Lei:	(Yes, here it is.)
Doganiere:	**Dove sta a Londra?**
Lei:	(You're not staying in London, you have to return to Rome straightaway.)
Doganiere:	**Mi mostri i documenti, per favore.**
Lei:	(Yes, here they are.)
Doganiere:	**Non ha niente da dichiarare?**
Lei:	(No, you already said...)
Doganiere:	**E queste tre bottiglie di whisky?**
Lei:	(They're for him. A little present...)

4. You always get a chatty taxi-driver when you least feel like talking – your London cabbie comes from Palermo.

(**Tassista**/Taxi-driver)

Lei:	(Sloane Avenue, Chelsea, please.)
Tassista:	**Ah, la signora è italiana?**
Lei:	(Yes, you're Italian.)
Tassista:	**Anch'io sono italiano.**
Lei:	(Oh yes, where does he come from?)
Tassista:	**Vengo da Palermo. Sono siciliano.**
Lei:	(How interesting.)
Tassista:	**E lei da dove viene?**
Lei:	(You have come from Rome and you're very tired.)
Tassista:	**Che bella giornata!**
Lei:	(Yes, you like rain. You have an appointment at 12.00. Will you arrive in time?)
Tassista:	**Sì, certo, signora, arriveremo anche in anticipo.**
Lei:	(Very good, thanks. Sorry, but you don't feel well.)

Mi mostri il passaporto.

Grammar

1. VERBS – PAST TENSES

The following verbs use **essere** in the perfect:

durare	**è durato**	**il viaggio è durato 45 minuti**
passare	**è passato**	**è passato al controllo passaporti**
diventare	**è diventato**	**sapeva di essere diventato pallido**
atterrare	**è atterrato**	**l'aereo è atterrato...**

Note the following past participle:

rispondere	**risposto**	**Peter non ha risposto**

Reflexives also go with **essere**:

girarsi	**si è girato**	**Peter si è girato sorpreso**

2. FEELINGS

To say how you feel, use **sentirsi**:

Present:
> **mi sento bene**
> **ti senti bene**
> **si sente bene,** etc.

Imperfect:
> **mi sentivo male**
> **ti sentivi male**
> **si sentiva male**

Story examples:
> **Peter si sentiva a disagio**
> **Peter si sentiva troppo confuso**

Other expressions of feelings use impersonal forms where English uses possessive forms:

aveva le mani bagnate di sudore	his hands were...
il cuore gli batteva forte	his heart was beating...
gli tremavano le mani	his hands were...

3. STARE

Uses of the verb **stare** include:

1. Staying: **Dove stai a Zurigo?**
    Lo sto sempre all'Hotel du Lac.

2. To be on the point of/be about to (+ **per...**):

    Sto per uscire.   I'm about to go out.
    Stava per uscire.   He was about to go out.

Story example: **Enrico stava per dire qualcosa**

4. EXPRESSIONS OF TIME

in anticipo	early
in ritardo	late
in punto	exactly (on time)
di tanto in tanto	from time to time

5. IDIOMS

come mai?	how come?
avere ragione (**aveva ragione** – he was right)	to be right
qualcosa non va (**qualcosa non andava** – something was up)	something's up

6. FUTURES

essere	**sarò**	**quando sarò**	(when I'm...)
avere	**avrò**	**quando avrò**	(when I've...)

Story examples: **quando avrò consegnato questi pacchetti**

    quando sarò di ritorno a Roma...

7. THE BIG ONE/THE SMALL ONE

il pacchetto grande	**quello grande**	**quello più grande**
il pacchetto piccolo	**quello piccolo**	**quello più piccolo**

Games

1. OPPOSITES

Though you may not know some of these words their opposite is to be found in the text.

1. 1	**Prima di...**
1. 2	**in ritardo**
1. 3	**femminile**
1. 4	**occupato**
1. 5	**tutto**
1. 6	**lontano**
1. 7	**cattivo**
1. 8	**debole**
1. 9	**raramente**
1.10	**mai**

2. FEELINGS

The following sentences express feelings. Complete the gap:

2. 1   **Peter _ _   _ _ _ _ _ _ _ a disagio.**

2. 2   **_ _   _ _ _ _ _ _ _ _ la fronte bagnata di sudore.**

2. 3   **_ _ _   _ _ _ _ _ _ _ _ _ le mani.**

2. 4   **Il cuore _ _ _   _ _ _ _ _ _ _ forte.**

2. 5   **_ _   _ _ _ _ _ _ _ _ troppo confuso.**

2. 6   **Peter _ _   _ _ _ _ _ _ _ più che mai confuso.**

3. CONVERSATION STOPPERS

People are always trying to pin you down on the phone. Avoid them by saying you're just about to ... Use **Scusi, sto per** or **stavo per** as appropriate:

3.`1	... go out.
3. 2	... go shopping.
3. 3	... phone your grandmother.
3. 4	... watch television.
3. 5	... run to the airport.
3. 6	... have a bath.
3. 7	... call a taxi to go to the station.
3. 8	... have dinner.
3. 9	... go to bed.
3.10	... finish your book.

4. TIMELESS

Unscramble the following expressions of time:

4. 1   **NUTOPIN**

4. 2   **CIPTIANONI**

4. 3   **NTOTAIDTONTANI**

4. 4   **DRATORINI**

4. 5   **PESSOS**

4. 6   **VVPROMIDSIO**

5. TOPLESS

The first words of the following lines from the story are missing. Find them and re-arrange them to discover a traveller's habit.

5. 1   _ _ _ _ _ _ _ _ _ **per l'aeroporto di Fiumicino.**

5. 2   _ _ _ _ _ _ _ **il volo.**

5. 3   _ _ _ _ _ _ _ **era buono e molto forte.**

5. 4   _ _ _ _ _ _ **spesso questo viaggio.**

5. 5   _ _ _ _ _ _ _ _ **due o tre volte al mese.**

What if...? **Se invece...**

A chance meeting on the plane (the ocean liner, the train, in space) could be boring, interesting, useful, lucrative, disastrous. It could be a cause for celebration, or commiseration. Perhaps it wasn't a chance meeting at all, but fate, or the result of a careful plan.

When the Customs Officer opens your case, and there are no documents inside, but... who knows what will happen next, and who is waiting for you at your final destination?

A REMINDER

Are you still doing the 'extra exercises' we described on page xxvii :

1. Making up post cards to revise with.

2. Acting out the Dialogues expressively.

3. Putting up post-it notes around the house or office or even in the car!

4. Representing at least 10 words visually.

5. Selecting the 10 most useful words per Act. (That gets you reviewing them all!)

6. Underlining, highlighting and <u>writing down</u> key words and sentences.

7. Describing the scenes out loud in your new language.

8. Making a Word Web for each Act.

Scene 1	**Scena 1**
The mystery is solved.	**Il mistero è risolto.**
It was mid-day exactly	**Era esattamente mezzogiorno**
when Peter got out of the taxi	**quando Peter è sceso dal taxi**
at 12 Bernestrasse.	**in Bernestrasse numero 12.**
The sign on the door said:	**La targa sulla porta diceva:**
Karl Braun, lawyer, third floor.	**Avvocato Karl Braun, terzo piano.**
The lift was out of order,	**L'ascensore non funzionava,**
so Peter climbed the stairs.	**così Peter è salito a piedi.**
A man of about fifty	**Un uomo sui cinquant'anni**
opened the door.	**gli ha aperto la porta.**

Lawyer:	Good morning.	**Buongiorno,**
	You must be Mr. West.	**lei deve essere il signor West.**
Peter:	Yes, I am.	**Sì, sono Peter West.**
	I've brought you	**Le ho portato**
	these two packages	**questi due pacchetti**
	from Signor Bruni.	**da parte del signor Bruni.**

Peter opened the briefcase	**Peter ha aperto la valigetta**
and put the two packages	**e ha messo i due pacchetti**
on the desk.	**sulla scrivania.**

Peter:	I'm sorry ..., they were opened	**Scusi ... sono stati aperti ...**
	at the customs ...	**alla dogana ...**

The lawyer didn't say a thing.	**L'avvocato non ha detto niente.**
He studied the documents in silence	**Ha studiato i documenti in silenzio**
for a few minutes.	**per alcuni minuti.**
Then he looked carefully at Peter.	**Poi ha guardato Peter attentamente.**

Lawyer:	Will you give me your passport,	**Mi dà il suo passaporto,**
	please?	**per favore?**

Peter hadn't expected this	**Questo Peter non se l'era aspettato**
but, without saying anything,	**ma, senza dire niente,**
he put his passport on the desk.	**ha messo il passaporto sulla scrivania.**
The lawyer continued	**L'avvocato ha continuato**
to study the documents,	**a studiare i documenti**
then Peter's passport,	**poi il passaporto di Peter,**
without a word.	**senza parlare.**
At last he lifted his head	**Finalmente ha alzato la testa**
and looked at him seriously.	**e lo la guardato serio.**

Era esattamente mezzogiorno.
È sceso dal taxi in.

BERNESTRASSE 12

Lawyer:	Congratulations, Mr. West!	**Congratulazioni, signor West!**
	I can now tell you	**Ora le posso dire**
	that you are a major shareholder	**che lei è un importante azionista**
	in the import-export company	**della ditta di importazioni ed esportazioni**
	Bruni and Sons.	**Bruni e Figli.**
	About three months ago	**Circa tre mesi fa**
	Mr. Ellrose	**il signor Ellrose**
	died in a plane crash	**è morto in un incidente aereo**
	in South America.	**nell'America del Sud.**
	I realise	**Mi rendo conto**
	you didn't know him,	**che lei non lo conosceva,**
	but, in fact,	**ma in realtà**
	he was a relative of yours.	**era infatti un suo parente.**
	Now you have inherited	**Ora lei ha ereditato**
	his estate.	**il suo patrimonio.**
	As a result you have become	**Di conseguenza, lei è diventato**
	the owner of 20% of the company	**proprietario del 20% della ditta**
	of Bruni and Sons ...	**Bruni e Figli."**

Peter looked at him open-mouthed.   **Peter lo guardava a bocca aperta.**

Peter:	It's not possible ...	**Non è possibile ...**
Lawyer:	That's not all, Mr. West.	**Questo non è tutto, signor West.**
	You have also inherited	**Lei ha ereditato anche**
	a little castle	**un piccolo castello**
	in the hills near Rome.	**sulle colline romane.**
Peter:	I can't believe it ...	**Non posso crederci ...**
	Are you sure about all this?	**È sicuro di tutto questo?**
Lawyer:	Quite sure. There are no doubts.	**Sicurissimo, non ci sono dubbi.**

	Once again	**Ancora una volta**
	Peter felt his hands and forehead	**Peter si sentiva le mani e la fronte**
	bathed in sweat.	**bagnate di sudore.**
	He had a strange taste	**Aveva uno strano sapore**
	in his mouth.	**in bocca.**

Peter:	May I have a glass of water?	**Posso avere un bicchiere d'acqua?**

	The lawyer opened	**L'avvocato ha aperto**
	a small fridge	**un piccolo frigorifero**
	and took out a bottle of champagne	**e ha preso una bottiglia di spumante**
	and two glasses.	**e due bicchieri.**
	He uncorked the bottle	**Ha tolto il tappo**
	and poured the champagne	**e ha versato lo spumante**
	into the glasses.	**nei bicchieri.**

Lawyer:	To your health, Mr. West,	**Alla sua salute, signor West,**
	and to your good fortune!	**e alla sua fortuna!**

	The champagne was refreshing.	**Lo spumante era rinfrescante:**
	After two glasses	**dopo due bicchieri**
	Peter felt better.	**Peter si sentiva meglio.**

	Scene 2	**Scena 2**
Peter:	But why all the mystery? Why didn't Bella and her uncle tell me all this?	**Ma perchè tanto mistero? Perchè non mi hanno detto tutto questo Bella e suo zio?**
Lawyer:	You mustn't forget that Bruni and Sons is a family firm. They wanted to see what sort of person you were, and whether you could work with them. Now they know that they will be very happy to work with you.	**Non deve dimenticare che la ditta Bruni e Figli è una ditta familiare. Volevano sapere che tipo di persona lei fosse, e se poteva lavorare con loro. Ora sanno che saranno molto felici di lavorare con lei.**

Peter stood up.
His head was spinning.
Perhaps it was the champagne,
or perhaps it was the thought
of working with Bella ...

**Peter si è alzato.
Gli girava la testa.
Forse era lo spumante,
o forse era il pensiero
di lavorare con Bella ...**

The voice of the lawyer
inviting him to sit down
in a large black leather armchair
seemed very distant.
The sound of the traffic
also seemed a long way away.

**La voce dell'avvocato
che lo invitava a sedere
in una grande poltrona di pelle nera,
sembrava molto lontana.
Anche i rumori del traffico
sembravano lontani.**

The whole room
was spinning around him:
the huge windows,
the long rows of books
on the high bookshelves,
the red velvet curtains ...

**Tutta la stanza
gli girava attorno:
le grandi finestre,
le lunghe file di libri
sugli scaffali alti,
le tende di velluto rosso ...**

Everything was spinning around him.
He closed his eyes and smiled.
The world was spinning around him,
and he was very, very happy.

**Tutto gli girava attorno.
Ha chiuso gli occhi e ha sorriso.
Il mondo girava attorno a lui,
e lui si sentiva felicissimo.**

Mr. Braun is no longer in the room.
Someone places a package
in his hands.
Two green eyes stare at him,
and a woman's voice whispers:
''This package is for signor Bruni ...''

**Il signor Braun non è più nella stanza.
Qualcuno gli mette un pacchetto
fra le mani.
Due occhi verdi lo guardano,
e una voce di donna gli sussurra;
"Questo pacchetto è per il signor Bruni..."**

ATTO 12 (i)

Era esattamente mezzogiorno quando Peter è sceso dal taxi

12 BERNESTRASSE

in Bernestrasse numero 12.

La targa sulla porta diceva:

AVVOCATO
KARL BRAUN
TERZO PIANO.

L'ascensore non funzionava,

non funzionava

così Peter è salito a piedi.

Buongiorno, lei deve èssere il signor West.

Un uomo sui cinquant'anni gli ha aperto la porta.

Peter ha aperto la valigetta e ha messo i due pacchetti sulla scrivania.

ATTO 12 (ii)

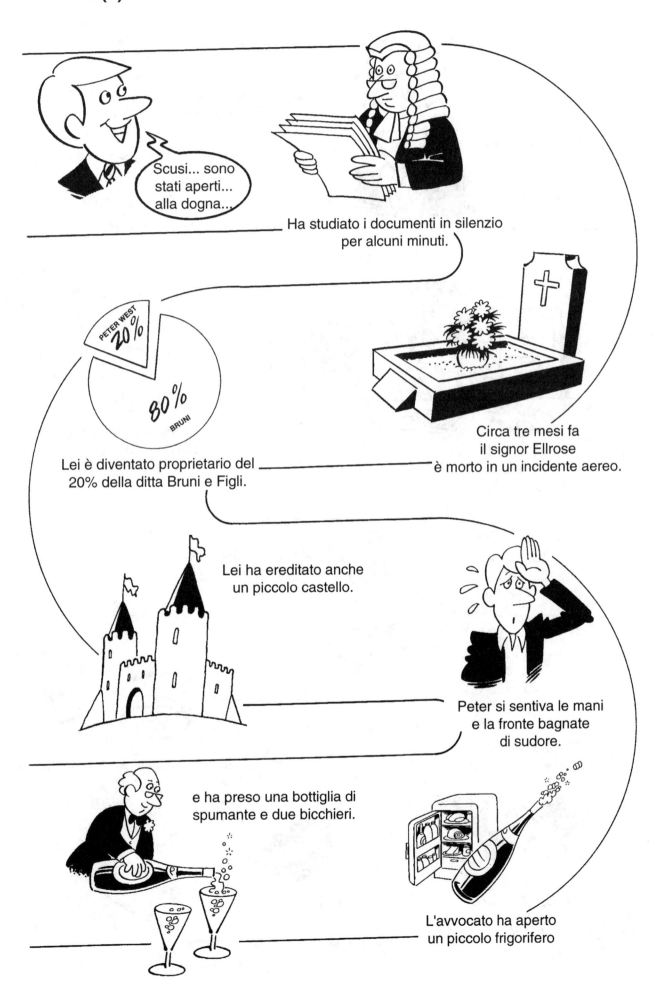

Scusi... sono stati aperti... alla dogna...

Ha studiato i documenti in silenzio per alcuni minuti.

Circa tre mesi fa il signor Ellrose è morto in un incidente aereo.

Lei è diventato proprietario del 20% della ditta Bruni e Figli.

Lei ha ereditato anche un piccolo castello.

Peter si sentiva le mani e la fronte bagnate di sudore.

e ha preso una bottiglia di spumante e due bicchieri.

L'avvocato ha aperto un piccolo frigorifero

Functional Dialogues

1.

Peter meets Lawyer Braun.

Peter incontra l'avvocato Braun.

Braun: Good morning. You must be Mr West.	**Buongiorno. Lei deve essere il signor West.**
Peter: Yes, I am Peter West.	**Sì, sono Peter West.**
Braun: Welcome to Zurich!	**Benvenuto a Zurigo!**
Peter: Thank you. I've brought you these two packages from signor Bruni.	**Grazie. Le ho portato questi due pacchetti da parte del signor Bruni.**
Braun: Ah, thank you, thank you.	**Ah, grazie, grazie.**
Peter: I'm sorry, they were opened at the customs.	**Scusi, sono stati aperti alla dogana.**
Braun: Mmm, will you give me your passport please.	**Mmm, mi dà il suo passaporte per favore.**
Peter: If you wish, but...	**Se vuole, ma...**
Braun: Congratulations Mr West. Unfortunately, about three months ago Mr Ellrose died in a plane crash in South America. He was a relative of yours. Now you have inherited his estate. You have become the owner of 20% of the company of Bruni & Sons.	**Congratulazioni, signor West. Purtroppo, circa tre mesi fa il signor Ellrose è morto in un incidente aereo nell'America del Sud. Era un suo parente. Ora lei ha ereditato il suo patrimonio. È diventato proprietario del 20% della ditta Bruni e Figli.**
Peter: It's not possible...	**Non è possibile...**

2.

Peter can't believe it.

Peter non può crederci.

Peter: It's not possible!	**Non è possibile!**
Braun: That's not all — you have also inherited a little castle in the hills near Rome.	**Questo non è tutto — lei ha anche ereditato un piccolo castello sulle colline romane.**
Peter: I can't believe it. Are you sure about all this?	**Non posso crederci. È sicuro di tutto questo?**
Braun: Quite sure. There are no doubts.	**Sicurissimo. Non ci sono dubbi.**
Peter: I feel strange. Can I have a glass of water?	**Mi sento strano. Posso avere un bicchiere d'acqua?**
Braun: Water no — *spumante!* To your health, Mr West, and your fortune.	**Acqua no — spumante! Alla sua salute, signor West, e alla sua fortuna.**
Peter: Thank you. I feel better now.	**Grazie. Ora mi sento meglio.**

Signor Ellrose è morto

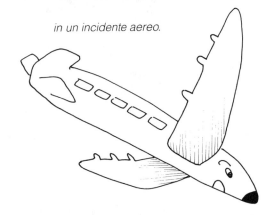

in un incidente aereo.

3.   Peter dreams about Bella.   **Peter sogna Bella.**

Peter:	But why so much mystery?	**Ma perchè tanto mistero?**
Bella:	You musn't forget that	**Non devi dimenticare che la ditta**
	Bruni & Sons is a family firm.	**Bruni e Figli è una ditta familiare.**
	We wanted to see	**Volevamo vedere**
	what sort of person you were.	**che tipo di persona tu fossi.**
Peter:	And now you know...	**E ora sapete...**
Bella:	Yes, we know.	**Sì, sappiamo.**
	We know we can work with you.	**Sappiamo di poter lavorare con te.**
Peter:	When do we start work?	**Quando cominciamo il lavoro?**
Bella:	Straight away.	**Subito.**
	We're leaving for Brazil this evening.	**Partiamo per il Brasile questa sera.**
Peter:	Brazil?	**Per il Brasile?**
Bella:	Yes, to Rio,	**Sì, per Rio,**
	because there is a carnival,	**perchè c'è il carnevale,**
	and then we're going	**e poi andiamo**
	to the Amazon region,	**nella zona amazzonica**
	where we have	**dove abbiamo**
	a very important client.	**un cliente molto importante.**
Peter:	Are you sure?	**Sei sicura?**
Bella:	Quite sure. I've already booked	**Sicurissima. Ho già prenotato**
	the flight and the hotel.	**il volo e l'albergo.**
Peter:	Is Enrico coming too?	**Viene anche Enrico?**
Bella:	No.	**No.**
Peter:	And Uncle Mario?	**E lo zio Mario?**
Bella:	No, we'll be alone.	**No, saremo soli.**
Bella:	Bella...	**Bella...**
Braun:	Mr West.... Mr West	**Signor West .... Signor West**
Peter:	Yes?	**Sì?**
Braun:	What happened?	**Cos'è successo?**
Peter:	I don't know... a dream.	**Non lo so... un sogno.**
Braun:	Do you feel unwell?	**Si sente male?**
Peter:	No, I feel very happy.	**No, mi sento felicissimo.**

Personalised Dialogues

1. Your lawyer has summoned you to an urgent meeting. He has a pleasant surprise for you.

(**Avvocato**/Lawyer)

Avvocato:	**Buongiorno, signora.**
Lei:	(Say hello, so what happened?)
Avvocato:	**Congratulazioni, signora – lei ha ereditato una fortuna.**
Lei:	(It's not possible.)
Avvocato:	**Un suo parente è morto circa due mesi fa nell'America del Sud. Era molto ricco. Lei ha ereditato il suo patrimonio.**
Lei:	(You can't believe it – how much?)
Avvocato:	**Dieci miliardi.**
Lei:	(Ten billion.)
Avvocato:	**Sì, e questo non è tutto. Ha ereditato anche un piccolo castello sulle colline romane.**
Lei:	(Is he sure about all this?)
Avvocato:	**Sicurissimo. Non ci sono dubbi.**
Lei:	(You feel strange. Can you have a glass of water?)
Avvocato:	**Acqua no – spumante! Alla sua salute, signora Ellrose, alla sua fortuna!**
Lei:	(Signora Ellrose? But you're not Mrs. Ellrose, you're Mrs. Rose.)
Avvocato:	**Lei non è la signora Ellrose? Allora c'è stato un errore!**

Ha tolto il tappo e ha versato lo spumante nei bicchieri.

Grammar

1. VERBS – PAST TENSES

Note the following past tenses with **essere**:

scendere	**è sceso**	**è sceso dal taxi**
salire	**è salito**	**è salito a piedi**

and with **avere:**

sorridere   **ha sorriso**
finalmente ha alzato la testa e ha sorriso.

togliere   **ha tolto**   **ha tolto il tappo**

2. DOUBLE NEGATIVES

In Italian negatives are usually double:

non ha detto niente
senza dire niente

3. GLI

Note the different uses of **gli**:

3.1   As article: **ha chiuso gli occhi.**

3.2   As indirect pronoun: **qualcuno gli mette un pacchetto fra le mani.**
un uomo gli ha aperto la porta.
una voce di donna gli sussurra.

3.3   As part of indirect impersonal statements:

tutto gli girava attorno.

4. UN SUO PARENTE

suo parente	your relative
un suo parente	a relative of yours
mio parente	my relative
un mio parente	a relative of mine
il mio amico	my friend
un mio amico	a friend of mine

Games

1. NO DOUBT ABOUT IT

A psychotherapist has helped you find a new brand of enthusiasm; she's just testing. Use **-issimo**!

1. 1   **È sicuro?**
1. 2   **È felice?**
1. 3   **È buono lo spumante?**
1. 4   **È bello il bambino?**
1. 5   **È nuovo il vestito?**
1. 6   **È cara la macchina?**
1. 7   **Il suo nuovo amante è giovane?**
1. 8   **È grande?**

2. TRUE OR FALSE

2. 1   **L'avvocato Karl Braun abita al terzo piano.**
2. 2   **L'ascensore funzionava.**
2. 3   **Peter ha messo i due pacchetti nella cassaforte.**
2. 4   **Il signor Ellrose è morto quattro mesi fa.**
2. 5   **Peter ha ereditato un grande castello.**
2. 6   **Le tende nella stanza dell'avvocato Braun erano di velluto rosso.**

3. OUT OF TIME

Fill in the gaps:

3. 1   **Era esattamente _ _ _ _ _ _ _ _ _ _ _ _ _ quando Peter è sceso dal taxi.**

3. 2   **Un uomo sui _ _ _ _ _ _ _ _ _ _ _ _ _ _ gli ha aperto la porta.**

3. 3   **Ha studiato i documenti in silenzio**

     _ _ _ _ _ _ _ _ _ _ _ _ _ _ _ _ _ _.

3. 4   **Circa _ _ _ _ _ _ _ _ _ _ _ il signor Ellrose è morto.**

3. 5   **Dopo _ _ _ _ _ _ _ _ _ _ _ _ _ _ Peter si sentiva meglio.**

225

4. CROSSWORD – **PAROLE INCROCIATE**

You will find most of the clues, and the answers, contained in the text of Act 12.

ACROSS

1. **Avvocato Karl Braun abita in Bernestrasse.**
2. **... esattamente mezzogiorno.**
4. **... voce di donna.**
5. You'll find one of these on the door.
6. Where the story takes place.
7. Peter had a strange one of these in his mouth.
8. Used to form the past, inverted.
9. Opposite of 'si'.
10. Nine inverted.
11. Then...
12. Is or and.

DOWN

1. **L'avvocato non ha detto...**
2. **... nonna è simpaticissima.**
3. **... lei ha ereditato il suo patrimonio.**
4. **Aveva ... strano sapore in bocca.**
5. **... uno strano sapore in bocca.**
6. Why? ...Because... (Anagram)
7. To be found in libraries and lawyers' offices.
8. More relative than parent.
9. What spins around, especially after too much *spumante*.
10. Half a double negative.
11. Inverted article.

What if...? **Se invece...**

Bring your alternative story to its conclusion in the most inventive way to make a dream come true...
buona fortuna!

Act 1

Answer Pages

PERSONALISED DIALOGUES

1. **Lei:** **Buona sera, signora. È questa la casa del Signor Visentini?**
    Cerco il Signor Visentini.
    Sono il Signor.../La Signora...
    Grazie.

2. **Lei:** **Mi chiamo.../Il mio nome è...**
    Vengo da ...
    Ecco il mio passaporto. Mi chiamo.../Il mio nome è... Sono...
    Sono... e ho... anni
    Grazie.

3. **Lei:** **No, è italiana.**
    No, abita a Roma.
    Si, è bella. Ha gli occhi azzurri e i capelli neri.
    Ha ventiquattro anni.

4. **Lei:** **Buongiorno, signora. Ha una camera?**
    Singola, per favore.
    Sì, mi chiamo... (Sì, il mio nome è...)
    Grazie, arrivederci.

5. **Lei:** **Buona sera. Ha una camera riservata a mio nome.**
    Mi chiamo... (Sono il Signor.../Sono la Signora.../
                Sono la Signorina...)
    È tranquilla?
    Grazie. Buonanotte.

GAMES

1. WORD CARDS

1. 1	**Peter guarda la casa**.
1. 2	**La casa è grande e bella**.
1. 3	**Una signora anziana apre la porta**.
1. 4	**Cerco il Signor Bruni**.
1. 5	**Peter entra in casa**.
1. 6	**La (donna) giovane prende il passaporto**.
1. 7	**Abito a Londra**.
1. 8	**Mi chiamo Bella Bruni (Il mio nome è B.B.)**
1. 9	**Ecco il pacchetto**.
1.10	**È un albergo piccolo ma comodo**.

Game 2.

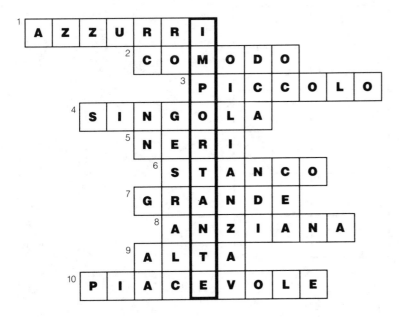

227

Game 2

Game 3

	VERO	FALSO
1	X	
2		X
3	X	
4		X
5		X
6	X	
7	X	
8		X
9	X	
10		X

Act 2

PERSONALISED DIALOGUES

1. **Lei:** **Buongiorno. (Pronto** = Hello, when answering the telephone.)
Buongiorno, Sandra.
È comodo e tranquillo.
È piccola, ma tranquilla.
Sono vecchi e belli.
Sì, è pulitissimo.
Sì, sono grandi e morbidi.
Arrivederci! (Ciao!)

2. **Lei:** **Buongiorno, che cosa c'è per colazione?**
C'è burro e marmellata?

Sì, grazie.
Vengo da Londra, sono inglese.
Sì, è bella e molto grande.

3. **Lei:** **Sono ...**
È molto interessante.
Sì, sono arrivato ieri, in aereo.
Grazie, però ho ancora molto da imparare.

4. **Lei:** **Benissimo, grazie. Il letto è molto comodo.**
A Londra fa freddo. E c'è la pioggia. (piove ...)

GAMES

1. WORD CARDS

1. 1 **Peter si sveglia, e si guarda intorno.**
1. 2 **I mobili della camera sono vecchi e belli.**
1. 3 **Peter si alza e apre la finestra.**
1. 4 **Peter apre la valigia, e prende il dentifricio e lo spazzolino da denti.**
1. 5 **Il bagno è pulitissimo.**
1. 6 **Peter si veste in fretta.**
1. 7 **Che cosa c'è per colazione?**
1. 8 **Vengo da Londra, sono inglese.**
1. 9 **Che cosa fa di professione?**
1.10 **Peter esce dall'albergo.**

2. Colours

2.1 **un tappeto rosso scuro**
2.2 **gli occhi marroni**
2.3 **i capelli biondi**
2.4 **una camicetta bianca**
2.5 **una gonna nera**

3. What's the opposite?

3.1. **nuovi e <u>brutti</u>**
3.2. **<u>chiude</u> la finestra**
3.3. **<u>chiude</u> le persiane**
3.4. **<u>spegne</u> la luce**
3.5. **sono <u>piccoli</u>**
3.6. **una <u>brutta</u> avventura**

4. Word Clusters

1. **si alza**
e
si veste

2. **pulitissimo**

3. **c'è un**
tappeto
rosso scuro

4. **sul**
pavimento

5. **ci sono**
la doccia
e
il gabinetto

6. **si lava**
i capelli

Act 3

PERSONALISED DIALOGUES

1. **Lei:** **Bene, grazie. E lei come sta?**
   Grazie.

2. **Lei:** **Mi piace moltissimo.**
   Sì, mi piace moltissimo. Amo i legumi.
   No, non mi piace. Io non mangio carne. Sono vegetariano.
   Preferisco vino bianco.
   Ottimo, ho già l'acquolina in bocca.

3. **Lei:** **Un chilo di pane fresco, per favore.**
   Mezzo chilo di tagliatelle all'uovo.
   Quanto costa quella torta?
   Va bene, ne prendo una.

   Lei: **Quanto costa il prosciutto?**
   Mi dia un etto di crudo, e un etto di cotto, per favore.
   Sì, vorrei 3 etti di formaggio locale, e una mozzarella.
   No, grazie, basta così.

   Lei: **Quanto costano le scaloppine di vitello?**
   (Sono molto care). Ne prendo quattro.

4. **Lei:** **Quanto costano i pomodori?**
   Un chilo, per favore.
   Quanto costano i funghi?
   Va bene, ne prendo tre etti.
   Sì, quanto costa un melone?
   Prendo questo.
   No, basta così, grazie.
   Quant'è in tutto?

5. **Lei:** **Vuole un aperitivo?**
   Anch'io ne prendo uno.
   Anche l'insalata (è pronta)!
   Che vino preferisce, bianco o rosso?
   C'è una bottiglia di vino bianco nel frigorifero.
   Grazie, altrettanto.

GAMES

1. I PREZZI

1. La torta di mele grande costa diecimila (10,000) lire.
2. La torta di mele piccola costa ottomila (8,000) lire.
3. Il prosciutto cotto costa tremila (3,000) lire.
4. Il melone costa ottomila (8,000) lire.
5. Le scaloppine di vitello costano diciottomila (18,000) lire.
6. Le fragole costano tremila (3,000) lire.

2. A Puzzle

1. *VANNO*
SUBITO
IN CUCINA
A *PREPARARE*
IL PRANZO

2. IN FONDO
ALLA STRADA
C'È
UN MERCATO
DI FRUTTA
E *VERDURA*

3. QUANTO *COSTA*
IL
PROSCIUTTO?

4. VANNO A *FARE*
LA SPESA

5. OGGI *FACCIAMO*
UNA BUONA
INSALATA
MISTA

6. RITORNANO
A CASA
STANCHI
E AFFAMATI

7. OTTIMO, *HO*
GIÀ
L'ACQUOLINA IN BOCCA!

8. NON *MANGIO* CARNE,
PERÒ QUALCHE VOLTA
MANGIO PESCE.

9. BELLA *CUOCE*
LA PASTA
MENTRE PETER
LAVA LA VERDURA
E *PREPARA*
L'INSALATA MISTA

10. BELLA PENSA
CHE *SONO*
MOLTO CARE
MA NE PRENDE QUATTRO
E VA A *PAGARE*
ALLA CASSA

11. BELLA *OFFRE*
A PETER UN
APERITIVO
E ANCHE LEI
NE *PRENDE* UNO

3. LET'S DO IT

3. 1 **Mangiamo!**
3. 2 **Facciamo la pasta!**
3. 3 **Pranziamo!**
3. 4 **Compriamo la frutta!**
3. 5 **Andiamo!**

4. LIKE IT OR NOT?

4. 1 **Mi piace la pasta (asciutta).**
4. 2 **Mi piacciono le ragazze.**
4. 3 **Mi piacciono i ragazzi.**
4. 4 **Mi piace la carne.**
4. 5 **Mi piace la frutta.**
4. 6 **Mi piacciono i legumi.**
4. 7 **Mi piacciono i diamanti.**
4. 8 **Mi piace il prosciutto.**
4. 9 **Mi piacciono le fragole.**
4.10 **Mi piace il vino bianco.**

5. 1 **Le piace il vino rosso?**
5. 2 **Le piace il pane?**
5. 3 **Le piacciono le fettucine?**
5. 4 **Le piace il formaggio locale?**
5. 5 **Le piacciono i funghi?**

Act 4

PERSONALISED DIALOGUES

1. **Lei:**   Devo telefonare a casa.
         Devo dire ai miei genitori che rimango a Roma ancora un paio di giorni.
         Devo andare a comprare un paio di pantaloni.
         ...e due camicie.
         Sì, ma prima devo andare in banca. Devo cambiare dei soldi.
         Arrivederci.

2. **Lei:**   Buongiorno.
         Vorrei cambiare dei soldi inglesi.
         ...in lire italiane.
         Quant'è il cambio oggi?
         Per travellers cheques.
         Vorrei cambiare 200 sterline, per favore.
         Oh no, è nell'albergo!

3. **Lei:**   Buona sera. Può mostrarmi qualche camicia sportiva, per piacere?
         Porto una taglia media, 40 o 42.
         Mi piace questo modello. Ha altri colori?
         Quanto viene?
         Va bene, prendo la camicia gialla.
         No, no, basta così. Non ho molti soldi.

4. **Lei:**   Non mi piacciono.
         Non mi piacciono quelli a righe.
         Non mi piacciono. Ha altri colori?
         Vorrei provare i neri.
         Va bene, li prendo. Quant'è in tutto?
         Ah, ma prima devo andare in banca!

GAMES

1. NUMBERS

1.	**Uno**	6.	**Sei**
2.	**Due**	7.	**Sette**
3.	**Tre**	8.	**Otto**
4.	**Quattro**	9.	**Nove**
5.	**Cinque**	10.	**Dieci**

2. COLOURS

Grigio   bianco   rosso   rosa   giallo   azzurro

3. OPERATOR

3. 1   **zero zero quattro quattro uno sette tre quattro otto zero zero uno**
3. 2   **nove nove quattro cinque sette**
3. 3   **sette cinque sei sei due sei**
3. 4   **due tre quattro otto zero**
3. 5   **sei nove due cinque uno**

4. IF THE PRICE IS RIGHT

4. 1   **Cinquantamila (50,000), diecimila (10,000)**
4. 2   **Duemila quattro cento (2,400) duemila trecento cinquanta (2,350)**
4. 3   **Quattrocento settantamila (470,000)**
4. 4   **Quaranta (40) quaranta due (42)**
4. 5   **Sessantaduemila (62,000)**
4. 6   **Centoduemila (102,000)**

5. INVENTORY

abito da uomo	**pantaloni**	**camicie**	**cravatte**
calzini	**slip**	**pullover**	**giacche** etc.

Act 5

Personalised Dialogies

1. **Lei:** È molto divertente qui. Mi piace guardare la gente.
   Io prendo un tè.
   Al limone, per piacere.

   Later: Non è possibile!
   Va bene, prendo una pasta al liquore.
   Mmm, è squisita!

2. **Lei:** Che cosa facciamo questa sera?
   Andiamo al cinema, o a teatro? Preferisce andare a ballare?
   Preferisce rimanere in casa a guardare la televisione?
   Allora, andiamo fuori a cena.
   Ottimo!

3. **Lei:** Ho mal di testa. Vorrei qualche pastiglia.
   Non sto molto male. Ma preferisco prendere qualcosa subito.
   Va bene, grazie.

4. **Lei:** Scusi, può indicarmi la strada per via Condotti?
   Va bene, grazie.

   Scusi, può indicarmi la strada per l'Hotel Ritz, (in) via Condotti?
   Fino al semaforo...
   ...la prima via a sinistra...
   Grazie. È lontana? (lontano?)

GAMES

2. SCRIPT EDITOR

2. 1	**...ha pagato...**
2. 2	**...ha chiamato...**
2. 3	**...conosceva...**
2. 4	**...ha messo...**
2. 5	**Hanno guardato...**
2. 6	**...c'era...**
2. 7	**...ha sorriso...**
2. 8	**...è tornato...**
2. 9	**...cantava...**
2.10	**...ha assaggiato...**

4. SIGN LANGUAGE

4. 1	**sul tavolo**
4. 2	**verso di lui**
4. 3	**fino al semaforo**
4. 4	**attorno a lui**
4. 5	**di fianco al caffè**
4. 6	**davanti al caffè**
4. 7	**è lontano?**
4. 8	**è vicino?**

3. AH! YES I REMEMBER IT WELL

3. 1	**c'era**
3. 2	**c'erano**
3. 3	**c'era**
3. 4	**c'era**
3. 5	**c'era**
3. 6	**c'erano**

6. MYSTERY

6. 1	**Perchè un tempo ci si incontravano artisti, scrittori e poeti.**
6. 2	**Perchè il Caffè degli Artisti è famoso.**
6. 3	**Perchè c'era molta gente.**
6. 4	**Perchè ha visto l'espressione sorpresa sul viso di Peter.**
6. 5	**Perchè non c'era niente d'interessante sul giornale. (sul l'elenco degli spettacoli.)**
6. 6	**Perchè il servizio era (è) già incluso.**
6. 7	**Perchè il sole cominciava a tramontare.**
6. 8	**Perchè aveva mal di testa.**

Act 6

PERSONALISED DIALOGUES

1. **Lei:**   **Ciao. Sono le nove in punto.**
    Si, è abbastanza lontano.
    Si, chiama "La Dolce Vita".
    Ho prenotato un tavolo per le nove e mezza.
    Andiamo!

Later: **E che atmosfera romantica! Ti piace mangiare fuori?**

2. **Lei:**   **Buonasera. Che cosa c'è di buono questa sera?**
    Io prendo il risotto. E tu che cosa prendi?
    E per secondo piatto che cosa ci consiglia?
    Sono vegetariano. Non mangio carne. Per me funghi arrosto con patate.
    Ci porti il suo vino bianco della casa, per piacere.

3. **Lei:**   **Parlami di te. Dove sei nata?**
    Da che città vieni?
    Dove abiti ora?
    E i tuoi genitori, dove abitano?
    E tuo padre, che cosa fa di professione?
    E tu che cosa fai di professione?
    Che interessante!

4. **Lei:**   **Che piani hai per il tuo futuro?**
    Ho studiato italiano.
    Ho studiato all'Università di Cambridge.
    Sono...
    Abito a Londra.

5. **Lei:**   **Ha fratelli o sorelle?**
    Ho un fratello e una sorella.
    È giornalista.
    È giornalista anche lei – lavora in televisione.

GAMES

1. DEAD OR ALIVE

1. 1	**è morto**
1. 2	**è viva**
1. 3	**è vivo**
1. 4	**è morto**
1. 5	**è morto**
1. 6	**è morta**
1. 7	**è vivo**
1. 8	**è morta**
1. 9	**è viva**
1.10	**è morta**

2. AD MAN

2. 1	**Il miglior vitello.**
2. 2	**La migliore pasta.**
2. 3	**I migliori antipasti.**
2. 4	**Il più bel cameriere.**
2. 5	**La più bella cameriera.**
2. 6	**Il miglior vino.**
2. 7	**Il miglior pane.**
2. 8	**I più grandi bicchieri.**
2. 9	**Il più bel giardino.**
2.10	**La migliore musica.**

3. SOUNDS FAMILIAR

3. 1	**sei**
3. 2	**hai**
3. 3	**Ti**
3. 4	**vieni**
3. 5	**fai**
3. 6	**Preferisci**
3. 7	**Hai**
3. 8	**Sei**
3. 9	**Hai**
3.10	**Sei**

4. **CHE ORE SONO?**

4. 1	**sono le otto**
4. 2	**sono le otto e mezza**
4. 3	**sono le nove**
4. 4	**sono le dieci**
4. 5	**sono le nove e mezza**

5. RESISTANCE

5. 1	**No, sto mangiando penne all'arrabbiata.**
5. 2	**No, sto bevendo il miglior vino di Roma.**
5. 3	**No, sto aspettando Godot.**
5. 4	**No, sto cercando Bella.**
5. 5	**No, sto scrivendo un libro.**
5. 6	**No, sto preparando l'insalata.**
5. 7	**No, sto studiando l'italiano.**
5. 8	**No, sto guardando la televisione.**

Act 7

PERSONALISED DIALOGUES

1. **Lei:**   **Sì, mi piacciono il cricket e il tennis.**
           Abbiamo tutti bisogno di fare un po' di sport.

           Io sto studiando l'italiano.
           La grammatica italiana non è facile, ma la pronuncia non è molto difficile.

           A cosa stai pensando?
           Andiamo a fare una gita domani, in collina, o al mare?
           Non è necessario. Possiamo andare con la mia macchina.

2. **Lei:**   **Che città meravigliosa!**
           Vorrei camminare tutta la notte!
           Andiamo a vedere la Fontana di Trevi.

   Later: **Che cos'è?**

           Mi piace molto. Sono senza parole. È squisito.

3. **Lei:**   **Sei pronto/a?**
           Allora, andiamo!
           Sì, certo.
           Sì, certo, ho la patente. Non ti fidi?
           No, non ho mai guidato a destra.
           Stai tranquillo, ho l'assicurazione globale.
           Sì, ho già fatto il pieno della benzina, e messo l'olio.

4. **Lei:**   **Va bene.**
           Sì, sì.
           Perchè, sto andando troppo forte?
           Qual'è il limite di velocità sulle autostrade?

5. **Lei:**   **Prendo la prossima uscita.**
           Al prossimo incrocio troverò un semaforo.
           Vado diritto.
           Ci sarà un caffè sulla sinistra.
           A destra vedrò un ospedale.
           Poi una piazza. Ah! ecco la piazza. Dove parcheggiamo?

GAMES

1. WITNESS

1. 1 **Hanno parlato molto.**
1. 2 **Hanno mangiato due affogati.**
1. 3 **Hanno bevuto il caffè.**
1. 4 **Hanno pagato il conto.**
1. 5 **Sono usciti dal ristorante.**
1. 6 **Hanno preso un taxi.**
1. 7 **Hanno preso il raccordo anulare.**
1. 8 **In poco tempo erano già sull'autostrada.**
1. 9 **Hanno fermato una macchina targata Roma.**
1.10 **Hanno preso una stradina stretta che saliva sulla collina.**

2. MALE/FEMALE

2. 1 **È uscito.**
2. 2 **È tornata.**
2. 3 **È uscita.**
2. 4 **È tornata.**
2. 5 **È andato in un caffè in piazza.**
2. 6 **È andata in un caffè in piazza.**
2. 7 **Si sono seduti.**
2. 8 **Si sono alzati.**
2. 9 **Hanno camminato tutta la notte.**
2.10 **Sono ritornati a casa in taxi.**

3. GUIDED TOUR

3. 1 **Possiamo vedere il Vaticano.**
3. 2 **Possiamo visitare il Colosseo.**
3. 3 **Possiamo guardare la Cappella Sistina.**
3. 4 **Possiamo ascoltare la musica a Trastevere.**
3. 5 **Possiamo noleggiare una macchina e andare a fare una gita al mare.**

3. 6 **Dobbiamo alzarci presto.**
3. 7 **Dobbiamo mangiare la colazione.**
3. 8 **Dobbiamo bere il caffè.**
3. 9 **Dobbiamo prendere l'aperitivo.**
3.10 **Dobbiamo mangiare un affogato.**

4. BEFORE AND AFTER

4. 1 **...prendere...prima di...**
4. 2 **...dopo; poco...prima.**
4. 3 **Dopo...ha portato.**
4. 4 **...dopo...è tornato...**
4. 5 **...fra poco...**
4. 6 **Poi...ci sarà...**

Act 8

1. **Lei:** Buongiorno. Vorrei tre panini, per favore.
Va bene, quattro panini. E vorrei anche una bottiglia di vino bianco.
Va bene, vorrei una bottiglia di vino rosso. Ha un formaggio locale?
Va bene, prendo due etti di formaggio francese – e una pizza fresca.
Va bene, prendo due fette di pizza. Che frutta c'è?
Vorrei un chilo di pesche, per favore.
Andiamo invece al ristorante.

2. **Lei:** Dove parcheggiamo? Lì?
Che pace!
Che bello!
Ho fame.
Ho sete.
Fermiamoci qui nel bosco?
Allora andiamo alla cascata.
Mmm, la pizza è buona.
Il formaggio è molto buono.
Le piace (ti piace) il vino?
Ti (le) piacciono i picnic?

3. **Lei:** Dove abita?
Abita in un appartamento?
Davvero?

Che cosa fa di professione? (Che lavoro fa?)
Davvero?
Ha fratelli o sorelle?
Davvero?
Mamma mia!

4. **Lei:** Ma non posso rimanere a Roma!
Ma non posso rilassarmi!
Ma non posso visitare la città!
Ma non posso guardare la televisione.
Perché non ho una televisione.

GAMES

1. TRUE OR FALSE?

1.	**Falso**
2.	**Falso**
3.	**Falso**
4.	**Falso**
5.	**Vero**
6.	**Vero**
7.	**Falso**
8.	**Falso**
9.	**Vero**
10.	**Falso**

2. TELEGRAM

2. 1	**Devo rimanere a Londra ancora un paio di giorni per ragioni d'affari.**
2. 2	**Ho mal di testa.**
2. 3	**Non mi piace Londra.**
2. 4	**C'è troppo rumore.**
2. 5	**L'albergo non è comodo.**
2. 6	**Non c'è sole.**
2. 7	**Vorrei ritornare a casa ma non posso.**
2. 8	**Buon compleanno!**

3. FUTURE STOCK

3. 1	**lavorare**
3. 2	**rimanere**
3. 3	**vivere**
3. 4	**piani hai**
3. 5	**essere**

4. COMPUTER BREAKDOWN

4. 1	**Hanno comprato...**
4. 2	**Sono entrati...**
4. 3	**Si è alzato...**
4. 4	**Hanno aspettato...**
4. 5	**Hanno mangiato...**
4. 6	**Sono ritornati...**

5. SECRET CODE

5. 1	**ANDIAMO ALLA CASCATA**
5. 2	**PARCHEGGIAMO LA MACCHINA**
5. 3	**FERMIAMOCI QUA**
5. 4	**DEVO RITARDARE ANCORA UN GIORNO**
5. 5	**PUÒ RIMANERE A ROMA?**

Act 9

PERSONALISED DIALOGUES

1. **Lei:** Buongiorno, bene grazie.
No, grazie, oggi prendo tè al limone.
Ha il giornale di oggi, per favore?
Vorrei vedere che tempo farà.
Che bello!
A Londra invece sarà nuvoloso, con vento e pioggia.

2. **Lei:** Buongiorno, sono...
Bene, grazie, e tu come stai?
Che cosa facciamo oggi?
Ah sì, avevo dimenticato. Ieri sera ho bevuto molto vino.
Da dove cominciamo?
Come ci andiamo?
Va bene, dove c'incontriamo?
Quando c'incontriamo?
Va bene, ciao, a fra poco.

3. **Lei:** Ciao, Silvana, hai già comprato i biglietti?
Oh no, ho lasciato il mio portafoglio all'albergo.
Grazie. Compro solo andata, o andata e ritorno?
Due andate per il Colosseo, per favore.
Grazie mille. Buongiorno. Andiamo!

4. **Lei:** Ho sempre sognato di visitare Roma.
Sì, c'è tanto da vedere. Vorrei visitare Caracalla, Tivoli, il Pincio, la Fontana di Trevi...
Che buon'idea!

Ho solo un desiderio.
Di ritornare a Roma.

GAMES

1. OPINIONS

1. 1	**No**
1. 2	**No**
1. 3	**No**
1. 4	**No**
1. 5	**No**
1. 6	**Sì**
1. 7	**No**
1. 8	**Sì**
1. 9	**Sì**
1.10	**No**

2. CHE SARÀ, SARÀ

2. 1	**farà**
2. 2	**sarà**
2. 3	**farà**
2. 4	**sarà**
2. 5	**sarà**
2. 6	**saranno**

3. ORDERS ARE ORDERS

3. 1	**Non compra...**
3. 2	**Non bere...**
3. 3	**Non entrare.**
3. 4	**Non andare...**
3. 5	**Non guardarmi!**
3. 6	**Non mangiare...**
3. 7	**Non entrare.**
3. 8	**Non mangiate...**

4. MORE OR LESS

4. 1	**più...di...**
4. 2	**più...di...**
4. 3	**meno del...**
4. 4	**più...dell'...**
4. 5	**più...della...**
4. 6	**più...dell'...**

5. CITY TOUR

5. 1	**LA CAPPELLA SISTINA**	5. 4	**IL FORO ROMANO**
5. 2	**IL COLOSSEO**	5. 5	**LA FONTANA DI TREVI**
5. 3	**PIAZZA SAN PIETRO**		

Act 10

PERSONALISED DIALOGUES

1. **Lei:**   **Mi dispiace di essere in ritardo.**
   Sono stata trattenuta fuori città dagli affari.
   Lo credo! Le piace Roma?
   Le piace la mia segretaria?
   Purtroppo ho un altro lavoro per lei.
   Voglio che lei porti la mia segretaria a pranzo.
   Non si preoccupi. Sì fidi di me, vedrà che tutto andrà bene.

2. **Lei:**   **Mi dispiace, ma purtroppo devo partire subito.**
   Ha già preparato il mio conto?
   No, non mi piacciono le carte di credito. Preferisco pagare subito.
   Il mio volo è prenotato per le dieci. Dove posso prendere un taxi?
   Grazie mille. Arrivederci.

3. **Lei:**   **Scusi, per favore, vorrei ritirare il mio biglietto di andata e ritorno per Londra.**
   Il mio nome è...
   In contanti. Non mi piacciono le carte di credito. Mi può dire se il volo è in orario?
   A che ora parte l'autobus per Fiumicino?
   No, solo bagagli a mano (un bagaglio a mano).
   No, non fumo. Odio il fumo.
   Posso confermare il volo di ritorno che parte da Londra alle diciotto (18.00).
   Grazie. Arrivederci.

4. **Lei:**   **Vorrei questa cartolina per favore. Quant'è? (Quanto viene?/Quanto costa?)**
   Sì, ha francobolli?
   Per l'Inghilterra. Un francobollo solo.
   Sì, ha un giornale inglese?
   Non importa. Basta così. Quanto viene?
   Ecco (li), grazie.

GAMES

1. INDENTIKIT

1. 1	**È grande.**
1. 2	**È grasso.**
1. 3	**È alto due metri.**
1. 4	**È ben vestito.**
1. 5	**Portava gli occhiali scuri.**
1. 6	**È brutto.**
1. 7	**È arrabbiato.**
1. 8	**È simpatico.**
1. 9	**È piuttosto piccolo.**
1.10	**È bello.**

2. INDENTIKIT Contd...

2. 1	**Era grande (e grossa).**
2. 2	**Era grassa.**
2. 3	**Era alto due metri.**
2. 4	**Era ben vestita.**
2. 5	**Portava gli occhiali scuri.**
2. 6	**Era brutta.**
2. 7	**Era arrabbiata.**
2. 8	**Era simpatica.**
2. 9	**Era piuttosto piccola.**
2.10	**Era bella.**

3. MINE, ALL MINE

3. 1	**...la mia...**
3. 2	**...la mia...**
3. 3	**...il mio...**
3. 4	**...il mio...**
3. 5	**...i miei...**
3. 6	**...i miei...**
3. 7	**...le mie...**
3. 8	**...le mie...**
3. 9	**...il mio...**
3.10	**...il mio...**

4. MIX-UP

4. 1	**preso**
4. 2	**comprato**
4. 3	**scritto**
4. 4	**detto**
4. 5	**preso**
4. 6	**aperto**
4. 7	**aperto**
4. 8	**prenotato**

Act 11

PERSONALISED DIALOGUES

1. **Lei:** **Giancarlo! Sono senza parole.**
   Va bene.
   Non per me grazie, e troppo presto. Però vorrei una tazza di caffè.
   Come mai vai a Londra?
   Ho un'appuntamento con un cliente importante. Faccio spesso questo viaggio.
   Non lo so ancora.
   Mi dispiace, ma devo visitare mia nonna.

2. **Lei:** **Ah sì, che ore sono?**
   Scusa, ma devo correre.
   Perchè devo essere ad un indirizzo in centro.
   Sì, ma devo arrivare per mezzogiorno.
   Grazie, ma mi dispiace, non voglio arrivare in ritardo. Ciao.

3. **Lei:** **Ma non ho niente da dichiarare.**
   Solo documenti.
   Sì, eccolo.
   Non rimango a Londra. Devo ritornare subito a Roma.
   Sì, eccoli.
   No, l'ho già detto.
   Sono per lei. Un piccolo regalo.

4. **Lei:** Sloane Avenue, Chelsea, **per favore.**
   Sì, sono italiana.
   Ah si, da dove viene?
   Che interessante!
   Vengo da Roma, e sono molto stanca.
   Sì, mi piace la pioggia. Ho un appuntamento alle dodici. Arriviamo in tempo?
   Benissimo grazie. Mi dispiace, ma non mi sento bene.

GAMES

1. OPPOSITES

1. 1 **dopo**
1. 2 **in anticipo**
1. 3 **maschile**
1. 4 **libero**
1. 5 **niente**
1. 6 **vicino**
1. 7 **buono**
1. 8 **forte**
1. 9 **spesso**
1.10 **sempre**

2. FEELINGS

2. 1 **...si sentiva...**
2. 2 **Si sentiva...**
2. 3 **Gli tremavano...**
2. 4 **...gli batteva...**
2. 5 **Si sentiva...**
2. 6 **...si sentiva...**

3. CONVERSATION STOPPERS

3. 1 **Scusi, sto per uscire.**
3. 2 **Scusi, sto per andare a fare la spesa.**
3. 3 **Scusi, sto per telefonare alla nonna.**
3. 4 **Scusi, sto per guardare la televisione.**
3. 5 **Scusi, sto per correre all'aeroporto.**
3. 6 **Scusi, sto per fare il bagno.**
3. 7 **Scusi, stavo per chiamare un taxi per andare alla stazione.**
3. 8 **Scusi, sto per cenare.**
3. 9 **Scusi, sto per andare a letto.**
3.10 **Scusi, sto per finire il tuo libro.**

4. TIMELESS

4. 1 **IN PUNTO**
4. 2 **IN ANTICIPO**
4. 3 **DI TANTO IN TANTO**
4. 4 **IN RITARDO**
4. 5 **SPESSO**
4. 6 **D'IMPROVVISO**

5. TOPLESS

5. 1 **Il viaggio...**
5. 2 **Durante...**
5. 3 **Il caffè...**
5. 4 **Faccio...**
5. 5 **Di solito...**

Durante il viaggio di solito faccio il caffè.

Act 12

PERSONALISED DIALOGUES

1. **Lei:** **Buongiorno, allora (che) cos'è successo?**
Non è possibile.
Non posso crederci – quanto?
Dieci milliardi!
E sicuro di tutto questo?
Mi sento strana. Posso avere un bicchiere d'acqua?
Signora Ellrose? Ma non sono la signora Ellrose, sono la signora Rose!

GAMES

1. NO DOUBT ABOUT IT

1. 1 **Sono sicurissimo/a!**
1. 2 **Sono felicissimo/a!**
1. 3 **E buonissimo!**
1. 4 **E bellissimo!**
1. 5 **E nuovissimo!**
1. 6 **E carissima!**
1. 7 **E giovanissimo/a**
1. 8 **E grandissimo/a!**

2. TRUE OR FALSE

2. 1 **Vero**
2. 2 **Falso**
2. 3 **Falso**
2. 4 **Falso**
2. 5 **Falso**
2. 6 **Vero**

3. OUT OF TIME

3. 1 **...mezzogiorno...**
3. 2 **...cinquant'anni...**
3. 3 **...per alcuni minuti.**
3. 4 **...tre mesi fa...**
3. 5 **...due bicchieri...**

4. CROSSWORD

Across
1. **numero**   2. **era**   3. **una**   4. **una**   5. **targa**   6. **Roma**
7. **sapore**   8. **ha**   9. **no**   10. **on**   11. **poi**   12. **è (e)**

Down
1. **niente**   2. **mia**   3. **ora**   4. **uno**   5. **aveva**   6. **perchè**
7. **scaffali**   8. **parente**   9. **mondo**   10. **non**   11. **nu**

ITALIAN – ENGLISH GLOSSARY

A

a	at
a buon prezzo	cheap
a piedi	on foot
a, contro	against
abbastanza	enough
abbellire (v)	to adorn
abbracciare (v)	to embrace, hug
abbronzatura	sunburn, suntan
abile	can, be able
abiti	clothes
abito	dress
abituare (v)	to accustom, used to
abitudine (f)	habit
accanto a	beside
accendere (v)	to switch on
accendersi	lit up
accettare (v)	to accept
accogliere (v)	to greet
accompagnare (v)	accompany
acino, chicco d'uva	grape
acqua	water
acquazzone (m)	shower
acquisti	shopping
adesso, ora	now
adorare (v)	to adore
aereo	plane
aereo/a	aerial
aeroporto	airport
affare (m)	bargain, matter
affari	business
afferrare (v)	to catch
affilato/a	sharp
agenzia	agency
aggiungere (v)	add
agire (v)	to do, to act
aglio	garlic
agnello	lamb
aiutare (v)	to help
al pianterreno	downstairs, groundfloor
albergo, hotel (m)	inn, hotel
albero	tree
alcolico/a	alcoholic
allegro/a	merry, jolly
allievo/a	student, pupil
allora	then
alto/a	tall, high
altro/a	other, the rest
amare (v)	to love
ambiente	setting
ambulanza	ambulance
americano/a	American
amicizia	friendship
amico/a	friend
ammalato/a	ill
amministrare (v)	to manage
ammirare (v)	to admire
ammirazione (f)	admiration
amore (m)	love
ananas (m)	pineapple
anatra	duck
anche	also, too
ancora un/a	another, still, yet
andare (v)	to go, attend
anello	ring
angolo	corner, angle
animale	animal
anni	age, years
anno	year
antico/a	ancient
antipatia	dislike
aprire (v)	to open
aperitivo	aperitif
aperto/a	open
apparizione (f)	appearance
appena	scarcely, just
apprezzare (v)	to appreciate
appuntamento	appointment, date
arancia	orange
area	area
aria	air
aroma (m)	aroma
arrabbiarsi (v)	to anger, make angry
arresto	stop
arrivare (v)	to arrive
arrivederci	goodbye
arrivo	arrival
arrosto	roast
arte (f)	art
artista (m/f)	artist
ascensore (m)	lift
ascesa, salita	climb
asciugamano	towel
aspettare (v)	to wait
aspirina	aspirin
aspro/a	tart, bitter, sour
assegno	cheque
assenza	absence
assicurare (v)	to assure, make certain
assicurazione (f)	insurance
assortito/a	mixed
assumere (v)	to engage
atmosfera	atmosphere
attaccare (v)	to join
attento/a	careful
attendere (v)	wait for
attorno	around

attraente	attractive	bisogno	need, want
attraversare (v)	to cross	bocca	mouth
attraverso	across, through	borsa, borsetta	handbag
autobus	bus	bottiglia	bottle
autorimessa	garage	braccio	arm
autorizzare (v)	to authorise	brillare (v)	to gleam, shine
autorizzazione (f)	permit, authorisation	brocca	jug
autostrada	motorway	buca	hole
autunno	autumn	buonanotte	goodnight
avere (v)	to have	buonasera	good evening
avere fame	to be hungry	buono/a	good
avvenimento	event	buongiorno	good day, good morning
avventura	adventure	burro	butter
avversione (f)	dislike	buttare (v) a terra	to knock down
avvertire (v)	to inform		
avvicinarsi (v)	to approach, come near		
avvocato/essa	solicitor, lawyer		
avvolgere (v)	to wrap up		
azienda, ditta	business, firm		
azionista (m/f)	shareholder		
azzurro/a	blue		

C

cabina	cabin
caffè (m)	coffee
cagna (f)	bitch
calcolatore (m)	calculator
calcolo	calculation
caldo/a	warm
calma	composure

B

baciare (v)	to kiss	calore	warmth
baffi (mpl)	moustache	calvo/a	bald
bagaglio	luggage	calza	stocking
bagno	bath, bathroom	calzino	sock
balcone (m)	balcony	calzoni	trousers
ballare (v)	to dance	cambiamento	change
ballo	dance	cambiare (v)	to change
bambina	girl	camera	room
bambino/a	child	cameriera	waitress
bambino	boy	cameriere (m)	waiter
banca	bank	camicetta	blouse
banconota	banknote	camicia	shirt
barba	beard	camion (m)	lorry
basso/a	low	camminare (v)	to walk
battere (v)	to beat	campagna	countryside
bello/a,	pretty, nice, beautiful	campanello	bell, doorbell
benché	although	candela	candle
bene	OK, fine, well	cane (m)	dog
benzina	petrol	cantante (m/f)	singer
bere (v)	to drink	cantare (v)	to sing
bestie feroci	wild animals	canzone (f)	song
bevanda (n)	drink	capace	capable
bianco/a	white	capelli (mpl)	hair
bicchiere (m)	glass (for drinking)	capire (v)	to understand
bicicletta	bicycle	capo	boss, head, chief
bidè (m)	bidet	capolavoro	masterpiece
biglietto	ticket, card	cappella	chapel
biondo/a	blonde, fair	cappello	hat
birra	beer	cappotto	coat

carattere (m)	character	cliente (m/f)	customer
carne (f)	meat	coda	queue, tail
carne di manzo	steak	codice (m)	code
caro/a	dear	coincidenza	coincidence
caro/a, costoso/a	dear, expensive	colazione (f)	breakfast
carta	paper	collaborazione (f)	collaboration
cartella	briefcase	collegare (v)	to connect
cartolina	postcard	collo	neck
casa	house	colonna	column
caseggiato	block	colore (m)	colour
caso	luck, chance	Colosseo	Colisseum
cassa	desk, counter	colpo	blow
cassetto	drawer	coltello	knife
cassiere/a	cashier	come	how
castano	chestnut brown	cominciare (v)	to begin, commence
castello	castle	commessa	saleswomen
cattedrale (f)	cathedral	commesso	salesman
cattivo/a	bad	comodo/a	comfortable
causa	cause	comparto	compartment
causare (v)	to cause	compassione (f)	pity
cavallo	horse	completamente	absolutely
cavolo	cabbage	completo (m)	suit
celebrare (v)	to celebrate	complicato/a	complicated
centrale	centre, middle	comprare (v)	to buy
cercare (v)	to look for	comprendere (v)	to understand
cerchio	circle	compressa	tablet
certamente	certainly, of course	con	with
certo/a	certain	concerto	concert
cestino	basket (small)	confermare (v)	to confirm
champagne (m)	champagne	congratularsi	to congratulate
che ha classe	stylish, smart	conoscenza	knowledge, information
chi	who	conoscere (v)	to know (a person)
chiamare (v)	to call	consecutivo/a	successive, following
chiaro/a	clear	consegnare (v)	to deliver
chiave (f)	key	consigliare (v)	to advise, recommend
chiedere (v)	to ask	contadino/a	peasant
chiedersi (v)	to wonder	contenere (v)	to contain
chiesa	church	contento/a	happy, glad, contented
chilo	kilo	continuare (v)	to continue
chiocciola	snail	continuo/a	continuous, unbroken
chitarra	guitar	contro	against
chiudere (v)	to close, shut	copertura	cover
ciascuno/a	each, everyone	coppia	couple
cibo	food	copriletto	cover, bedspread
ciclomotore (m)	moped	coprire (v)	to cover
cielo	sky	corpo	body
cima	top	correre (v)	to run
cinema	cinema	corriera	coach
cintura	belt	cortese	polite
cintura di sicurezza	safety belt	cortile (m)	courtyard
cioccolato	chocolate	corto/a	short
cipolla	onion	cosa	thing
circondare (v)	to surround	così	so
città	town, city	costare (v)	to cost

costituire (v)	to establish, set up	dipendente (m/f)	employee
costo	cost	dipingere (v)	to paint
costruzione (f)	building	dipinto	painting, painted
cotone (m)	cotton	dire	to say
cravatta	tie	direttore (m)	director, manager
credere (v)	to believe	direzione (f)	direction, management
credible	credible	dirigere (v)	to manage
crepuscolo	dusk	disco	record
criminale (m/f)	criminal	disgrazia	accident
crisi (f)	crisis	disponibile	available
cristallo	crystal	ditta	business
crocicchio	crossroads	divano	sofa, settee
cucchiaio	spoon	diventare (v)	to become
cucina	cooker, kitchen	diversamente	otherwise
cugino/a	cousin	divertente	amusing, funny
cuoco/a	cook, chef	dividere (v)	to divide
cuore (m)	heart	divorziare (v)	to divorce
		documento	document
		Dogana	Customs

D

		dolce (m)	sweet, pudding
		dollaro	dollar
d'oro	golden	domanda (f)	question
da	from	domandare (v)	to ask
da allora	since	domani	tomorrow
dappertutto	everywhere	domenica	Sunday
dare (v)	to give	donare (v)	to give
decidere (v)	to decide	donna	woman, lady
dedicare (v)	to devote	donna d'affari	business woman
del (m), della (f)	of	dono	gift
del/della	some, any	dopo, più tardi	after, afterwards
delizioso/a	delicious, charming	dormire (v)	to sleep
denaro, soldi	money	dottore/essa	doctor
dentifricio	toothpaste	dove	where
dentista (m/f)	dentist	dovere (v)	to have to, ought
dentro	within	dozzina	dozen
deserto/a	empty	dubbio	doubt
desiderare (v)	to desire, want	durare (v)	to last
destarsi (v)	to wake up	duro/a	hard
destro/a	right		
dettagliato/a	detailed		
deviazione (f)	diversion		
di fronte	in front of, opposite		
di legno	wooden		
di mezzo	middle	## E	
di moda	smart, fashionable		
di solito	usually	e, ed	and
diamante (m)	diamond	ecco	here is
dichiarare (v)	to declare	edicola	newspaper kiosk
dietro	behind	edificio	building
differenza	difference	educato/a	polite
difficile	difficult	effetto	result
dimensione (f)	size	elegante	elegant
dimenticare (v)	to forget	elenco	list
Dio	God	ella, lei	she, her
		emozionante	exciting
		enorme	large, huge
		entrare (v)	to enter

equilibrio	balance	forno	oven
erede (m/f)	heir, heiress	forse	perhaps
ereditare (v)	to inherit	forte	loud, strong
errore (m)	error	foschia	mist
esattamente	exactly	fotografia	photograph
esclamare (v)	to cry out	fra	between
esempio	sample	fragola	strawberry
esercizio	exercise	francese (m)	French
esitare (v)	to hesitate	francobollo	stamp
esportazione (f)	export	fratello	brother
esposizione	show, exhibition	freddo/a	cold
esprimere (v)	to express	fresco/a	fresh
essere (v)	to be	frìggere (v)	to fry
essere d'accordo	to agree	frigorìfero, frigo	fridge
esso/a, lo/la	it	frittata	omelette
estate (f)	summer	frittella	pancake
estremità	end	frutti di mare	seafood
evadere (v)	to escape	fruttivendolo/a	greengrocer
		frutto	fruit
		fumante	smoking
		fumatore/trice	smoker
		fungo	mushroom
		fuoco	fire

F

		fuori	outside
		futuro	future
fabbricare (v)	to make		
faccia	face		
facile	easy		
fame (f)	hunger		
famiglia	family		
famoso/a, celebre	famous		

G

fare (v)	to do, make		
fare il numero (v)	to dial	gallina	hen
fare la spesa	shopping for food	gamba	leg
farina	flour	gàmbero	crayfish
farmacia	pharmacy, chemist	garage	garage
fatica	fatigue	gatto/a	cat
fatto	fact	gelato	ice cream
fattura	bill, invoice	gente (f)	people
felice	happy	genitore/i	parent/s
ferire (v)	to hurt, wound	gentile	kind
ferito/a	wounded	gesto	sign
fianco	side	gesticolare (v)	to gesticulate
figlio/a	son, daughter	gettare (v)	to throw
filo	string, thread	ghiacciao	glacier
fine settimana	weekend	già	already, yet
finestra	window	giacca	jacket
finire (v)	to finish	giallo/a	yellow
fino	up to, until, till	giardino	garden
fiore (m)	flower	gigante	giant
fiume (m)	river	ginocchio	knee
fondo	bottom	giocare (v)	to play
forchetta	fork	gioco	game
foresta	forest	giornale (m)	newspaper
formaggio	cheese	giorno	day
fornaio	baker's	giòvane	young
fornire (v)	to provide	gioviale	merry

giovedi	Thursday	in ritardo	late
giovinezza	youth	incertezza	suspense
giro	turn	incidente (m)	accident
giù	down	incontrare (v)	to meet
giurare (v)	to swear	incontro	meeting
giusto/a	just	incredibile	incredible
gonna	skirt	incrocio	crossroads
gradito/a	welcome, pleasant	indicazione (f)	indication
grammo	gram	indirizzo	address
grande	big	infermiere/a	nurse
gratuito/a	free	informare (v)	to inform
grazie	thank you	Inghilterra	England
grazioso/a	pretty, lovely	inghiottire (v)	to swallow
gridare (v)	to cry, shout	inglese	English
grigio/a	grey	inglese (m)	English language
grosso/a, spesso/a	thick, big	iniziare (v)	to begin
gruppo	group	inizio, principio	beginning
guancia	cheek	insalata	salad
guardare (v)	to look at	insegnante	teacher
guardaroba (m)	wardrobe	insetto	insect
guida	guide	insieme	together
gusto	taste	insòlito/a	unusual
		intelligente	intelligent
		interessante	interesting

H

		interesse (m)	interest
hostess (f)	air hostess	interno	inside
		intorno	around
		introdurre (v)	to introduce

I

		inventare (v)	to invent
		inverno	winter
idea	Idea	invitare (v)	to invite
ideale (m)	ideal	io	I, myself
identificazione (f)	identification	isola	island
identico/a	identical	ispettore/trice	inspector
ieri	yesterday	ispezionare (v)	to inspect, examine
ieri sera, ieri notte	last night	Italia	Italy
il, (lo), la, i	the	italiano	Italian language
resto	the rest, the remainder	italiano/a	Italian
illegale	illegal	itinerario	route
immaginazione (f)	imagination		
immediatamente	immediately, at once		
impaziente	impatient		
Imperatore	Emperor		

L

impiegato/a	clerk		
importante	important	là, lì	there
importanza	significance, meaning	la, l', lei	her
importare (v)	to import	lago	lake
improvvisamente	suddenly	lampo	flashlight
impresa	business, company, firm	lampada	lamp
in	in	lana	wool
in fretta	rapidly, hurriedly	lanciare(v)	to throw
in nessun posto	nowhere	largo/a	broad, wide
in realtà	reality	lasciare (v)	to leave, to go
		latte (m)	milk
		latteria	dairy

lattuga	lettuce	martedi	Tuesday
lavare (v)	to wash	matemàtica	maths
lavoro, posto	work, job	matita	pencil
leggere (v)	to read	matrimonio	marriage
leggero/a	light, small	mattina	morning
legno/a	wood	mazzo	bunch
lentamente	slowly	medicina	medicine
lento/a	slow	medievale	medieval
lenzuolo	sheet	medio/a	average
lettera	letter	mela	apple
letto	bed	melone	melon
libero/a	free	meno	less
libreria	bookshop, bookcase	mente (f)	mind
libro	book	mentre	as, while
limite (m)	limit	menu	menu
limone (m)	lemon	meraviglioso/a	marvellous
linguaggio	language	mercato	market
liquore (m)	liqueur	mercoledi	Wednesday
lista	list, note	merletto	lace
litro	litre	mese (m)	month
lo, l', lui, gli	him	messaggio	message
Londra	London	metà (f)	half
lontano/a	far, distant	metallo	metal
lui, egli	he	metro	metre
luna	moon	metropolitana	underground
lunedi (m)	Monday	mezzanotte (f)	midnight
lungo/a	long	mezzo	half
luogo	place	mi piace	I like
		mi scusi!	excuse me
		migliore	better
		minuto	minute
		mio/a, miei	my, mine

M

ma	but	misterioso/a	misterious
macchina	car	mistero	mistery
macelleria	butcher's	mite	mild
madre	mother	mobilio (mpl)	furniture
maggiore	elder	moda	way, fashion
magnifico/a	magnificent	modello	model
magro/a	slim	moderno/a	modern
mal di testa (m)	headache	modo	way, method
malato/a	sick, ill	moltiplicare (v)	multiply
mancanza	lack, shortage	molto/a	much. many, very
mancia	tip	momento	moment
mandare (v)	to send	mondo	world
mangiare (v)	to eat	montagna	mountain
maniera	manner	monumento	monument
mano (f)	hand	morire (v)	to die
marciapiede (m)	pavement	morte (m)	death
marinaio	sailor	mostra	show
marito	husband	mostrare (v)	to show
marmellata	jam	moto (f)	motorbike
marmellata (d'arance)	marmalade	motore (m)	engine
marmo	marble	mucca, vacca	cow
marrone	brown	murale	mural, wall painting

muro	wall	olfatto	smell
museo	museum	olio	oil
musica	music	oltre a	besides
mutande (fpl)	pants, underpants	ombrello	umbrella
		onore (m)	honour
		opinione (f)	opinion
		opposto/a,	opposite
N		ora	hour
		ordinato/a	tidy, orderly
nascere(v)	to be born	ordine (m)	order
nascita	birth	orecchio	ear
nascondere (v)	to hide	orfanotrofio	orphanage
naso	nose	organizzare (v)	to organise
natale, nativo/a	native	orologio	clock, watch
natura	nature	orribile	terrible, horrible, awful
naturale	natural	ortaggio	vegetable
necessario/a	necessary	ospite (f)	hostess
necessità	need, necessity	ospite (m/f)	guest
negozio	shop, store	ostinato	obstinate
nero/a	black	ottimo/a	best, excellent
nascondere	to hide		
nessuno/a	none		
niente (m), nulla (m)	nothing		
nipote	nephew, niece, grandson, granddaughter	**P**	
no	no		
noleggio, a nolo	hire, for hire	pacchetto	packet
nome (m)	name	pacco	package
non	not	pacifico/a	peaceful
non ... mai	never	padre	father
nonna	grandmother	paese (m)	country
nonno	grandfather	pagare (v)	to pay
nord (m)	north	pagina	page
normale	normal	pagnotta	loaf
nostro/a, nostri/e (pl)	our, ours	paio	pair
nota	note	palazzo	palace
notévole	impressive	palla	ball
notte (f)	night	pane (m)	bread
nube (f)	cloud	pane tostato	toast
nùmero	number	panna	cream
numeroso/a	numerous	pantaloni	trousers
nuotare (v)	to swim	Papa	Pope
nuovo/a	new	Papà	Daddy
nùvola	cloud	parcheggio	parking space
		parco	park
		parere (v)	to appear, seam
		parecchi/ie	several
		parlante	speaking
O		parlare (v)	to speak, talk
		parrucchiere/a	hairdresser
obbligatorio/a	compulsory	parte (f)	part
obbligo	obligation, duty	partenza	departure
occhiali	spectacles	particolare	special
occhio	eye	particolarmente	especially
occupato/a	busy, engaged	pascolo	meadow
odorare	to smell	passante (m/f)	passerby
oggi	today		
ognuno	everyone		

passaporto	passport	piuttosto	rather, fairly
passare (v)	to pass, go by	pizzicare (v)	to pinch
passatempo	pastime	pizzo	lace
passeggero/a	passenger	polizia	police
passeggiatina	stroll	poliziotto	policeman
pasticcino	small cake, pastry	pollo	chicken
pasto	meal	pomeriggio	afternoon
patata	potato	pomodoro	tomato
patatina fritta	potato chips	pompelmo	grapefruit
pâté (m)	pâté	ponte (m)	bridge
patente de guida	driving licence	porta	door
pazienza	patience	portafoglio	wallet
pecora	sheep	portare,indossare (v)	to carry, take,wear, bring
pedone (m)	pedestrian	portiere/a	porter
pelle (f)	skin, leather	posizione (f)	situation
pensare (v)	to think	possibile	possible
pensionato/a	retired(person)	posta	post
pepe (m)	pepper	posto, luogo	place
per	for, through	potere (v)	to be able, can
per antipasto	starter	povero/a	poor
per di più, inoltre	moreover	pranzare (v)	to dine
per favore	please	pranzo	lunch
per piacere	please	prato, pascolo	meadow
pera	pear	precario/a	uneasy
perché	why, because	precipitarsi (v)	to rush
perciò	therefore, thus	preferire (v)	to prefer
perdere (v)	to lose	prendere (v)	to take, catch
pericoloso/a	dangerous	prenotare(b)	to book, reserve
permettere (v)	to allow, permit	prenotato/a	booked, reserved
però	however	prenotazione (f)	reservation
persona	person	preoccupato/a	worried
personalmente	personally	preoccupazione (f)	worry
persone (fpl)	people	preparare (v)	to prepare
persuadere (v)	to persuade	presentazione (f)	presentation
pesante	heavy	pressione (f)	pressure
pesca	peach	presto	soon
pesce (m)	fish	previsione (f)	forecast
peso	weight	prezioso/a	precious
pettine (m)	comb	prima di	before
pezzo/a	piece	primavera	spring
piacere (m)	pleasure	primo/a	first, early
piano	plan	principale	principal, main
piatto	plate	principiante (m/f)	beginner
piccolo/a	small, little	principio	beginning
picnic (m)	picnic	privato/a	private
piede (m)	foot	probabilmente	probably
pieno/a	full	problema	problem
pioggia	rain	prodotto	product
pipa	pipe (smoker's)	profumo	perfume
piscina	swimming pool	progetto	plan
pisello	pea	programma	programme
pittura	picture	proibire (v)	to forbid
più	more	pronto/a	ready, early
più di tutti	most		

proprietà	property	rilassare (v)	to relax
proprietario/a	owner	rimanere (v)	to remain, rest
prosciutto	ham	rimettere (v)	to replace
prossimo/a	next	ringraziare	to thank
prova	proof	riposo	rest
provare (v)	to prove	riservato/a,	reserved
pubblicità (f)	publicity	rispondere (v)	to reply, answer
pulito/a	clean	ristorante (m)	restaurant
punto	point	ritardo	delay
puro/a	pure	ritirarsi (v)	to retire, withdraw
purtroppo	unfortunately	ritornare (v)	to return, come back
		rivista	magazine
		roccia	rock
		Roma	Rome

Q

qua e là	about
quadrato	square
qualche cosa	something
qualche volta	sometimes
qualcosa	something
qualcuno	someone
quale	which, what
qualità	quality
quando	when
quanto	how much
quarto	quarter
quasi	almost
quei, quella, quello	that, those
questo/a	this, these
qui, qua	here
quindi	therefore
quindici giorni	fortnight

rosa	pink
rosa (m)	rose
rosso/a	red
rotto/a	broken
rubinetto	tap
rullino	film
rumore (m)	noise

S

sabato	Saturday
sala	room
sala da pranzo	dining room
sale (m)	salt
salice (m)	willow
salire (v)	to go up, ascend
salone (m)	hall, sitting room
salsiccia	sausage
saltare (v)	to jump
salute (f)	health
salutare (v)	to greet
salvietta	serviette, napkin
santo/a	saint
sapere (v)	to know (a fact)
sapone (m)	soap
sbagliato/a	wrong
sbrigarsi	to hurry up
scacchi	chess
scala	staircase
scalino	stair
scambio	exchange
scansare (v)	to avoid
scappare (v)	to escape, disappear
scarico	drain
scarsità	need, lack
scarpa	shoe
scegliere (v)	to choose
scendere (v)	to go down, descend
schiena	back

R

raccogliere (v)	to collect
radere, rasare (v)	to shave
ragazzo	boy
rapidamente	quickly, rapidly
rasoio	razor
rassomiglianza	resemblance
reception (f)	reception
registrazione (f)	registration
relativo/a	relative
resistere (v)	to resist
restare (v)	to remain, rest
ricco/a	rich
ricevere (v)	to receive
richiedere (v)	to request
riconoscere (v)	to recognise
ricordare (v)	to remember
ridere (v)	to laugh
rifiutare (v)	to refuse

schivare (v)	to avoid	snello/a	company
sciarpa	scarf	società	slim
scintillante	sparkling	soddisfare (v)	to satisfy
scolaro/a	pupil, student	soffitto	ceiling
sconosciuto/a	strange, unkown	sogno (v)	to dream
sconto	discount	soldo	money, coin
scopo	purpose, intention	sole (m)	sun
scrivania	desk	sollievo/a	relief
scrivere (v)	to write	solo/a, unico/a	alone, single
scuola	school	somiglianza	similarity
scuro/a	dark	sopra	on, over
scusa	excuse, apology	sopracciglio	eyebrow
se	if	sordo/a	deaf
secchio	bucket	sorella	sister
secco/a	dry	sorgere (v)	to rise up, get up
secolo	century	sorprendere (v)	to surprise
secondario/a	secondary	sorridere (v)	to smile
secondo, stando a	according to	sotto	under, below
secondo/a	second	sottrarre (v)	to subtract
sedersi (v)	to sit down	spagnolo	Spanish
sedia	seat, chair	spalla	shoulder
segno, gesto	sign	spazzolino da denti	toothbrush
segretario/a	secretary	speciale	special
seguente	following	spedire per posta	to post
selvaggio	wild	spendere (v)	to spend
sembrare	to seem, appear	spesa	expense, expenditure
semplice	simple	spesso	often
sempre	always	spettacolo	show (theatre)
sentiero	path	spiacevole	unpleasant
sentire (v)	to feel, to hear	spiaggia	beach
senza	without	spiegare (v)	to explain, spell out
sera	evening	spiegazione (f)	explanation
serie (f)	set	splendido/a	splendid, magficent
serio/a	serious	sport	sport
serpente	snake	sportivo/a	sporting
servire (v)	to service	sposato/a	married
servizio	service, duty	sprazzo	flash
sessanta	sixty	spuntimo	snack
seta	silk	stalla	stall
sete (f)	thirst	stanchezza	fatigue
settimana	week	stanco/a	tired
sgradevole	unpleasant	stando a	according to
si	yes	stanza	room
sicurezza	safety	Stati Uniti	United States
sicuro/a	sure, certain	statua	statue
sigaretta	cigarette	stazione (f)	station
Signora	Mrs	stazione (f) di	petrol station
Signore	Mr	servizio	stereo
Signorina	Miss	stereo (m)	pound (money)
silenzio	silence, quiet	sterlina	same
silenzioso/a	silent, tranquil	stesso/a	style, manner
simile	like, same	stile (m)	stomach
simpatico/a	nice, likeable	stomaco	history, story
sinistro/a	left	storia	road, street

strada	main road	terminale (m)	end
strada principale	lane	terrapieno	embankment
stradina, straniero/a	foreign	terrazzo	terrace
stringere (v)	to tighten, close	terribile	horrible
strofinare (v)	to rub	terzo/a	third
studente/essa	student	testa	head
studiato/a	studied	testimonianza	evidence
studio	studio	timido/a	shy, timid
stupido/a	stupid, silly	tipo	type, class
su	on, over	toccare (v)	to touch
succedere (v)	to succeed	togliere (v)	to remove
successivo/a	later	tono	tone
succo	juice	topo	mouse
sufficiente	sufficient, enough	torta	cake, tart
suolo	floor	tosse (f)	cough
suonare (v)	to ring up, phone	tovaglia	tablecloth
superficie (f)	area	tovagliolo	serviette, napkin
supermercato	supermarket	tra	between
superstite (m/f)	survivor	traffico	traffic
svago	leisure	tramezzino	sandwich
svegliarsi,	to wake up	tramontare (v)	to go down
svolgimento	performance	tranquillo/a	quiet, peaceful
		tremendo/a	terrible, horrible
		treno	train
		trenta	thirty
		triste	sad

T

		troppo	too
tabaccaio	tobacconist	trovare (v)	to find
tagliente	sharp	tu, voi	you
taglio (v)	to cut	turista (m/f)	tourist
tappeto	carpet	tutti/e e due	both
tappo	cork	tutto	all, every, whole
tariffa	fare		
tasca	pocket		
tastare (v)	to feel, to touch		
tavola calda	snack bar		
tavolo	table		
taxi (m)	taxi		
tazza	cup		

U

tè (m)	tea		
teatro	theatre	uccello	bird
tedesco	German	ufficio	office
teiera	teapot	uguale/a	equal
telefonare (v)	to telephone	ultimo/a	last
telefono	telephone	umido/a	damp
telegramma	telegram	un (m) una (f)	a, an, one
televisione (f)	television	unghia	nail, claw
temere (v)	to fear	unire	to join
temperatura	temperature	unito/a	united
tempesta	storm	università	university
tempo	weather, time	uomo	man
tenda	curtain	uomo d'affari	businessman
tenere (v)	to hold, keep	uovo	egg
tenero/a	tender	usare (v)	to use
tennis (m)	tennis	uscire (v)	to go out
		uscita	exit

V

vacanza	holiday
valigia	suitcase
valoroso/a	gallant
vaniglia	vanilla
vaso	vase
vassoio	tray
vecchio/a	old
vedere (v)	to see
vela	sail
velluto	velvet
velocità	speed
vendere (v)	to sell
venerdì	Friday
venire (v)	to come
venti	twenty
vento	wind
veramente	really
verde	green
verdura	vegetables
verità	truth
vero/a	true
verso	towards
vestire (v)	to dress, wear
vestiti	clothes
vestito	dress
via	road, highway
viaggiare (v)	to travel
viaggio	journey
viale (m)	avenue
vicino	next
vicino/a	neighbour
villaggio	village
vincere (v)	to win
vincitore/trice	winner
vino	wine
visitare (v)	to visit
vista	view
vita	life
vivere (v)	to live
voce (f)	voice
voi	you
volere (v)	to wish, want
volo	flight
vuoto/a	empty

Z

zio	uncle
zucchero	sugar
Zurigo	Zurich

Y

yogurt	yoghurt

ENGLISH – ITALIAN GLOSSARY

A

a, an	un (m) una (f)
able, capable	capace
to be able	poter fare (v), essere in grado di fare
about	que e là, in giro
absence	assenza
absolutely	completamente
accept	accettare (v)
accident	incidente (m), disgrazia
accompany	accompagnare (v)
according to	secondo, stando a
accustomed to, used to	abituato/a (v)
across	attraverso
act, do	agire (v)
add	aggiungere (v)
address	indirizzo
admiration	ammirazione (f)
admire	ammirare (v)
adore	adorare (v)
adorn	abbellire (v)
adventure	avventura
advertisement	pubblicità (f)
advise	consigliare (v)
aerial	aereo/a
after	dopo
afternoon	pomeriggio
afterwards	dopo, più tarde
against	a, contro
age	anni
agency	agenzia
agree	essere d'accordo
air	aria
airport	aeroporto
alcoholic	alcolico/a
all, every, whole	tutto
allow	permettere (v)
almost	quasi
alone, on its own	solo/a
along	lungo
already	gia
also, too	anche
altogether	tutto
although	benché
always	sempre
ambulance	ambulanza
amusing	divertente
American	americano/a
ancient	antico/a
and	e, ed
animal	animale
another	ancora un/a
any	dei (m), della (f)
anything	niente, qualcosa
aperitif	aperitivo
appearance	apparizione (f)
apple	mela
appointment, date	appuntamento
appreciate	apprezzare (v)
approach	avvicinarsi (v)
area	area, superficie (f)
arm	braccio
aroma	aroma (m)
around	attorno, intorno
arrive	arrivare (v)
arrival	arrivo
art	arte (f)
artist	artista (m/f)
as	mentre
ask	domandare (v)
aspirin	aspirina
assure, make certain	assicurare (b)
at	a
atmosphere	atmosfera
attend	andare (v)
attractive	attraente, interessante
authorise	autorizzare (v)
autumn	autunno
available	disponibile
avenue	viale (m)
average	medio/a
avoid	scansare, schivare (v)
away	lontano
awful	terribile, orribile

B

back	schiena
bad	cattivo/a
baker's	fornaio
balance	equilibrio
balcony	balcone (m)
bald	calvo/a
ball	palla
banana	banana
bank	banca
bank-note	banconota
bargain	affare (m)
basket	cestino
bath	bagno
bathroom	(stanza da) bagno
be	essere (v)
beach	spiaggia
beard	barba
beat	colpo (v)
beautiful	bello/a, splendido/a
because	perché
become	diventare, divenire (v)
become angry	arrabbiarsi (v)
bed	letto

beer	**birra**	butter	**burro**
before	**prima di**	buy	**comprare (v)**
begin	**cominciare, iniziare (v)**		
beginner	**principiante (m/f)**		
beginning	**inizio, principio**	# C	
behind	**dietro**		
believe	**credere (v)**	cab, taxi	**cabina**
bell, doorbell	**campanello**	cabbage	**cavolo**
below	**sotto**	cake (large)	**torta**
belt	**cintura**	cake (small)	**pasticcino**
bench	**panchina**	calculation	**calcolo**
beside	**accanto a**	calculator	**calcolatore (m)**
besides	**altre a**	call	**chiamare (v)**
better	**migliore**	can, be able	**potere (v)**
between	**tra, fra**	candle	**candela**
bicycle	**bicicletta**	capable	**capace, abile**
bidet	**bidè (m)**	car	**macchina**
big	**grande**	card	**biglietto**
bill, invoice	**fattura**	careful	**attento/a**
bird	**uccello**	carpet	**tappeto**
birth	**nascita**	carry, take	**portare (v)**
blonde	**biondo/a**	cashier	**cassiere/a**
black	**nero/a**	castle	**castello**
block	**caseggiato**	cat	**gatto/a**
blouse	**camicetta**	catch	**afferrare, prendere (v)**
blue	**azzurro/a**	cathedral	**cattedrale (f)**
body	**corpo**	cause	**causa, causare (v)**
book	**libro**	ceiling	**soffitto**
bookcase	**libreria**	celebrate	**celebrare (v)**
bookshop	**libreria**	century	**secolo**
born	**nascere(v)**	certain	**certo/a, sicuro/a**
boss	**capo, padrone**	certainly, of course	**certamento, certo**
both	**tutti/e e due**	champagne	**champagne (m)**
bottle	**bottigilia**	chance, luck	**caso**
bottom	**fondo**	change	**cambiamento**
boy	**ragazzo. bambino**	change (v)	**cambiare (v)**
bread	**pane (m)**	chapel	**cappella**
breakfast	**colazione (f)**	character	**carattere (m)**
bridge	**ponte (m)**	charming	**delizioso/a**
briefcase	**cartella**	cheap	**a buon prezzo**
bring	**portare (v)**	check	**limitazione (f)**
broad, wide	**largo/a**	cheek	**guancia**
broken	**rotto/a**	cheer	**grido (v)**
brother	**fratello**	cheese	**formaggio**
brown	**marrone, castano/a**	chemist, pharmancy	**farmacia**
bucket	**secchio**	cheque, check	**assegno**
building	**costruzione (f), edificio**	chess	**scacchi**
bunch	**mazzo**	chicken	**pollo**
bus	**autobuses**	child	**bambino/a**
business	**affari**	chip (potato)	**patatina fritta**
businessman	**uomo d'affari**	chocolate	**cioccolato, cioccolata**
businesswoman	**donna d'affari**	choose	**scegliere (v)**
busy	**occupato/a**	church	**chiesa**
but	**ma**	cigarette	**sigaretta**
butcher's	**macelleria**	cinema	**cinema**

circle	**cerchio**	cover, bedspread	**copriletto**
city	**città**	cow	**mucca, vacca**
class	**tipo**	crayfish	**gambero**
clean	**pulito/a**	cream	**crema**
clear	**chiaro/a**	cream (whipped)	**panna**
clerk	**impiegato/a**	credible	**credible**
climb	**ascesa, salita (v)**	criminal	**criminale (m/f)**
clock	**orologio**	crisis	**crisi (f)**
close, shut	**chiudere (v)**	cross	**attraversare (v)**
clothes	**vestiti, abiti**	crossing	**attraversamento**
cloud	**nuvola, nube**	cross-roads	**incrocio, crocicchio**
clue	**indicazione (f)**	cry	**gridare (v)**
coach	**corriera**	crystal	**cristallo**
coat	**cappotto**	cup	**tazza**
code	**codice (m)**	curtain	**tenda**
coffee	**caffè (m)**	customer	**cliente (m/f)**
coin	**soldo**	Customs	**Dogana**
coincidence	**coincidenza**	cut	**taglio (v)**
cold	**freddo/a**		
collaboration	**collaborazione (f)**		
collect	**raccogliere (v)**		
Colosseum	**Colosseo**	**D**	
colour	**colore (m)**		
column	**colonna**	Dad, Daddy	**Papà**
comb	**pettine (m)**	dairy	**latteria**
come	**venire (v)**	dance	**ballo**
comfortable	**comodo/a**	dance	**ballare (v)**
company	**società**	danger	**pericoloso/a**
compartment	**comparto**	dark	**scuro/a**
complicated	**complicato/a**	daughter	**figlia**
composure	**calma**	day	**giorno**
compulsory	**obbligatorio/a**	deaf	**sordo/a**
concert	**concerto**	dear	**caro/a**
confirm	**confermare (v)**	death	**morte (m)**
congratulate	**congratularsi con**	decide	**decidere (v)**
connect	**collegare (v)**	declare	**dichiarare (v)**
contain	**contenere (v)**	delay	**ritardo**
content	**contenuto**	delicious	**delizioso/a**
continue	**continuare (v)**	deliver	**consegnare**
continuous, unbroken	**continuo/a**	dentist	**dentista (m/f)**
cook	**cuoco/a**	departure	**partenza**
cooker	**cucina**	design	**modello**
cork	**sughero**	desire	**desiderio (v)**
corner	**angolo**	desk	**scrivania**
cost	**costo**	desk,counter	**cassa**
cost	**costare (v)**	dessert	**dolce (m)**
cotton	**cotone (m)**	detailed	**dettagliato/a**
cough	**tosse (f)**	devote	**dedicare (v)**
country	**paese (m)**	dial	**fare il numero (v)**
countryside	**campagna**	diamond	**diamante (m)**
couple	**coppia**	die	**morire (v)**
courtyard	**cortile (m)**	difference	**differenza**
cousin	**cugino/a**	difficult	**difficile**
cover	**coprire (v)**	dine	**pranzare (v)**
cover	**copertura**	dining-room	**sala da pranzo**
		direction	**direzione (f)**

discount	**sconto**	escape, disappear	**scappare (v), evadere (v)**
dislike	**antipatia, avversione (f)**	especially	**particolarmente**
distant	**lontano/a**	establish, set up	**costituire (v)**
diversion	**deviazione (f)**	evening	**sera**
divide	**dividere (v)**	event	**avvenimento**
divorce	**divorziare (v)**	everybody	**ognuno, ciascuno**
do	**fare (v)**	everywhere	**dappertutto**
doctor	**dottore/essa**	evidence	**testimonianza**
document	**documento**	exactly	**esattamente, in punto**
dog	**cane (m), cagna (f)**	examine, inspect	**ispezionare (v)**
dollar	**dollaro**	example	**esempio**
door	**porta**	excellent	**ottimo**
doubt	**dubbio**	exchange	**scambio**
down	**giù**	exciting	**emozionante**
downstairs, ground floor	**al pianterreno**	exclaim, cry out	**esclamare (v)**
		excuse	**scusa**
dozen	**dozzina**	excuse me	**mi scusi!**
drain	**scarico**	exercise	**esercizio**
drawer	**cassetto**	exit	**uscita**
dream	**sogno (v)**	expenditure	**spensa**
dress	**vestito, abito**	expense	**spesa**
dress, put on	**vestire (v)**	expensive	**caro/a, costoso/a**
drink	**bevanda (n), bere (v)**	explain	**spiegare (v)**
drinking glass	**bicchiere (m)**	explanation	**spiegazione (f)**
driving licence	**patente de guida**	export	**esportazione (f)**
dry	**secco/a**	express	**esprimere (v)**
duck	**anantra**	eye	**occhio**
dusk	**crepuscolo**	eyebrow	**sopracciglio**

E

each	**ciascuno/a**
ear	**orecchio**
early	**primo/a, pronto/a**
easy	**facile**
eat	**mangiare (v)**
elder	**maggiore**
effect, result	**effetto**
egg	**uovo**
elegant	**elegante**
embankment	**terrapieno**
embrace	**abbraccio (v)**
employee	**dipendente (m/f)**
empty	**vuota/a, deserto/a**
emperor	**l'imperatore**
end	**estremità**
engage	**assumere (v)**
engine	**motore (m)**
England	**Inghilterra**
English	**inglese**
English language	**inglese**
enough, sufficient	**abbastanza**
enter, go into	**entrare (v)**
equal, the same	**uguale**

F

face	**faccia**
fact	**fatto**
fairly	**abbastanza, piuttosto**
family	**famiglia**
famous	**famoso/a, celebre**
far	**lontano**
fare	**tariffa**
fashion	**moda**
fatigue	**stanchezza, fatica**
father	**padre**
fear, be afraid	**temere (v), avere paura**
feel, touch	**tastare (v), toccare (v)**
film	**rullino**
find	**trovare (v)**
fine, O.K.	**bene**
fine, elegant	**ottimo/a, elegante**
finish, complete	**finire (v), terminare (v)**
fire	**fuocco**
firm, business	**azienda, ditta, impresa**
first	**primo/a**
fish	**pesce (m)**
flash	**sprazzo, lampo**
flight	**volo**

floor	**suolo**	gram	**grammo**
flower	**fiore (m)**	granddaughter	**nipotina**
following, next	**seguente**	grandfather	**nonno**
food	**cibo**	grandmother	**nonna**
foot	**piede (m)**	grandson	**nipote**
for	**per**	grape	**acino, chicco d'uva**
forbid	**proibire (v)**	grapefruit	**pompelmo**
forecast	**previsione**	green	**verde**
foreign	**straniero/a**	greengrocer	**fruttivendolo/a**
forest	**foresta**	greet	**accogliere, salutare (v)**
forget	**dimenticare (v)**	grey	**grigio/a**
fork	**forchetta**	group	**gruppo**
fortnight	**quindici giorni**	guest	**ospite (m/f)**
free	**gratuito/a, libero/a**	guide	**guida**
French language	**francese**	guitar	**chitarra**
fresh	**fresco/a**		
Friday	**venerdì**		
fridge	**frigorifero, frigo**		
friend	**amico**	**H**	
friendship	**amicizia**		
from	**da**	habit	**abitudine (f)**
fruit	**frutto**	hair	**capelli (mpl)**
fry	**friggere (f)**	hairdresser	**parrucchiere/a**
full	**pieno/a**	half	**metà (f)**
funny	**divertente**	hall, sitting room	**salone (m)**
furniture	**mobili (mpl)**	ham	**prosciutto**
future	**futuro/a**	hand	**mano (f)**
		handbag	**borsa, borsetta**
		happy	**contento/a, felice**
		hard	**duro/a**
G		hat	**cappello**
		have	**avere (v)**
gallant	**valorosa/a**	have to, ought	**dovere (v)**
game	**gioco**	he	**lui, egli**
garage	**garage, autorimessa**	head	**testa, capo**
garden	**giardino**	headache	**mal (m) di testa**
garlic	**aglio**	health	**salute (f)**
garment	**articolo di vestiario**	hear	**sentire (v)**
German language	**tedesco**	heart	**cuore (m)**
giant	**gigante, colosso**	heavy	**pesante**
girl	**bambina, ragazzina**	heir, inheritor	**erede (m/f)**
give	**dare (v)**	hello	**hullo**
glad	**contento/a**	help	**aiutare (v)**
glass	**bicchiere (m)**	hen	**gallina**
gleam	**brillare (v)**	her	**la, l', lei**
go	**andare (v)**	here	**qui, qua**
go out	**uscire (v)**	here is	**ecco**
go down, descend	**tramontare, scendere (v)**	hesitate	**esitare (v)**
go up, ascend	**salire, andare (v)**	hide, conceal	**nascondere (v)**
God	**Dio**	high	**alto/a**
golden	**d'oro**	him	**lo, l', lui**
good	**buono/a**	hire, for hire	**noleggio, a nolo**
goodbye	**arrivederci**	history, story	**storia**
good morning/day	**buonogiorno**	hold	**tenere (v)**
good evening	**buonasera**	hole	**buca**
good night	**buonanotte**	holiday	**vacanza**

honour	onore (m)	Italian	italiano/a
horse	cavallo	Italian language	italiano
hostess	ospite (f), hostess, air (f)	Italy	Italia
hotel	albergo, hotel (m)		
hour	ora		
house	casa	**J**	
how, how much	come, quanto/a		
however	però	jacket	giacca
hug	abbraccio (v)	jam	marmellata
huge, vast	enorme	job	lavoro, posto
hunger	fame (f)	join	unire, attaccare (v)
hungry	aver fame	jolly	allegro/a, gioviale
hurriedly	in fretta	journey	viaggio
hurry up	sbrigarsi	jug	brocca
hurt	ferire (v)	juice	succo
husband	marito	jump	saltare (v)
		just	giusto/a

I

I, myself	io
ice	ghiacciao
ice cream	gelato
idea	idea
ideal	ideale (m)
identical	identico/a
identification	identità
if	se
ill	ammalato/a malato/a
illegal	illegale
imagination	immaginazione (f)
immediately, at once	immediatamente
impatient	impaziente
import	importare (v)
important	importante
impressive	notevole
in	in
include	comprendere (v)
income	reddito
incredible	incredibile
indeed	veramente
inform	informare, avvertire (v)
inherit	ereditare (v)
insect	insetto
inside	interno
inspector	ispettore/trice
insurance	assicurazione (f)
intelligent	intelligente
interest	interesse (m)
interesting	interessante
introduce	introdurre (v)
invent	inventare (v)
invite	invitare (v)
island	isola
it	esso/a, lo/la

K

keep	tenere (v)
key	chiave (f)
kilo	chilo
kind	gentile
kiosk	edicola
kiss	bacio
kitchen	cucina
knee	ginocchio
knife	coltello
knock down	buttare a terra
know (a fact)	sapere (v)
know (a person)	conoscere (v)
knowledge, information	conoscenza

L

lace	pizzo, merletto
lack, be missing	mancanza, scarsità
lady	signora
lake	lago
lamb	agnello
lamp	lampada
lane	stradina
language	linguaggio
last	ultimo/a
last night	ieri sera, ieri notte
late	in ritardo
later	successivo/a
laugh	ridere (v)
lawyer	avvocato, legale
leather	pelle (f)
leave, go	lasciare (v)
left	sinistro/a

leg	**gamba**	meadow	**prato, pascolo**
leisure	**svago**	meal	**farina**
lemon	**limone**	meal (to have a), eat	**mangiare (v)**
less	**meno**	meat	**carne (f)**
letter	**lettera**	medicine	**medicina**
lettuce	**lattuga**	medieval	**medievale**
life	**vita**	medium, average	**medio/a**
lift	**ascensore (m)**	meet	**incontrare (v)**
light, small	**leggero/a**	meeting	**incontro**
like, same	**simile**	melon	**melone**
like	**mi piace**	menu	**menù**
limit	**limite (m)**	merry	**allegro/a**
liqueur	**liquore (m)**	message	**messagio**
list	**lista, elenco**	metal	**metallo**
lit up, lighted	**accendersi**	metre	**metro**
litre	**litro**	middle, centre	**di mezzo, centrale**
little, few	**piccolo/a**	midnight	**mezzanotte (f)**
live	**vivere (v)**	mild	**mite**
loaf	**pagnotta, pane (m)**	milk	**latte (m)**
London	**Londra**	mind	**mente (f)**
long	**lungo/a**	minute	**minuto**
look at	**guardare (v)**	Miss	**Signorina**
look for	**cercare (v)**	mist	**foschia, nebbiolina**
lorry	**camion (m)**	mistake	**errore (m)**
lose	**perdere (v)**	mixed	**assortito/a**
loud	**forte**	modern	**moderno/a**
love	**amore (m)**	moist	**umido/a**
love	**amare (v)**	moment	**momento**
low	**basso/a**	Monday	**lunedi (m)**
luggage	**bagagli, bagaglio**	money	**denaro, soldi**
lunch	**pranzo**	month	**mese (m)**
		monument	**monumento**
		moon	**luna**
		moped	**ciclomotore (m)**
		more	**più, altro/a, ancora**

M

		moreover	**per di più, inoltre**
magazine	**rivista**	morning	**mattina**
magnificent, great	**magnifico/a**	most	**più di tutti**
main	**principale**	mother	**madre**
main road	**strada principale**	motorbike	**moto (f)**
make	**fare, fabbricare (v)**	motorway	**autostrada**
man	**uomo**	mountain	**montagna**
manage	**dirigere,amministrare (v)**	moustache	**baffi (mpl)**
management	**direzione (f)**	mouse	**topo**
manager	**direttore (m)**	mouth	**bocca**
manner, way	**modo, maniera**	Mr	**Signore**
mansion	**palazzo, villa**	Mrs	**Signora**
map	**carta, pianta**	much,many	**molto/a**
marble	**marmo**	multiply	**moltiplicare (v)**
market	**mercato**	mural, wall painting	**murale, pittura murale**
marmalade	**marmellata di arance**	museum	**museco**
marriage	**matrimonio**	mushrooom	**fungo**
married	**sposato/a**	music	**musica**
marvellous, wonderful	**meraviglioso/a**	must, ought	**dovere (v)**
masterpiece	**capolavoro**	my, mine	**mio/a, miei**
mathematics	**matematica**		

mysterious	**misterioso/a**
mystery	**mistero**

N

nail (finger)	**unghia**
name	**nome (m)**
napkin, serviette	**tovagliolo, salvietta**
native	**natale, natio/a**
natural	**naturale**
nature	**natura**
near, close to	**vicino**
necessary	**necessario/a**
neck	**collo**
need, want	**bisogno, necessità**
neighbour	**vicino/a**
nephew	**nipote (m)**
never	**non ... mai**
new	**nuovo/a**
newspaper	**giornale (m)**
next	**vicino/a**
nice	**bello/a,**
nice, likeable	**simpatico/a**
niece	**nipote (f)**
night	**notte (f)**
no	**no**
noise	**rumore (m)**
none	**nessuno/a**
normal	**normale**
north	**nord (m)**
nose	**naso**
not	**non**
note	**nota**
nothing	**niente (m), nulla (m)**
now	**adesso, ora, allora**
nowhere	**in nessun posto**
number	**numero**
numerous	**numeroso/a**
nurse	**infermiere/a**

O

obligation, duty	**obbligo**
obstinate	**ostinato**
office	**ufficio**
often	**spesso**
oil	**olio**
old	**vecchio/a**
omelet	**frittata, omelette (f)**
on	**su**
on foot	**a piedi**
onion	**cipolla**
only, single	**solo/a, unico/a**

open	**aperto/a**
open	**aprire (v)**
opinion	**opinione (f)**
opposite	**opposto/a, contrario/a**
opposite, facing	**di fronte**
orange	**arancia**
order	**ordine (m)**
organize	**organizzare (v)**
orphanage	**orfanotrofio**
others, the rest	**altro/a**
otherwise	**diversamente**
our	**nostro/a, nostri/e (pl)**
outside	**fuori**
oven	**forno**
over, on	**su**
over here, here	**qui**
owner	**proprietario/a**

P

package	**pacco**
packet	**pacchetto**
page	**pagina**
paint	**dipingere (v)**
painting	**dipinto, pittura**
pair	**paio, coppia**
pancake	**frittella**
pants	**mutande (fpl)**
paper	**carta**
parent/s	**genitore/i**
park	**parco**
parking	**parcheggio**
part	**parte (f)**
pass	**passare (v)**
passenger	**passeggero/a**
passerby	**passante (m/f)**
passport	**passaporto**
pastime	**passatempo**
paté	**pâté (m)**
path	**sentiero**
patience	**pazienza**
pavement	**marciapiede (m)**
pay	**pagare (v)**
pea	**pisello**
peaceful	**pacifico/a**
peach	**pesca**
pear	**pera**
peasant	**contadino/a**
pedestrian	**pedone (m)**
pencil	**matita**
people	**persone (fpl)**
pepper	**pepe (m)**
performance	**svolgimento**
perfume	**profumo**

permit	**autorizzazione (f)**	purpose, intention	**scopo, intenzione (f)**
perhaps	**forse**		
person	**persona**		
personally	**personalmente**		
persuade	**persuadere (v)**	**Q**	
petrol	**benzina**		
petrol station	**stazione (f) di servizio**	quality	**qualità**
photograph	**fotografia**	quarter	**quarto**
picnic	**picnic (m)**	question	**domanda**
piece	**pezzo**	queue	**coda**
pinch	**pizzicare (v)**	quickly	**in fretta, rapidamente**
pineapple	**ananas**	quiet	**silenzioso/a, tranquillo/a**
pink	**rosa**		
pipe (smoker's)	**pipa**		
pity	**compassione (f)**	**R**	
place	**posto, luogo**		
plain, clear	**chiaro/a**	rain	**pioggia**
plan	**piano, progetto**	razor	**rasoio**
plane	**aereo**	read	**leggere (v)**
plate	**piatto**	ready	**pronto/a**
play	**giocare (v)**	reality	**in realtà**
please	**per piacere, per favore**	really	**veramente**
pleasure	**piacere (m)**	receive	**ricevere (v)**
pocket	**tasca**	reception	**reception (f)**
point	**punto**	recognize	**riconoscere (v)**
police	**polizia**	recommend	**consigliare (v)**
policeman	**poliziotto**	record	**disco**
polite	**educato/a, garbato/a**	red	**rosso/a**
poor	**povero/a**	refuse	**rifiutare (v)**
Pope	**Papa**	registration	**registrazione (f)**
porter	**portinaio/a**	regret	**essere (v) desolato/a**
possible	**possibile**	relative	**relativo/a**
post	**posta**	relax	**rilassare (v)**
post, send	**spedire per posta**	relief	**sollievo/a**
postcard	**cartolina**	remain, stay	**rimanere, restare (v)**
potato	**patata**	remember	**ricordare (v)**
pound (sterling)	**sterlina**	remove	**togliere (v)**
precious	**prezioso/a**	replace	**rimettere (v)**
prefer	**preferire (v)**	reply, answer	**rispondere (v)**
prepare	**preparare (v)**	request	**richiedere (v)**
present, gift	**dono**	resemblance	**somiglianza**
presentation	**presentazione (f)**	reservation	**prenotazione (f)**
pressure	**pressione (f)**	reserve, book	**prenotare, riservare (v)**
pretty, lovely	**grazioso/a**	reserved	**riservato/a, prenotato/a**
principle	**principio**	resist	**resistere (v)**
private	**privato/a**	rest	**riposo**
probably	**probabilmente**	rest, remainder	**il resto, gli/le, altri/e**
problem	**problema**	restaurant	**ristorante (m)**
product	**prodotto**	retire, withdraw	**ritirarsi (v)**
programme	**programma**	retired	**pensionato/a**
proof	**prova**	return, come back	**ritornare (v)**
property	**proprietà**	rich	**ricco/a**
provide	**fornire (v)**	right	**destro/a**
pupil, student	**allievo/a, scolaro/a**	ring	**anello**
pure	**puro/a**	ring, phone	**suonare (v)**
		rise, get up	**sorgere (v)**

river	**fiume (m)**	sheet, bedsheet	**lenzuolo**
road, highway	**strada, via**	shirt	**camicia**
roast	**arrosto**	shoe	**scarpa**
rock	**roccia**	shop, store	**negozio**
Rome	**Roma**	shopping	**acquisti**
room	**stanza, sala**	shopping for food	**spesa**
rose (flower)	**rosa**	short	**corto/a**
route	**itinerario**	shoulder	**spalla**
rub	**strofinare (v)**	show	**mostrare (v)**
run	**correre (v)**	show, exhibition	**esposizione, mostra**
rush	**precipitarsi (v)**	show (theatre)	**spettacolo**
		shower	**acquazzone (m)**
		shy	**timido/a**

S

		side	**fianco**
		sign	**segno, gesto**
sad	**triste**	significance, meaning	**importanza**
safety	**sicurezza**	silence	**silenzio**
safetybelt	**cintura di sicurezza**	silk	**seta**
sailing	**vela**	simple	**semplice**
sailor	**marinaio**	since	**da allora**
saint	**santo/a**	sing	**cantare (v)**
salad	**insalata**	singer	**cantante (m/f)**
salesman	**commesso**	singing	**canto**
saleswoman	**commessa**	single	**solo/a**
salt	**sale (m)**	sister	**sorella**
same	**stesso/a**	sit down	**sedersi (v)**
sandwich	**tramezzino, sandwich**	situation	**posizione (f)**
satisfy	**soddisfare (v)**	sixty	**sessanta**
Saturday	**sabato**	size	**dimensioni**
sausage	**salsiccia**	skin	**pelle (f)**
scarcely	**appena**	skirt	**gonna**
scarf	**sciarpa**	sky	**cielo**
school	**scuola**	sleep	**dormire (v)**
seafood, shellfish	**frutti di mare**	slim	**magro/a, snello/a**
seat	**sedia**	slow	**lento/a**
second	**secondo/a**	slowly	**lentamente**
secondary	**secondario/a**	small, little	**piccolo/a**
secretary	**segretario/a**	smart, pretty	**di moda**
see	**vedere (v)**	smell	**olfatto, odorato (v)**
seem, appear	**sembrare, parere (v)**	smile	**sorriso (v)**
self	**l'io**	smoker	**fumatore/trice**
sell	**vendere (v)**	smoking	**fumante**
send	**mandare (v)**	snack	**spuntimo**
serious	**serio/a**	snackbar	**tavola calda**
serve	**servire (v)**	snail	**chiocciola**
service	**servizio**	snake	**serpente**
set	**serie (f)**	so	**così**
setting	**ambiente**	soap	**sapone (m)**
several	**parecchi/ie**	sock	**calzino**
share	**parte (f)**	sofa	**divano**
shareholder	**azionista (m/f)**	solicitor	**avvocato/essa**
sharp	**tagliente, affilato/a**	some, any	**del/della**
shave	**radere, rasare (v)**	somebody, someone	**qualcuno**
she	**ella, lei**	something	**qualcosa, qualche cosa**
sheep	**pecora**	sometimes	**qualche volta**

song	**canzone (f)**	surprise, amaze	**sorprendere (v)**
soon	**presto**	surround	**circondare (v)**
Spanish language	**spagnolo**	survivor	**superstite (m/f)**
sparkling	**scintillante**	suspense	**incertezza**
speak	**dire, parlare (v)**	swallow	**inghiottire (v)**
speaking	**parlante**	swear	**giurare (v)**
special	**particolare, speciale**	swim	**nuotare (v)**
spectacle	**occhiali**	swimming pool	**piscina**
speed	**velocità**	switch on	**accendere (v)**
spell out	**spiegare (v)**		
spend	**spendere (v)**		
splendid	**splendido/a**		
spoon	**cucchiaio**	**T**	
sport	**sport**		
sporting	**sportivo/a**	table	**tavolo**
square	**quadrato**	tablet	**compressa**
spring	**primavera**	tablecloth	**tovaglia**
stair	**scalino**	take	**prendere (v)**
staircase	**scala**	take away, subtract	**sottrarre (v)**
stall	**stalla**	talk	**parlare (v)**
stamp	**francobollo**	tall	**alto/a**
starter	**per antipasto**	tap	**rubinetto**
station	**stazione (f)**	tart, bitter, sour	**aspro/a**
statue	**statura**	taste	**gusto**
steak	**carne di manzo**	taxi	**taxi (m)**
stereo	**stereo (m)**	tea	**tè (m)**
stewardess	**hostess (f)**	teapot	**teiera**
stomach	**stomaco**	teacher	**insegnante**
stop	**arresto**	telegram	**telegramma**
storm	**tempesta**	telephone	**telefono**
strange	**sconosciuto/a**	telephone	**telefonare (v)**
strawberry	**fragola**	television	**televisione (f)**
street	**strada**	temperature	**temperatura**
string	**filo**	tender	**tenero/a**
stroll	**passeggiatina**	tennis	**tennis (m)**
strong	**forte**	terminal	**terminale (m)**
student	**studente/essa**	terrace	**terrazza, terrazzo**
studied	**studiato/a**	terrible	**terribile, tremendo/a**
study	**studio**	testimony, evidence	**testimonianza**
stupid	**stupido/a**	thank	**ringraziare**
style, manner	**stile (m)**	thank you	**grazie**
stylish, smart	**che ha classe**	that, those	**quei, quello, quella**
succeed	**succedere (v)**	the	**il (lo), la, i**
successive, following	**consecutivo/a**	theatre	**teatro**
suddenly	**improvvisamente**	then	**allora**
sufficient, enough	**sufficiente**	there	**là, lì**
sugar	**zucchero**	therefore	**perciò, quindi**
suit	**completo (m)**	thick, big	**grosso/a, spesso/a**
suitcase	**valigia**	thing	**cosa**
summer	**estate (f)**	think	**pensare (v)**
sun	**sole (m)**	third	**terzo/a**
sunburn, suntan	**abbronzatura**	thirst	**sete (f)**
Sunday	**domenica**	thirty	**trenta**
supermarket	**supermercato**	this, these	**questo/a**
sure, certain	**sicuro/a**	through	**attraverso**
		throw	**lanciare, gettare (v)**

Thursday	**giovedi**	up to, until	**fino**
thus	**perciò**	use	**usare (v)**
ticket	**biglietto**	usually	**di solito**
tidy	**ordinato/a**		
tie	**cravatta**		
tighten, close	**stringere (v)**		
time	**tempo**		

tip	**mancia**	vanilla	**vaniglia**
tired	**stanco/a**	vase	**vaso**
toast	**pane tostato**	vegetable	**ortaggio**
tobacconist	**tabaccaio**	velvet	**velluto**
today	**oggi**	very	**molto**
together	**insieme**	view	**vista**
tomato	**pomodoro**	village	**paeze (m)**
tomorrow	**domani**	visit	**visitare (v)**
tone	**tono**	voice	**voce (f)**
too	**troppo**		
toothbrush	**spazzolino da denti**		
toothpaste	**dentifricio**		

W

top	**cima**	wait	**aspettare,attendere (v)**
touch	**toccare (v)**	waiter	**cameriere (m)**
tourist	**turista (m/f)**	waitress	**cameriera**
towards	**verso**	wake	**svegliarsi, destarsi (v)**
towel	**asciugamano**	walk	**camminarea (v)**
town	**città**	wall	**muro**
traffic	**traffico**	wallet	**portafoglio**
train	**treno**	wardrobe	**guardaroba (m)**
travel	**viaggiare (v)**	warm	**caldo/a**
tray	**vassoio**	warmth	**calore**
tree	**albero**	wash	**lavare (v)**
trousers	**pantaloni, calzoni**	watch	**orologio**
true	**vero/a**	water	**acqua**
truth	**verità**	wave	**gesticolare (v)**
try	**provare (v)**	way, method	**mezzo, modo**
Tuesday	**martedi**	wear	**portare, indossare (v)**
turn	**giro**	weather	**tempo**
twenty	**venti**	Wednesday	**mercoledi**
type	**tipo**	week	**settimana**
		weekend	**fine settimana**
		weight	**peso**
		welcome	**gradito/a**

U

		well	**bene**
umbrella	**ombrello**	what	**quale**
uncle	**zio**	when	**quando**
under	**sotto**	where	**dove**
Underground	**metropoliana**	which	**quale**
underpants	**mutande**	(a) while	**un pó**
understand	**capire (v)**	while	**mentre, nel frattempo**
uneasy	**precario/a, agitato/a**	white	**bianco/a**
unfortunately	**purtroppo**	who	**chi**
united	**unito/a**	why	**perché**
United States	**Stati Uniti**	wild	**selvatico/a**
tniversity	**università**	wild animals	**bestie feroci**
unpleasant	**sgradevole,spiacevole**	will, wish	**volere (v)**
unusual	**insolito/a**		

willow	**salice (m)**
win	**vincere (v)**
wind	**vento**
window	**finestra**
wine	**vino**
wineglass	**bicchiere (m) da vino**
winner	**vincitore/trice**
winter	**inverno**
wish	**volere, desiderare (v)**
with	**con**
within	**dentro**
without	**senza**
woman	**donna**
wonder	**chiedersi (v)**
wonderful	**meraviglioso/a**
wood	**legno**
wooden	**di legno**
wool	**lana**
work	**lavoro**
world	**mondo**
worried	**preoccupato/a**
worry	**preoccupazione (f)**
wounded	**ferito/a**
wrap up	**avvolgere (v)**
write	**scrivere (v)**
wrong	**sbagliato/a**

Y

year	**anno**
yellow	**giallo/a**
yes	**sì**
yesterday	**ieri**
yet	**già**
yoghurt	**yogurt**
you	**tu, voi**
young	**giovane**
youth	**giovinezza**

Z

Zurich	**Zurigo**